PREDATOR™

RACE WAR

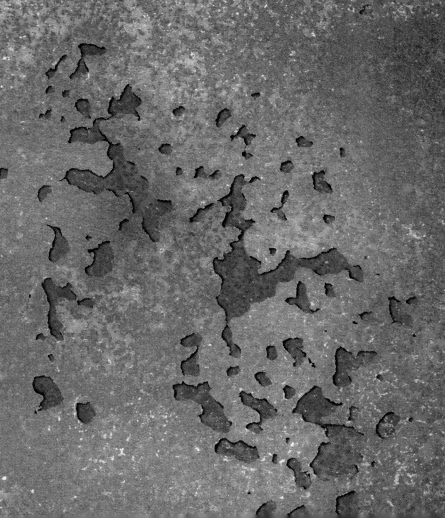

JERRY PROSSER
SERIES EDITOR

LYNN ADAIR
COLLECTION EDITOR

BRIAN GOGOLIN
BOOK DESIGN MANAGER

TEENA GORES
COLLECTION DESIGNER

CARY GRAZZINI
LOGO DESIGNER

PREDATOR™
RACE WAR

ANDREW VACHSS
STORY

RANDY STRADLEY
ADAPTATION

RAY LAGO
COVER

**JORDAN RASKIN
& LAUCHLAND PELLE**
PENCILS

RICK BRYANT
INKS

**MATT HOLLINGSWORTH
& PAMELA RAMBO**
COLORS

CLEM ROBINS
LETTERING

DARK HORSE COMICS®

MIKE RICHARDSON
PUBLISHER

NEIL HANKERSON
EXECUTIVE VP

DAVID SCROGGY
VP OF PUBLISHING

LOU BANK
VP OF SALES & MARKETING

ANDY KARABATSOS
VP OF FINANCE

MARK ANDERSON
GENERAL COUNSEL

DIANA SCHUTZ
EDITOR IN CHIEF

RANDY STRADLEY
CREATIVE DIRECTOR

CINDY MARKS
DIRECTOR OF PRODUCTION & DESIGN

MARK COX
ART DIRECTOR

SEAN TIERNEY
COMPUTER GRAPHICS DIRECTOR

CHRIS CREVISTON
DIRECTOR OF ACCOUNTING

MICHAEL MARTENS
MARKETING DIRECTOR

TOD BORLESKE
SALES & LICENSING DIRECTOR

MARK ELLINGTON
DIRECTOR OF OPERATIONS

DALE LAFOUNTAIN
DIRECTOR OF M.I.S.

Published by Dark Horse Comics
10956 SE Main Street
Milwaukie, OR 97222

ISBN:1-56971-112-7
First edition: August 1995

10 9 8 7 6 5 4 3 2

Printed in Canada

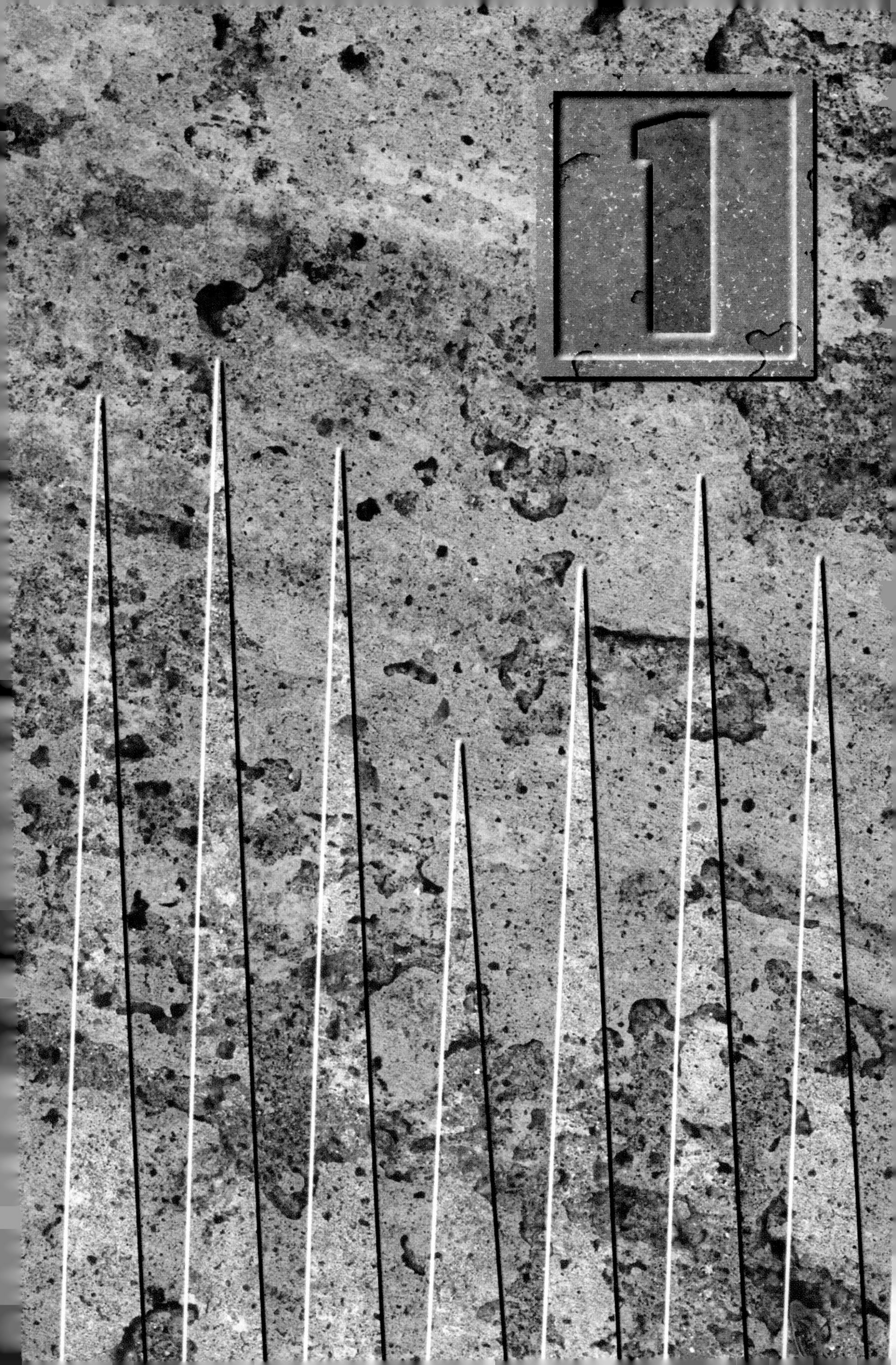
1

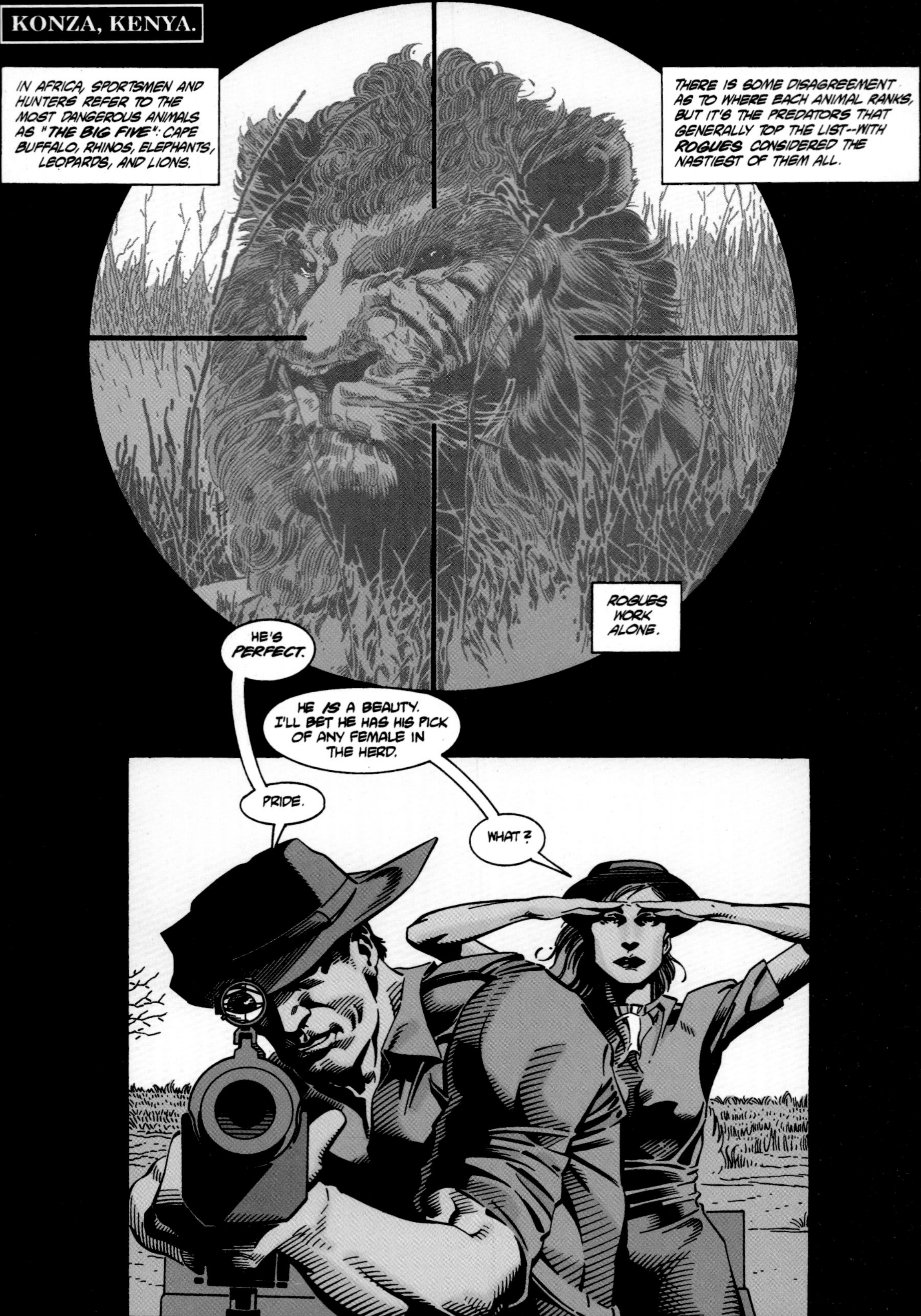
KONZA, KENYA.
IN AFRICA, SPORTSMEN AND HUNTERS REFER TO THE MOST DANGEROUS ANIMALS AS "THE BIG FIVE": CAPE BUFFALO, RHINOS, ELEPHANTS, LEOPARDS, AND LIONS.
THERE IS SOME DISAGREEMENT AS TO WHERE EACH ANIMAL RANKS, BUT IT'S THE PREDATORS THAT GENERALLY TOP THE LIST--WITH ROGUES CONSIDERED THE NASTIEST OF THEM ALL.
ROGUES WORK ALONE.
HE'S PERFECT.
HE IS A BEAUTY. I'LL BET HE HAS HIS PICK OF ANY FEMALE IN THE HERD.
PRIDE.
WHAT?

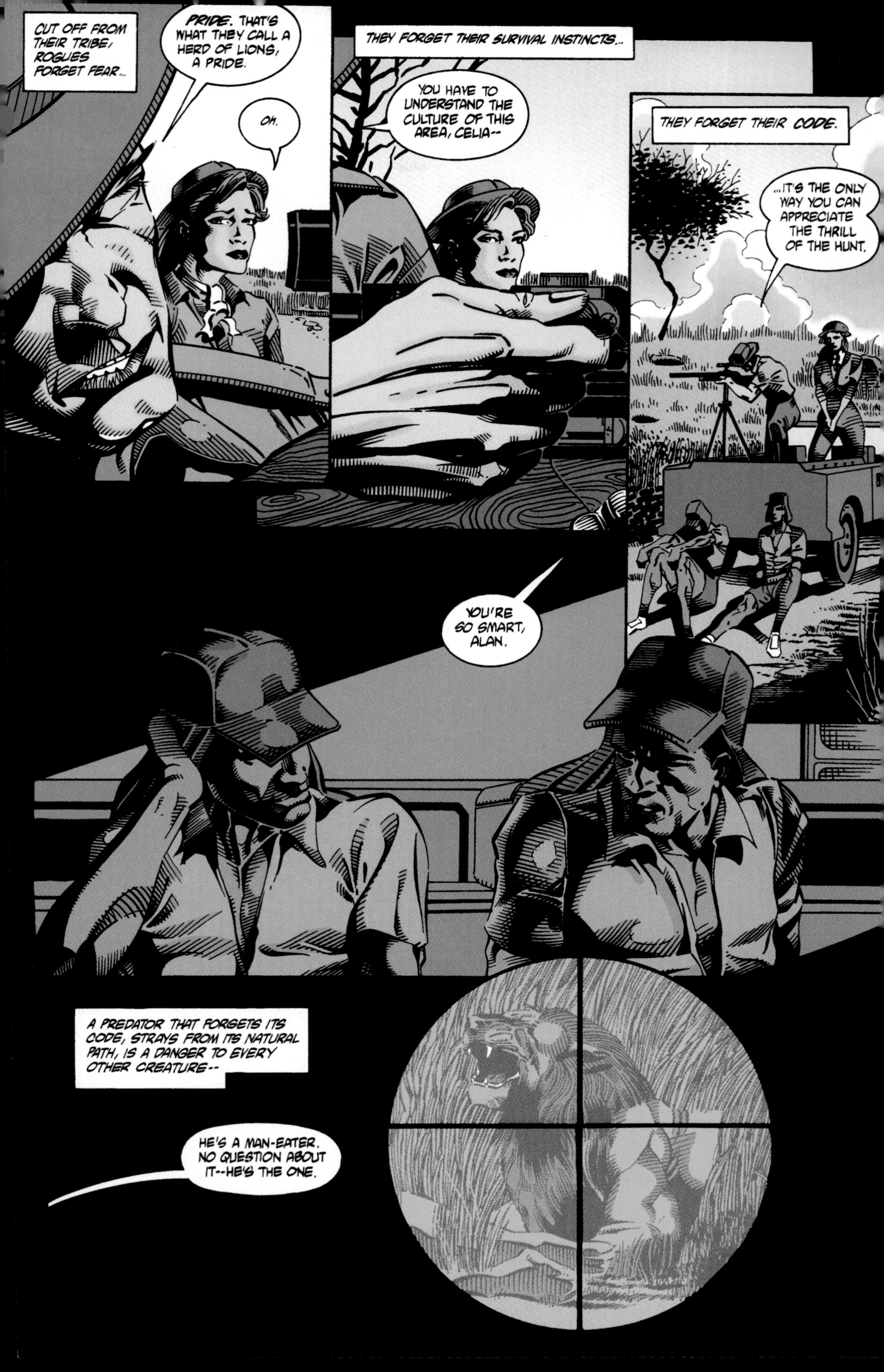
CUT OFF FROM THEIR TRIBE, ROGUES FORGET FEAR...
PRIDE. THAT'S WHAT THEY CALL A HERD OF LIONS, A PRIDE.
OH.
THEY FORGET THEIR SURVIVAL INSTINCTS...
YOU HAVE TO UNDERSTAND THE CULTURE OF THIS AREA, CELIA--
THEY FORGET THEIR CODE.
...IT'S THE ONLY WAY YOU CAN APPRECIATE THE THRILL OF THE HUNT.
YOU'RE SO SMART, ALAN.
A PREDATOR THAT FORGETS ITS CODE, STRAYS FROM ITS NATURAL PATH, IS A DANGER TO EVERY OTHER CREATURE--
HE'S A MAN-EATER. NO QUESTION ABOUT IT--HE'S THE ONE.

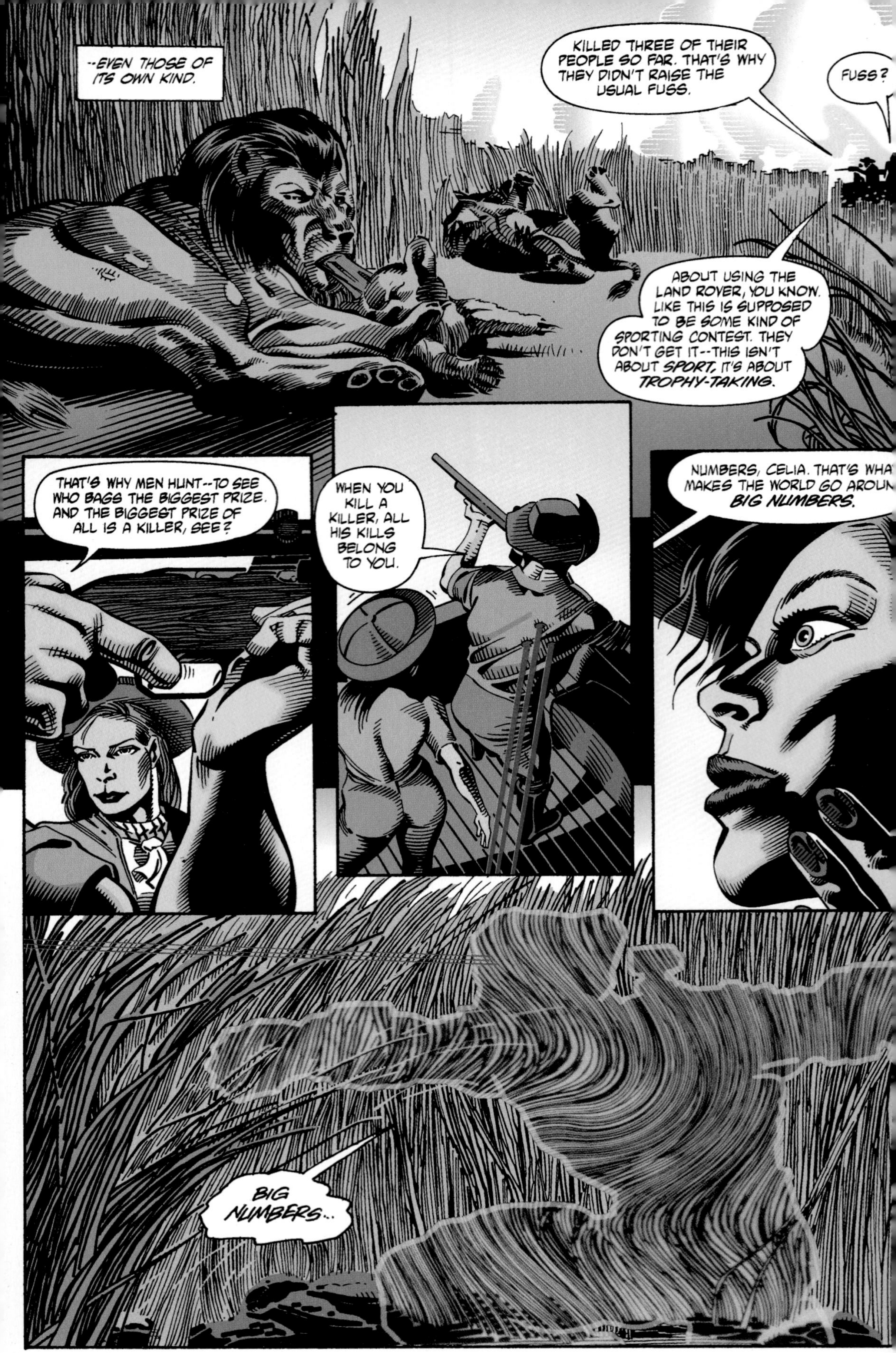
--EVEN THOSE OF ITS OWN KIND.
KILLED THREE OF THEIR PEOPLE SO FAR. THAT'S WHY THEY DIDN'T RAISE THE USUAL FUSS.
FUSS?
ABOUT USING THE LAND ROVER, YOU KNOW. LIKE THIS IS SUPPOSED TO BE SOME KIND OF SPORTING CONTEST. THEY DON'T GET IT--THIS ISN'T ABOUT SPORT, IT'S ABOUT TROPHY-TAKING.
THAT'S WHY MEN HUNT--TO SEE WHO BAGS THE BIGGEST PRIZE. AND THE BIGGEST PRIZE OF ALL IS A KILLER, SEE?
WHEN YOU KILL A KILLER, ALL HIS KILLS BELONG TO YOU.
NUMBERS, CELIA. THAT'S WHAT MAKES THE WORLD GO AROUN BIG NUMBERS.
BIG NUMBERS..

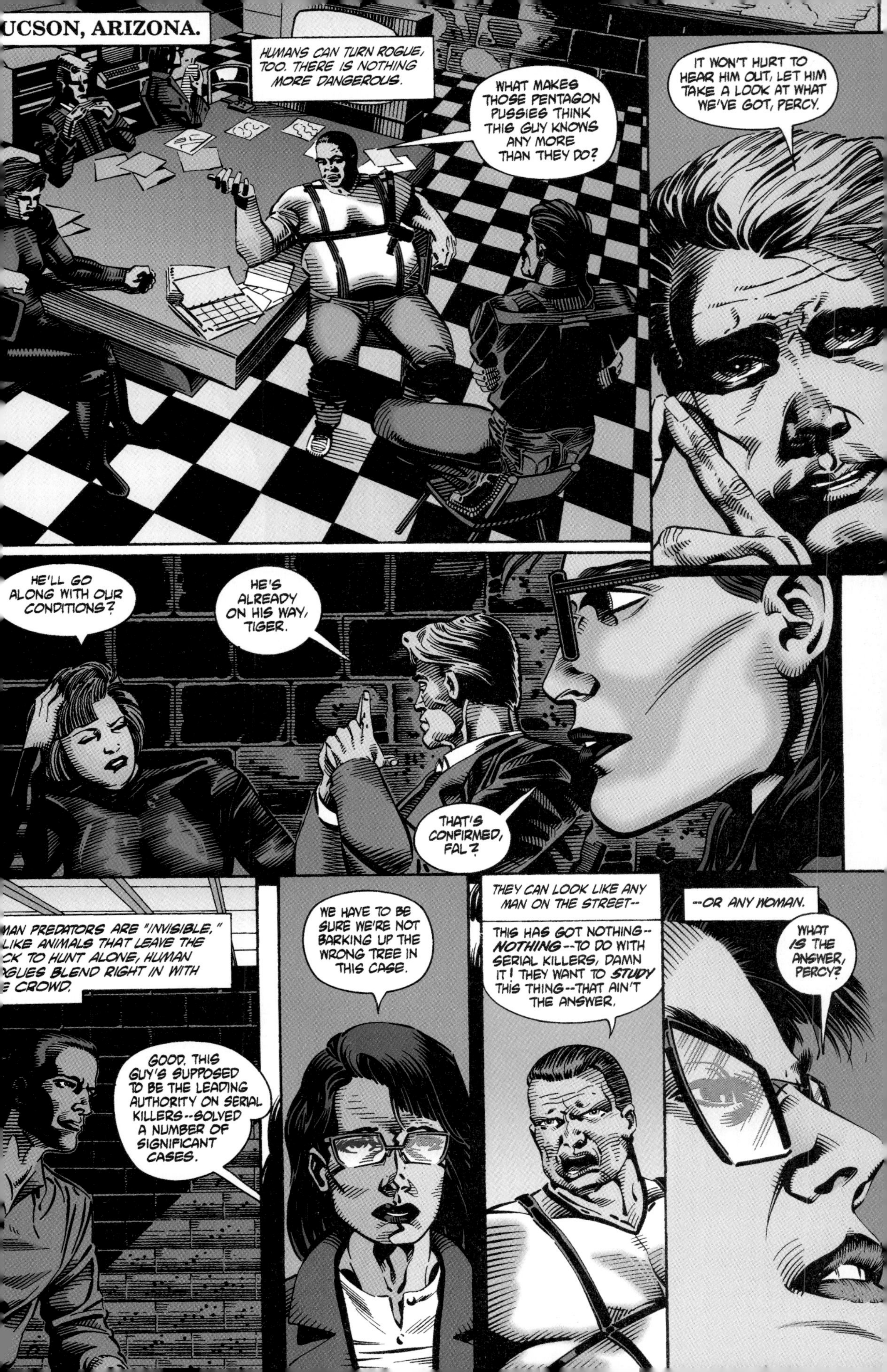
UCSON, ARIZONA.
HUMANS CAN TURN ROGUE, TOO. THERE IS NOTHING MORE DANGEROUS.
WHAT MAKES THOSE PENTAGON PUSSIES THINK THIS GUY KNOWS ANY MORE THAN THEY DO?
IT WON'T HURT TO HEAR HIM OUT, LET HIM TAKE A LOOK AT WHAT WE'VE GOT, PERCY.
HE'LL GO ALONG WITH OUR CONDITIONS?
HE'S ALREADY ON HIS WAY, TIGER.
THAT'S CONFIRMED, FAL?
MAN PREDATORS ARE "INVISIBLE." LIKE ANIMALS THAT LEAVE THE CK TO HUNT ALONE, HUMAN OGUES BLEND RIGHT IN WITH E CROWD.
GOOD. THIS GUY'S SUPPOSED TO BE THE LEADING AUTHORITY ON SERIAL KILLERS--SOLVED A NUMBER OF SIGNIFICANT CASES.
WE HAVE TO BE SURE WE'RE NOT BARKING UP THE WRONG TREE IN THIS CASE.
THEY CAN LOOK LIKE ANY MAN ON THE STREET--
THIS HAS GOT NOTHING--NOTHING--TO DO WITH SERIAL KILLERS, DAMN IT! THEY WANT TO STUDY THIS THING--THAT AIN'T THE ANSWER.
--OR ANY WOMAN.
WHAT IS THE ANSWER, PERCY?

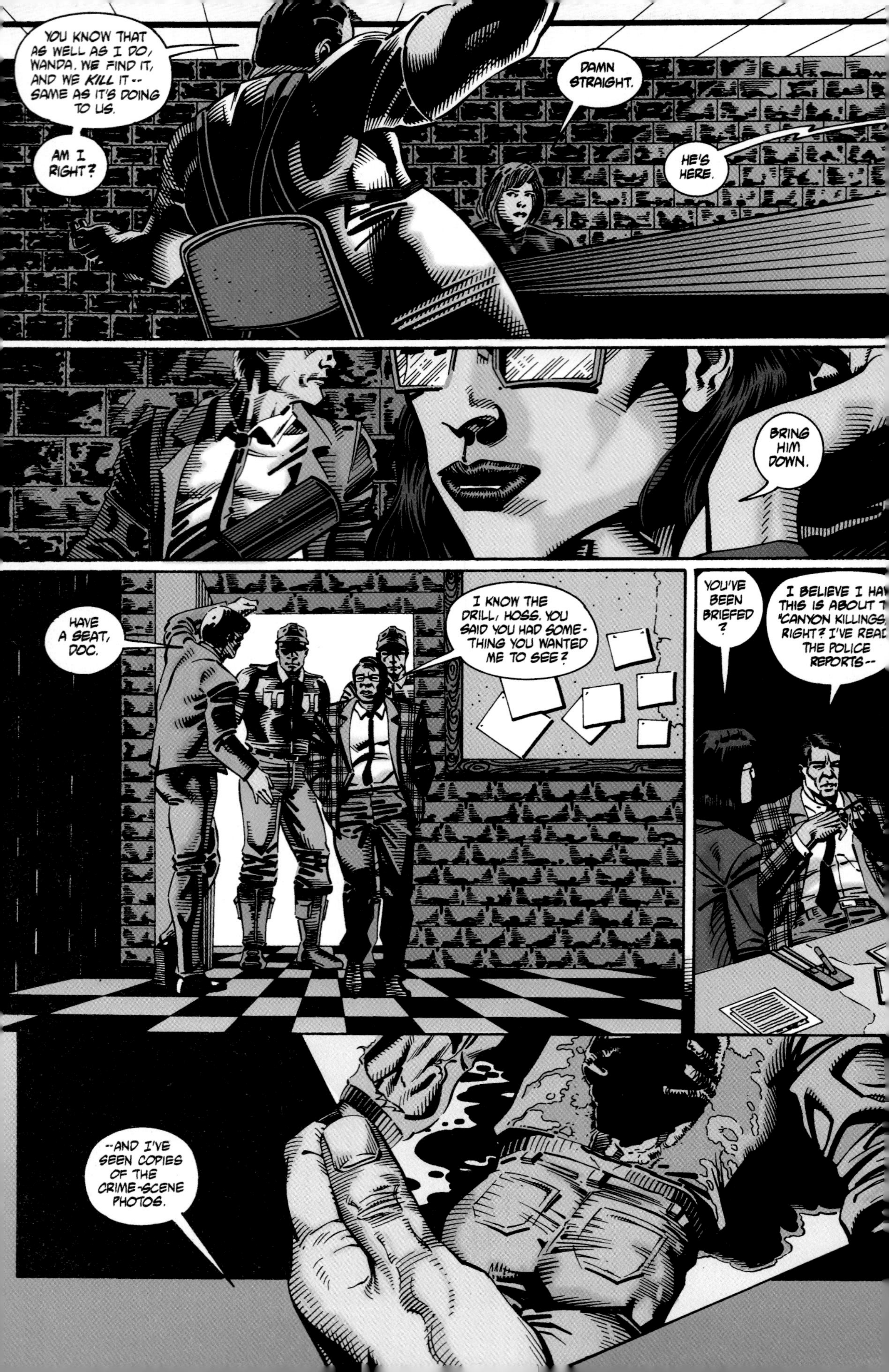
YOU KNOW THAT AS WELL AS I DO, WANDA. WE FIND IT, AND WE KILL IT -- SAME AS IT'S DOING TO US.
AM I RIGHT?
DAMN STRAIGHT.
HE'S HERE.
BRING HIM DOWN.
HAVE A SEAT, DOC.
I KNOW THE DRILL, HOSS. YOU SAID YOU HAD SOME-THING YOU WANTED ME TO SEE?
YOU'VE BEEN BRIEFED?
I BELIEVE I HAV THIS IS ABOUT T "CANYON KILLINGS, RIGHT? I'VE READ THE POLICE REPORTS--
--AND I'VE SEEN COPIES OF THE CRIME-SCENE PHOTOS.

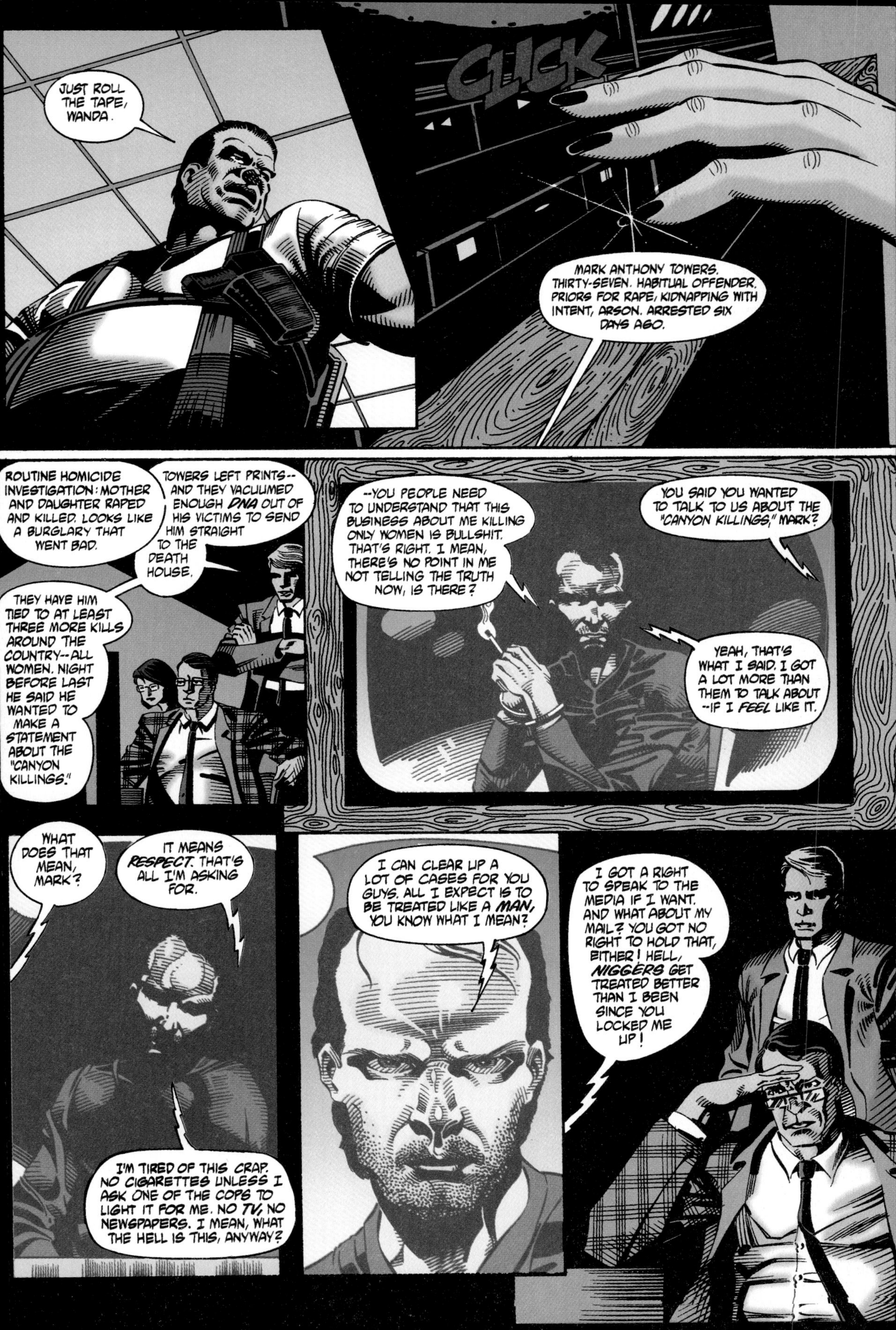

JUST ROLL THE TAPE, WANDA.
CLICK
MARK ANTHONY TOWERS. THIRTY-SEVEN. HABITUAL OFFENDER. PRIORS FOR RAPE, KIDNAPPING WITH INTENT, ARSON. ARRESTED SIX DAYS AGO.
ROUTINE HOMICIDE INVESTIGATION: MOTHER AND DAUGHTER RAPED AND KILLED. LOOKS LIKE A BURGLARY THAT WENT BAD.
TOWERS LEFT PRINTS-- AND THEY VACUUMED ENOUGH DNA OUT OF HIS VICTIMS TO SEND HIM STRAIGHT TO THE DEATH HOUSE.
THEY HAVE HIM TIED TO AT LEAST THREE MORE KILLS AROUND THE COUNTRY--ALL WOMEN. NIGHT BEFORE LAST HE SAID HE WANTED TO MAKE A STATEMENT ABOUT THE "CANYON KILLINGS."
YOU SAID YOU WANTED TO TALK TO US ABOUT THE "CANYON KILLINGS," MARK?
--YOU PEOPLE NEED TO UNDERSTAND THAT THIS BUSINESS ABOUT ME KILLING ONLY WOMEN IS BULLSHIT. THAT'S RIGHT. I MEAN, THERE'S NO POINT IN ME NOT TELLING THE TRUTH NOW, IS THERE?
YEAH, THAT'S WHAT I SAID. I GOT A LOT MORE THAN THEM TO TALK ABOUT --IF I FEEL LIKE IT.
WHAT DOES THAT MEAN, MARK?
IT MEANS RESPECT. THAT'S ALL I'M ASKING FOR.
I'M TIRED OF THIS CRAP. NO CIGARETTES UNLESS I ASK ONE OF THE COPS TO LIGHT IT FOR ME. NO TV, NO NEWSPAPERS. I MEAN, WHAT THE HELL IS THIS, ANYWAY?
I CAN CLEAR UP A LOT OF CASES FOR YOU GUYS. ALL I EXPECT IS TO BE TREATED LIKE A MAN, YOU KNOW WHAT I MEAN?
I GOT A RIGHT TO SPEAK TO THE MEDIA IF I WANT. AND WHAT ABOUT MY MAIL? YOU GOT NO RIGHT TO HOLD THAT, EITHER! HELL, NIGGERS GET TREATED BETTER THAN I BEEN SINCE YOU LOCKED ME UP!

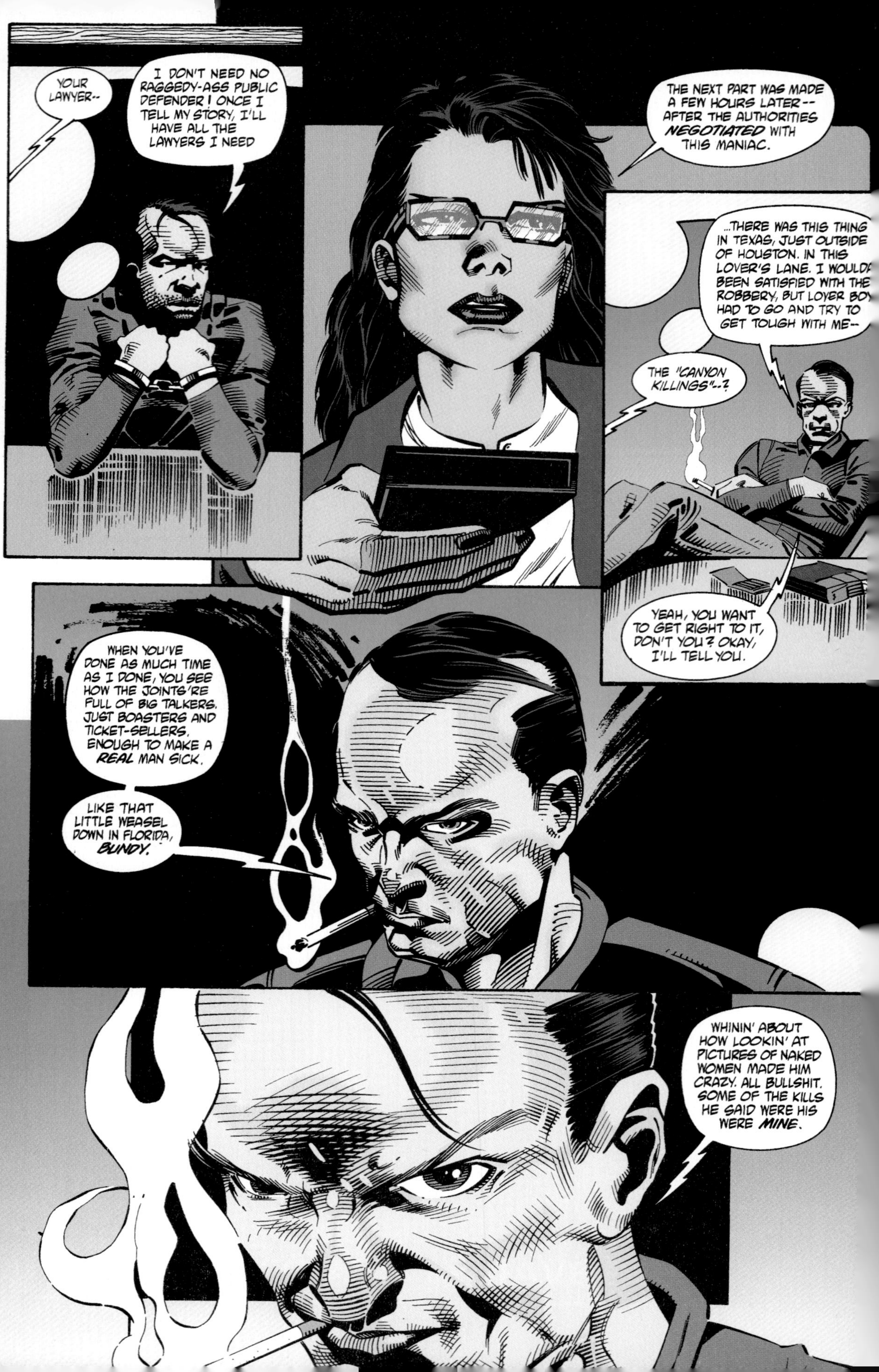
YOUR LAWYER--
I DON'T NEED NO RAGGEDY-ASS PUBLIC DEFENDER! ONCE I TELL MY STORY, I'LL HAVE ALL THE LAWYERS I NEED
THE NEXT PART WAS MADE A FEW HOURS LATER-- AFTER THE AUTHORITIES NEGOTIATED WITH THIS MANIAC.
...THERE WAS THIS THING IN TEXAS, JUST OUTSIDE OF HOUSTON. IN THIS LOVER'S LANE. I WOULDA BEEN SATISFIED WITH THE ROBBERY, BUT LOVER BOY HAD TO GO AND TRY TO GET TOUGH WITH ME--
THE "CANYON KILLINGS"--?
YEAH, YOU WANT TO GET RIGHT TO IT, DON'T YOU? OKAY, I'LL TELL YOU.
WHEN YOU'VE DONE AS MUCH TIME AS I DONE, YOU SEE HOW THE JOINTS'RE FULL OF BIG TALKERS. JUST BOASTERS AND TICKET-SELLERS. ENOUGH TO MAKE A REAL MAN SICK.
LIKE THAT LITTLE WEASEL DOWN IN FLORIDA, BUNDY.
WHININ' ABOUT HOW LOOKIN' AT PICTURES OF NAKED WOMEN MADE HIM CRAZY. ALL BULLSHIT. SOME OF THE KILLS HE SAID WERE HIS WERE MINE.

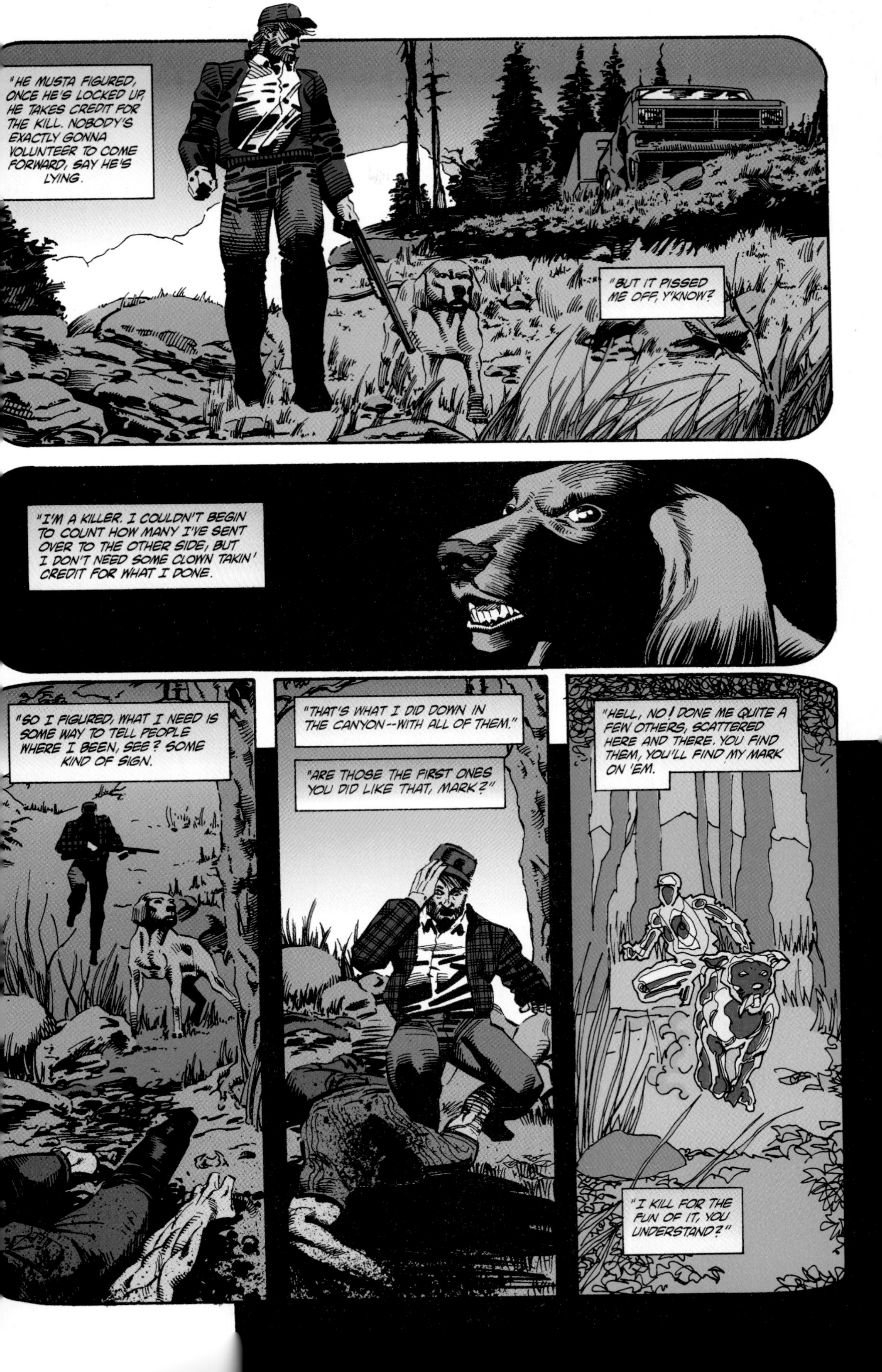
"HE MUSTA FIGURED, ONCE HE'S LOCKED UP, HE TAKES CREDIT FOR THE KILL. NOBODY'S EXACTLY GONNA VOLUNTEER TO COME FORWARD, SAY HE'S LYING.
"BUT IT PISSED ME OFF, Y'KNOW?
"I'M A KILLER. I COULDN'T BEGIN TO COUNT HOW MANY I'VE SENT OVER TO THE OTHER SIDE, BUT I DON'T NEED SOME CLOWN TAKIN' CREDIT FOR WHAT I DONE.
"SO I FIGURED, WHAT I NEED IS SOME WAY TO TELL PEOPLE WHERE I BEEN, SEE? SOME KIND OF SIGN.
"THAT'S WHAT I DID DOWN IN THE CANYON--WITH ALL OF THEM."
"ARE THOSE THE FIRST ONES YOU DID LIKE THAT, MARK?"
"HELL, NO! I DONE ME QUITE A FEW OTHERS, SCATTERED HERE AND THERE. YOU FIND THEM, YOU'LL FIND MY MARK ON 'EM.
"I KILL FOR THE FUN OF IT, YOU UNDERSTAND?"

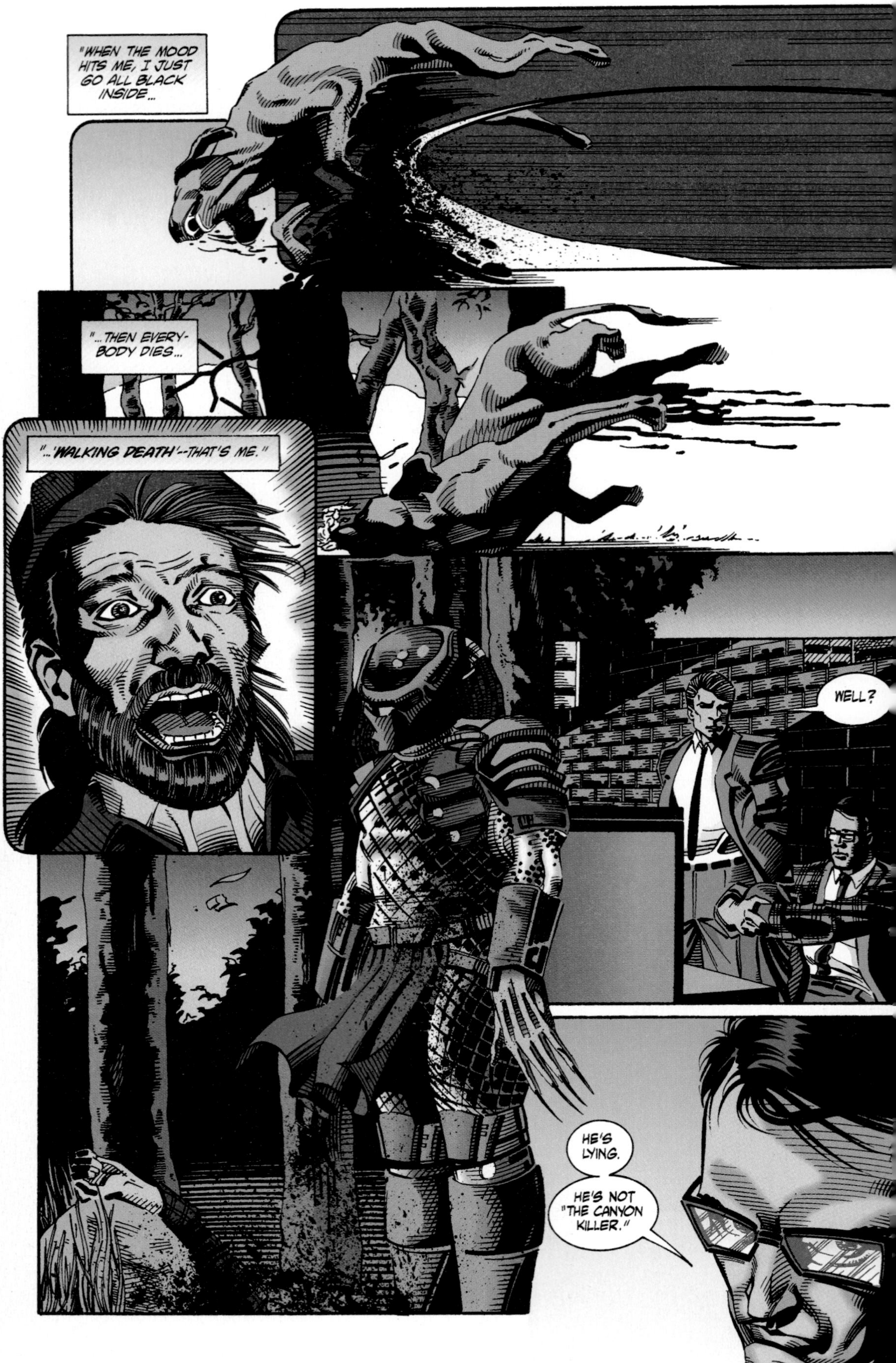
"WHEN THE MOOD HITS ME, I JUST GO ALL BLACK INSIDE...
"...THEN EVERYBODY DIES...
"...'WALKING DEATH'--THAT'S ME."
WELL?
HE'S LYING.
HE'S NOT "THE CANYON KILLER."

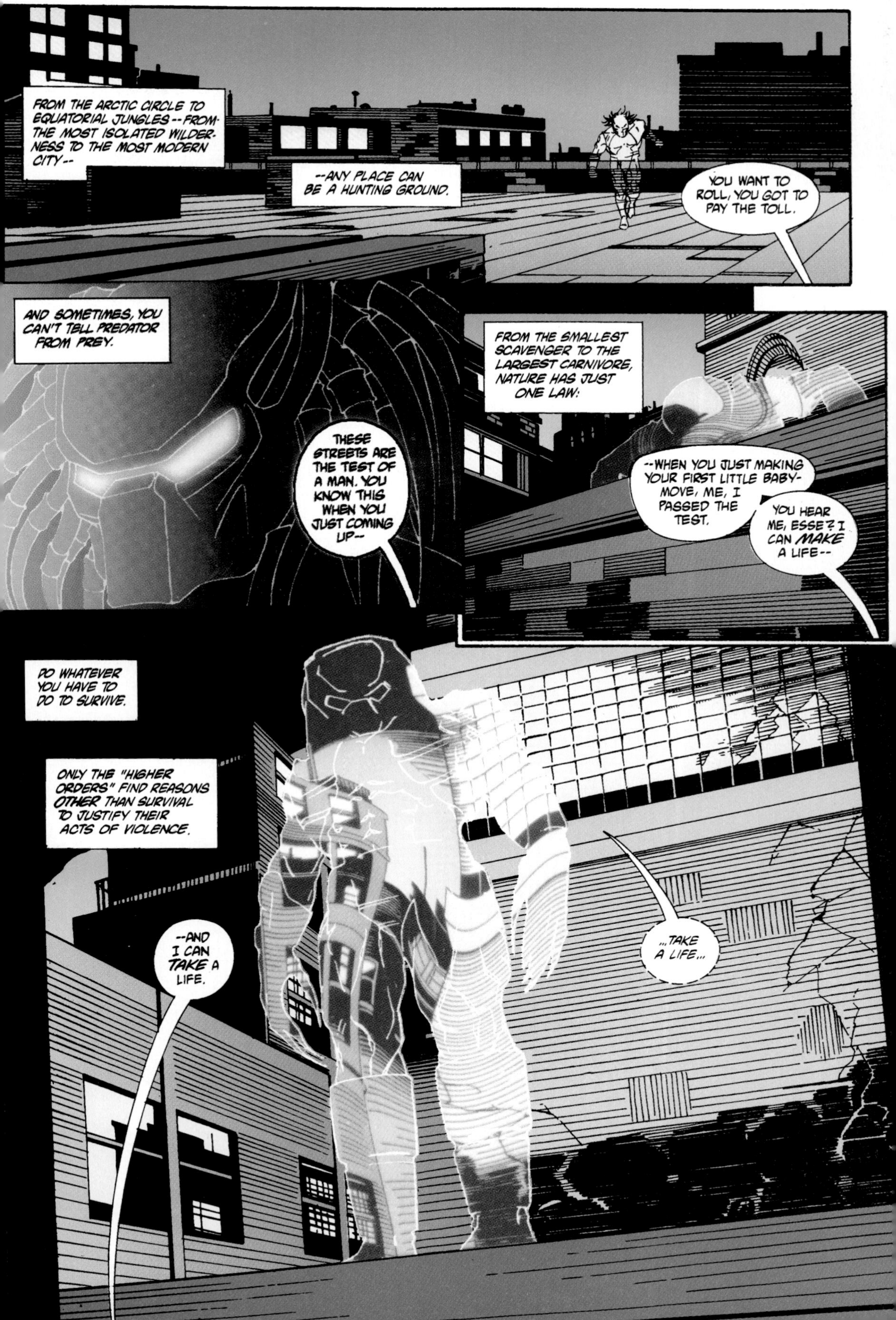

FROM THE ARCTIC CIRCLE TO EQUATORIAL JUNGLES--FROM THE MOST ISOLATED WILDERNESS TO THE MOST MODERN CITY--
--ANY PLACE CAN BE A HUNTING GROUND.
YOU WANT TO ROLL, YOU GOT TO PAY THE TOLL.
AND SOMETIMES, YOU CAN'T TELL PREDATOR FROM PREY.
THESE STREETS ARE THE TEST OF A MAN. YOU KNOW THIS WHEN YOU JUST COMING UP--
FROM THE SMALLEST SCAVENGER TO THE LARGEST CARNIVORE, NATURE HAS JUST ONE LAW:
--WHEN YOU JUST MAKING YOUR FIRST LITTLE BABY-MOVE, ME, I PASSED THE TEST.
YOU HEAR ME, ESSE? I CAN MAKE A LIFE--
DO WHATEVER YOU HAVE TO DO TO SURVIVE.
ONLY THE "HIGHER ORDERS" FIND REASONS OTHER THAN SURVIVAL TO JUSTIFY THEIR ACTS OF VIOLENCE.
--AND I CAN TAKE A LIFE.
...TAKE A LIFE...

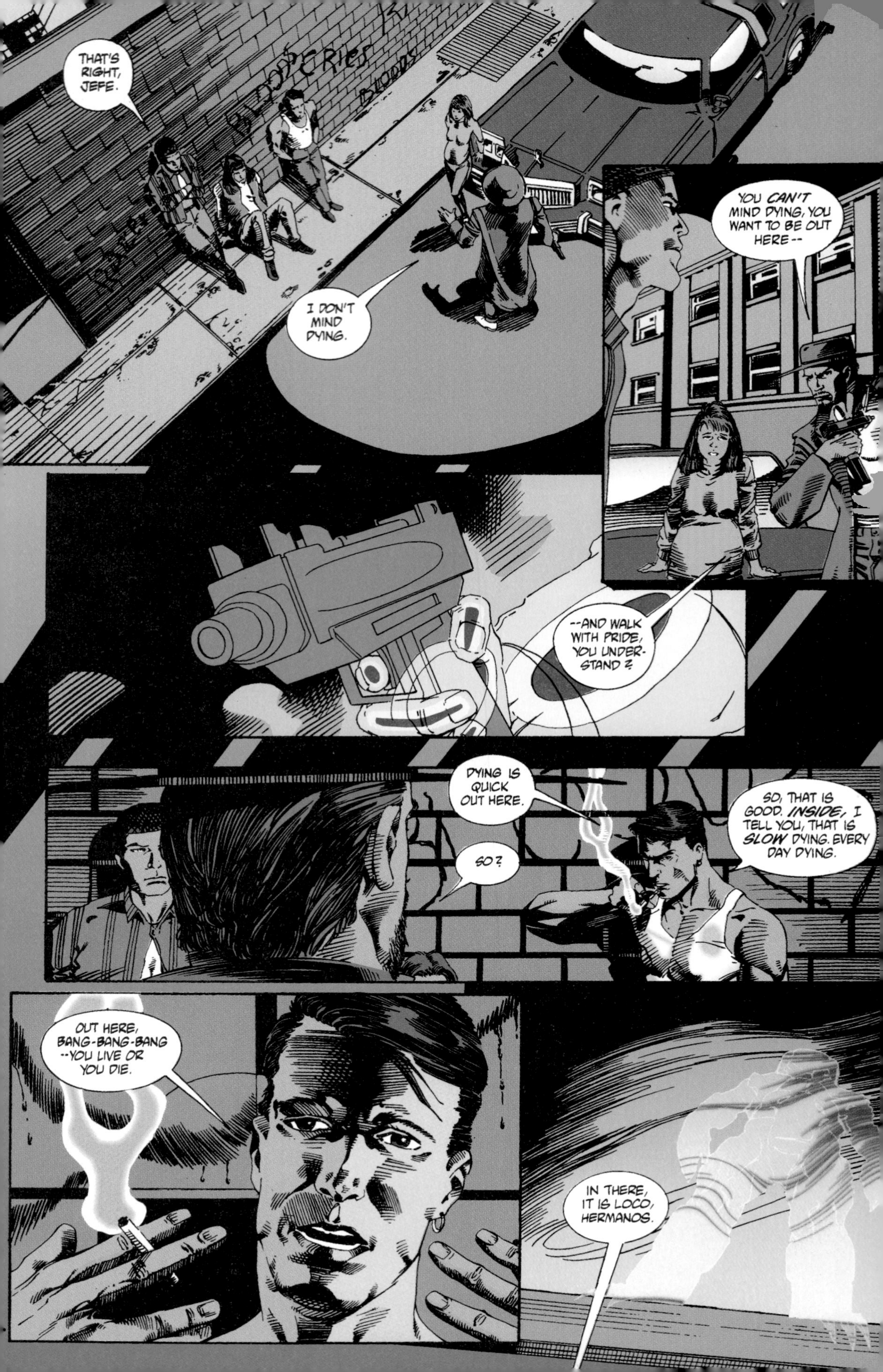
THAT'S RIGHT, JEFE.
I DON'T MIND DYING.
YOU CAN'T MIND DYING, YOU WANT TO BE OUT HERE--
--AND WALK WITH PRIDE, YOU UNDER-STAND?
DYING IS QUICK OUT HERE.
SO?
SO, THAT IS GOOD. INSIDE, I TELL YOU, THAT IS SLOW DYING. EVERY DAY DYING.
OUT HERE, BANG-BANG-BANG --YOU LIVE OR YOU DIE.
IN THERE, IT IS LOCO, HERMANOS.

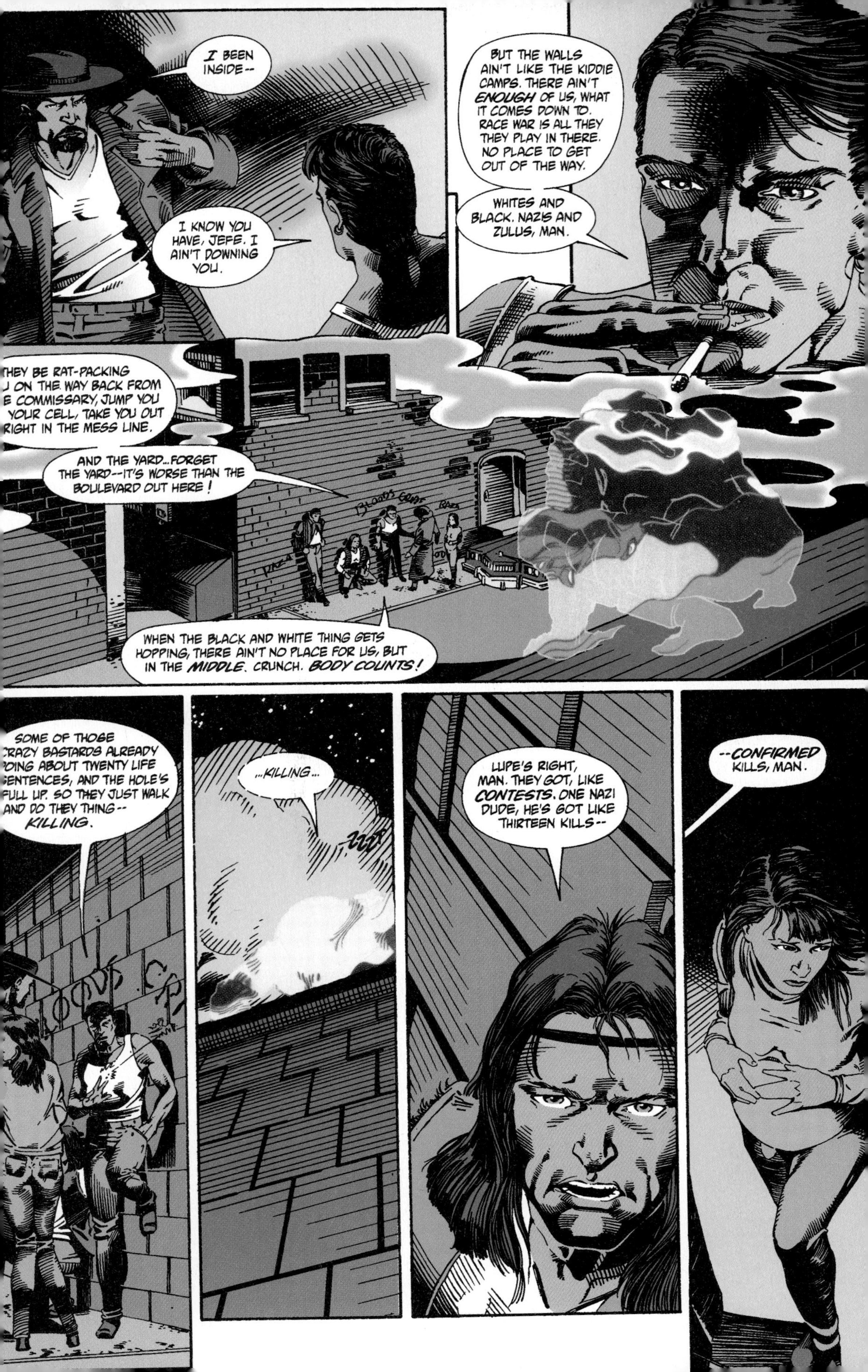
I BEEN INSIDE--
I KNOW YOU HAVE, JEFE. I AIN'T DOWNING YOU.
BUT THE WALLS AIN'T LIKE THE KIDDIE CAMPS. THERE AIN'T ENOUGH OF US, WHAT IT COMES DOWN TO. RACE WAR IS ALL THEY THEY PLAY IN THERE. NO PLACE TO GET OUT OF THE WAY.
WHITES AND BLACK. NAZIS AND ZULUS, MAN.
THEY BE RAT-PACKING U ON THE WAY BACK FROM E COMMISSARY, JUMP YOU YOUR CELL, TAKE YOU OUT RIGHT IN THE MESS LINE.
AND THE YARD... FORGET THE YARD--IT'S WORSE THAN THE BOULEVARD OUT HERE!
WHEN THE BLACK AND WHITE THING GETS HOPPING, THERE AIN'T NO PLACE FOR US, BUT IN THE MIDDLE. CRUNCH. BODY COUNTS!
SOME OF THOSE CRAZY BASTARDS ALREADY DOING ABOUT TWENTY LIFE SENTENCES, AND THE HOLE'S FULL UP. SO THEY JUST WALK AND DO THEY THING-- KILLING.
...KILLING...
LUPE'S RIGHT, MAN. THEY GOT, LIKE CONTESTS. ONE NAZI DUDE, HE'S GOT LIKE THIRTEEN KILLS--
--CONFIRMED KILLS, MAN.

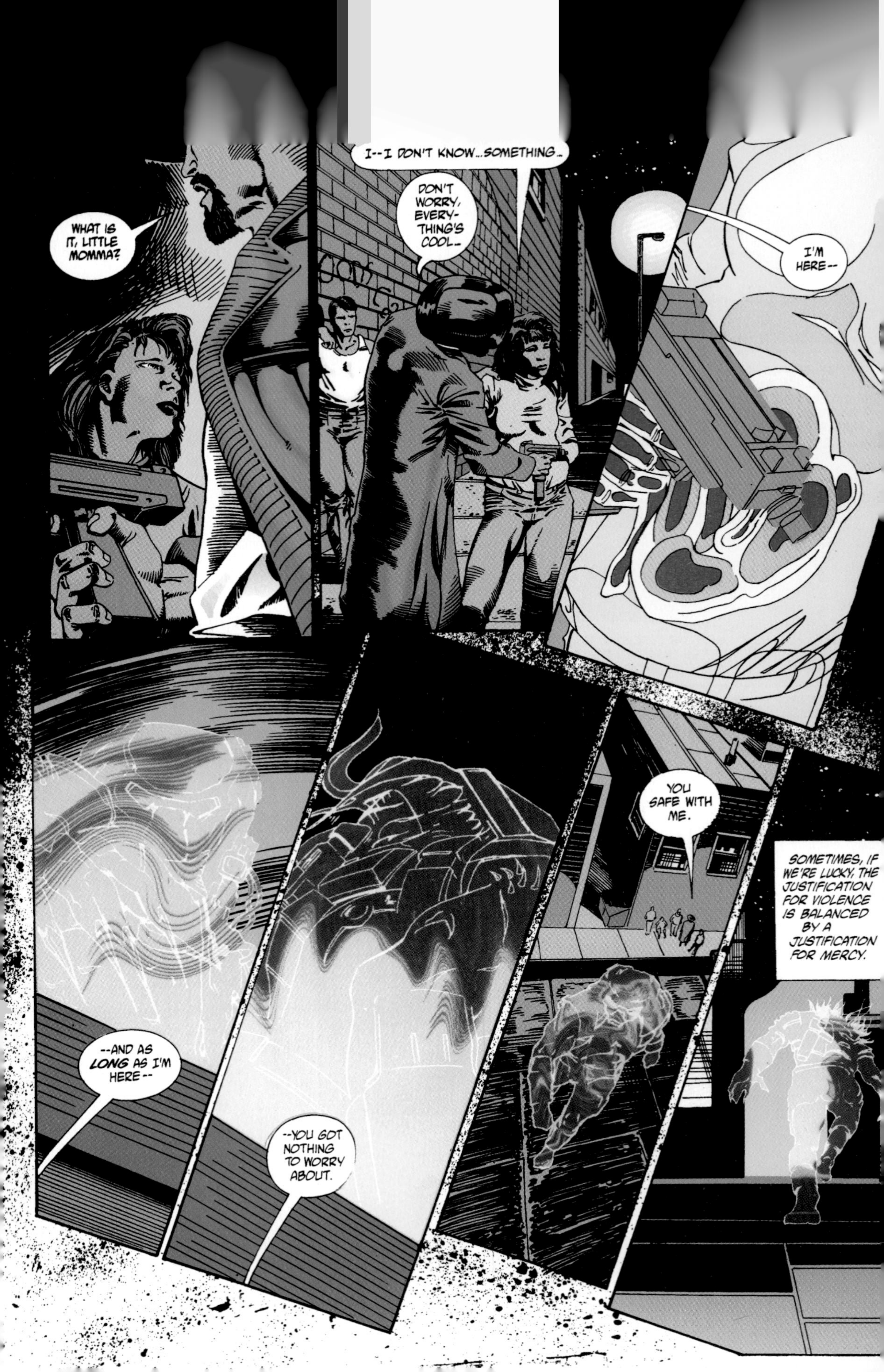
WHAT IS IT, LITTLE MOMMA?
I--I DON'T KNOW...SOMETHING...
DON'T WORRY, EVERY-THING'S COOL...
I'M HERE--
--AND AS LONG AS I'M HERE--
--YOU GOT NOTHING TO WORRY ABOUT.
YOU SAFE WITH ME.
SOMETIMES, IF WE'RE LUCKY, THE JUSTIFICATION FOR VIOLENCE IS BALANCED BY A JUSTIFICATION FOR MERCY.

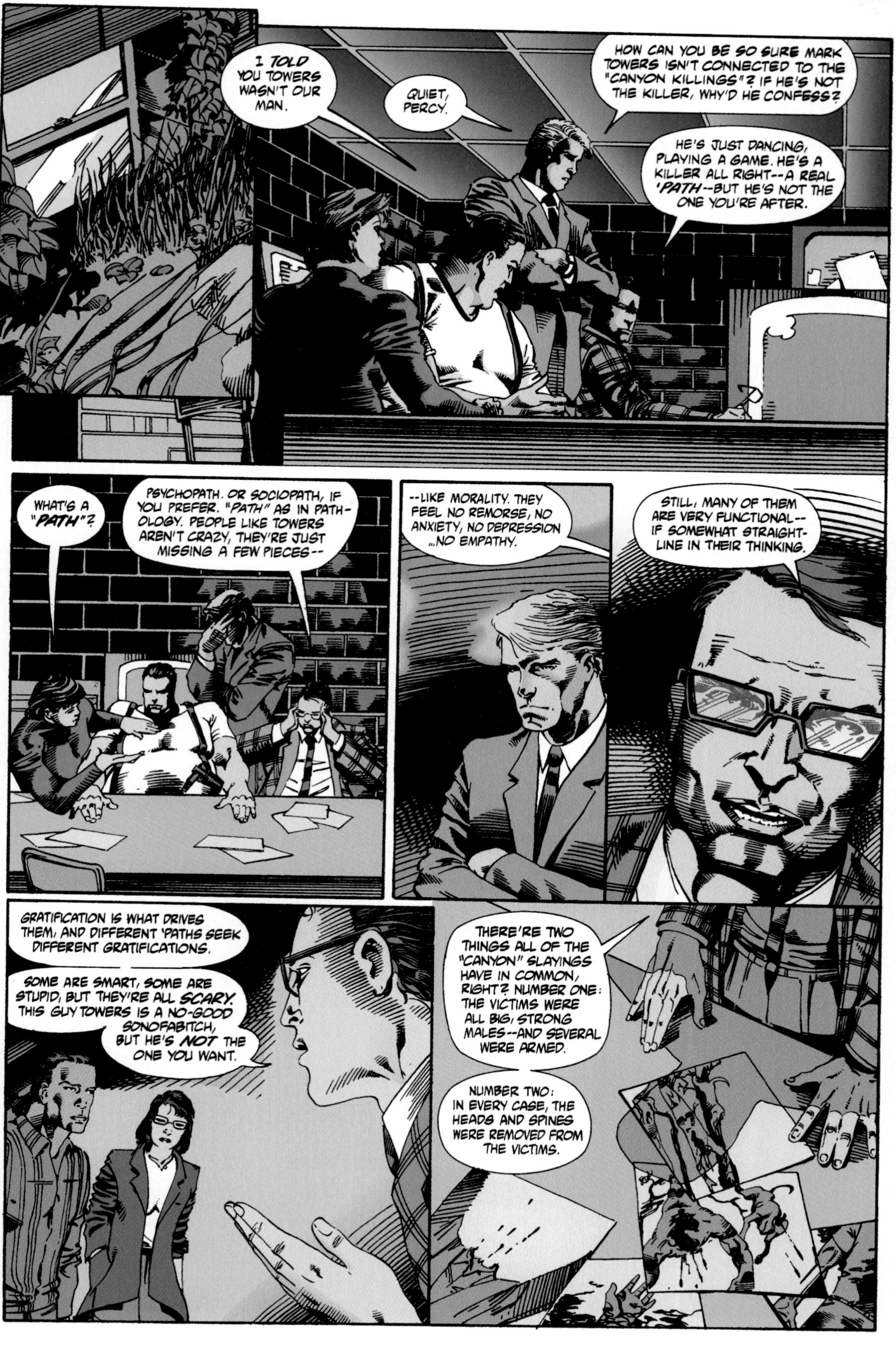
I *TOLD* YOU TOWERS WASN'T OUR MAN.
QUIET, PERCY.
HOW CAN YOU BE *SO SURE* MARK TOWERS ISN'T CONNECTED TO THE "CANYON KILLINGS"? IF HE'S NOT THE KILLER, WHY'D HE CONFESS?
HE'S JUST DANCING, PLAYING A GAME. HE'S A KILLER ALL RIGHT--A REAL *'PATH*--BUT HE'S NOT THE ONE YOU'RE AFTER.
WHAT'S A "*PATH*"?
PSYCHOPATH. OR SOCIOPATH, IF YOU PREFER. "*PATH*" AS IN PATH-OLOGY. PEOPLE LIKE TOWERS AREN'T CRAZY, THEY'RE JUST MISSING A FEW PIECES--
--LIKE MORALITY. THEY FEEL NO REMORSE, NO ANXIETY, NO DEPRESSION ...NO EMPATHY.
STILL, MANY OF THEM ARE VERY FUNCTIONAL-- IF SOMEWHAT STRAIGHT-LINE IN THEIR THINKING.
GRATIFICATION IS WHAT DRIVES THEM, AND DIFFERENT 'PATHS SEEK DIFFERENT GRATIFICATIONS.
SOME ARE SMART, *SOME* ARE STUPID, BUT THEY'RE ALL *SCARY*. THIS GUY TOWERS IS A NO-GOOD SONOFABITCH, BUT HE'S *NOT* THE ONE YOU WANT.
THERE'RE TWO THINGS ALL OF THE "CANYON" SLAYINGS HAVE IN COMMON, RIGHT? NUMBER ONE: THE VICTIMS WERE ALL BIG, STRONG MALES--AND SEVERAL WERE ARMED.
NUMBER TWO: IN EVERY CASE, THE HEADS AND SPINES WERE REMOVED FROM THE VICTIMS.

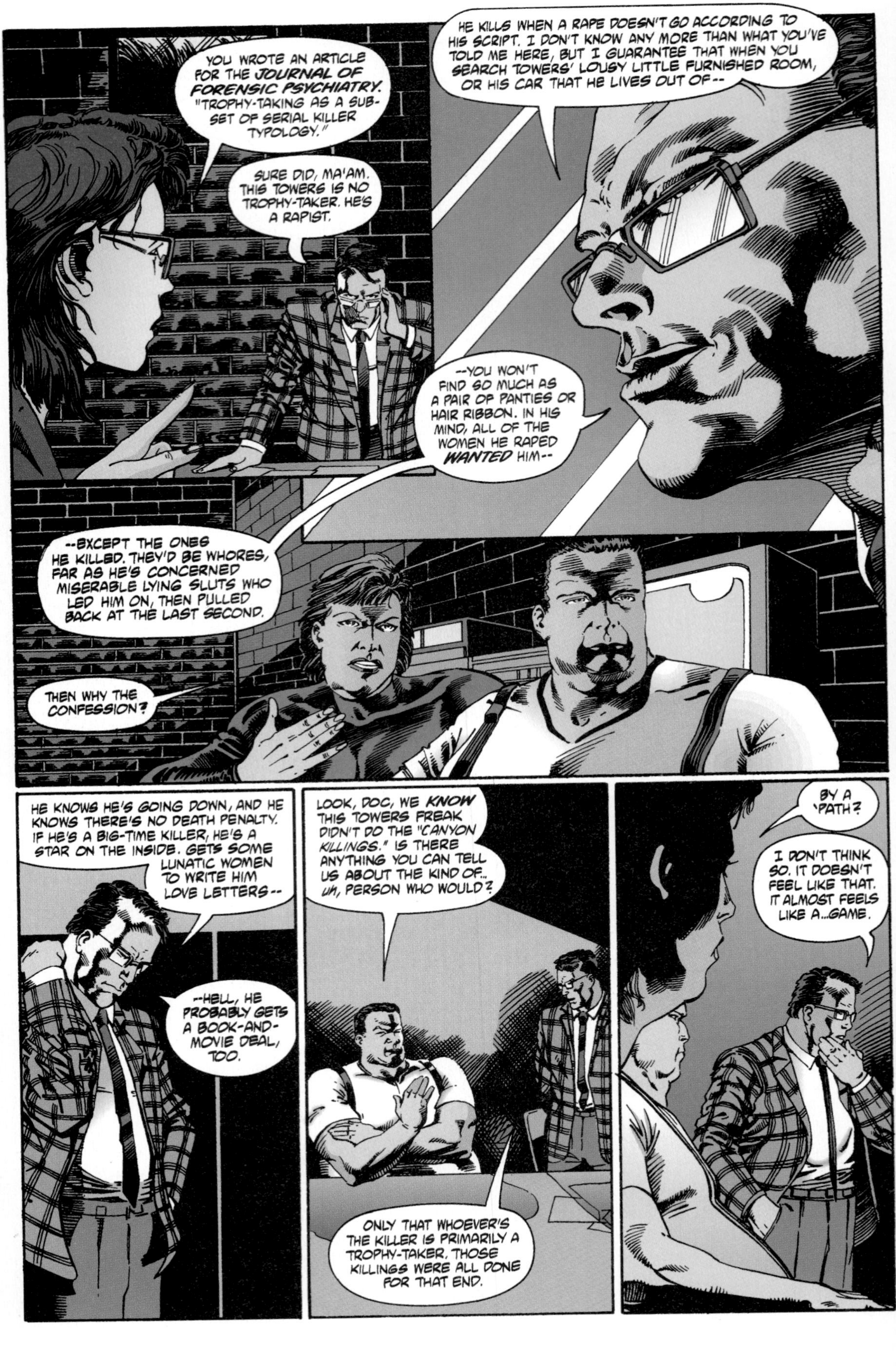
YOU WROTE AN ARTICLE FOR THE JOURNAL OF FORENSIC PSYCHIATRY. "TROPHY-TAKING AS A SUBSET OF SERIAL KILLER TYPOLOGY."
SURE DID, MA'AM. THIS TOWERS IS NO TROPHY-TAKER. HE'S A RAPIST.
HE KILLS WHEN A RAPE DOESN'T GO ACCORDING TO HIS SCRIPT. I DON'T KNOW ANY MORE THAN WHAT YOU'VE TOLD ME HERE, BUT I GUARANTEE THAT WHEN YOU SEARCH TOWERS' LOUSY LITTLE FURNISHED ROOM, OR HIS CAR THAT HE LIVES OUT OF--
--YOU WON'T FIND SO MUCH AS A PAIR OF PANTIES OR HAIR RIBBON. IN HIS MIND, ALL OF THE WOMEN HE RAPED WANTED HIM--
--EXCEPT THE ONES HE KILLED. THEY'D BE WHORES, FAR AS HE'S CONCERNED MISERABLE LYING SLUTS WHO LED HIM ON, THEN PULLED BACK AT THE LAST SECOND.
THEN WHY THE CONFESSION?
HE KNOWS HE'S GOING DOWN, AND HE KNOWS THERE'S NO DEATH PENALTY. IF HE'S A BIG-TIME KILLER, HE'S A STAR ON THE INSIDE. GETS SOME LUNATIC WOMEN TO WRITE HIM LOVE LETTERS--
--HELL, HE PROBABLY GETS A BOOK-AND-MOVIE DEAL, TOO.
LOOK, DOC, WE KNOW THIS TOWERS FREAK DIDN'T DO THE "CANYON KILLINGS." IS THERE ANYTHING YOU CAN TELL US ABOUT THE KIND OF... UH, PERSON WHO WOULD?
ONLY THAT WHOEVER'S THE KILLER IS PRIMARILY A TROPHY-TAKER. THOSE KILLINGS WERE ALL DONE FOR THAT END.
BY A 'PATH?
I DON'T THINK SO. IT DOESN'T FEEL LIKE THAT. IT ALMOST FEELS LIKE A...GAME.

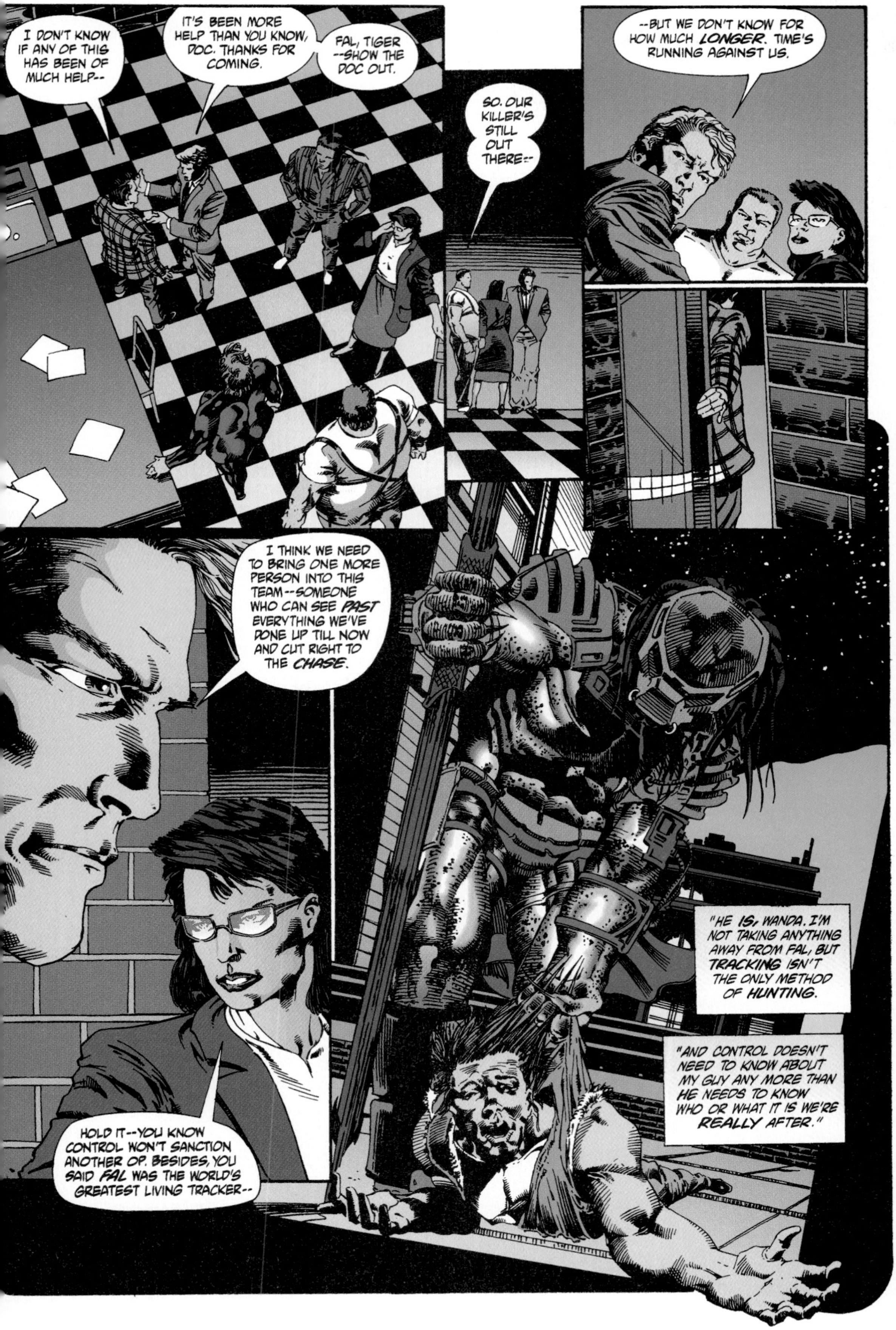

I DON'T KNOW IF ANY OF THIS HAS BEEN OF MUCH HELP--
IT'S BEEN MORE HELP THAN YOU KNOW, DOC. THANKS FOR COMING.
FAL, TIGER --SHOW THE DOC OUT.
SO. OUR KILLER'S STILL OUT THERE--
--BUT WE DON'T KNOW FOR HOW MUCH LONGER. TIME'S RUNNING AGAINST US.
I THINK WE NEED TO BRING ONE MORE PERSON INTO THIS TEAM--SOMEONE WHO CAN SEE PAST EVERYTHING WE'VE DONE UP TILL NOW AND CUT RIGHT TO THE CHASE.
HOLD IT--YOU KNOW CONTROL WON'T SANCTION ANOTHER OP. BESIDES, YOU SAID FAL WAS THE WORLD'S GREATEST LIVING TRACKER--
"HE IS, WANDA. I'M NOT TAKING ANYTHING AWAY FROM FAL, BUT TRACKING ISN'T THE ONLY METHOD OF HUNTING.
"AND CONTROL DOESN'T NEED TO KNOW ABOUT MY GUY ANY MORE THAN HE NEEDS TO KNOW WHO OR WHAT IT IS WE'RE REALLY AFTER."

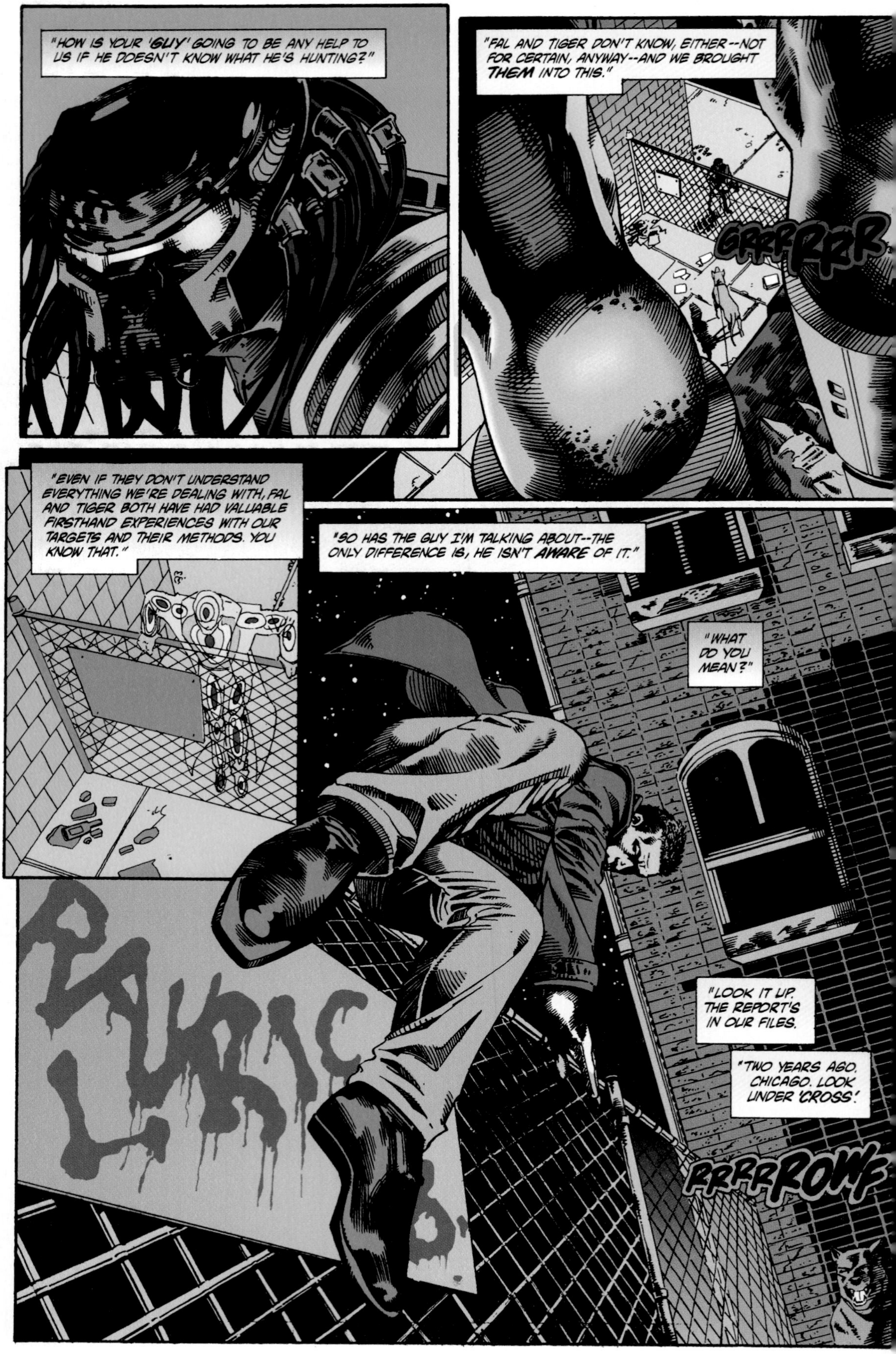
"HOW IS YOUR 'GUY' GOING TO BE ANY HELP TO US IF HE DOESN'T KNOW WHAT HE'S HUNTING?"
"FAL AND TIGER DON'T KNOW, EITHER--NOT FOR CERTAIN, ANYWAY--AND WE BROUGHT THEM INTO THIS."
GRRRRRR
"EVEN IF THEY DON'T UNDERSTAND EVERYTHING WE'RE DEALING WITH, FAL AND TIGER BOTH HAVE HAD VALUABLE FIRSTHAND EXPERIENCES WITH OUR TARGETS AND THEIR METHODS. YOU KNOW THAT."
"SO HAS THE GUY I'M TALKING ABOUT--THE ONLY DIFFERENCE IS, HE ISN'T AWARE OF IT."
"WHAT DO YOU MEAN?"
"LOOK IT UP. THE REPORT'S IN OUR FILES.
"TWO YEARS AGO. CHICAGO. LOOK UNDER 'CROSS'.
RRRRROWF

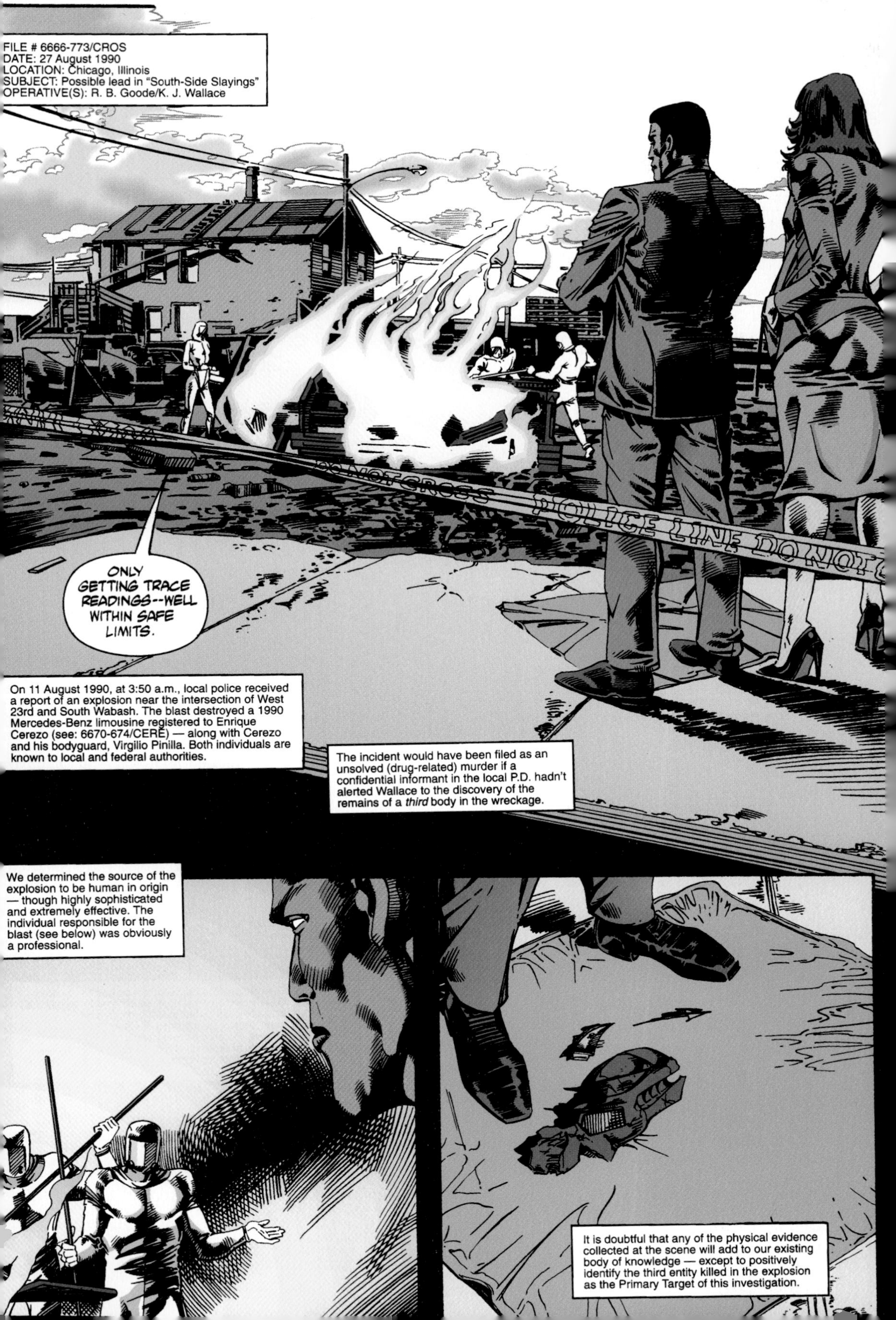
FILE # 6666-773/CROS
DATE: 27 August 1990
LOCATION: Chicago, Illinois
SUBJECT: Possible lead in "South-Side Slayings"
OPERATIVE(S): R. B. Goode/K. J. Wallace
DO NOT CROSS
POLICE LINE DO NOT
ONLY GETTING TRACE READINGS--WELL WITHIN SAFE LIMITS.
On 11 August 1990, at 3:50 a.m., local police received a report of an explosion near the intersection of West 23rd and South Wabash. The blast destroyed a 1990 Mercedes-Benz limousine registered to Enrique Cerezo (see: 6670-674/CERE) — along with Cerezo and his bodyguard, Virgilio Pinilla. Both individuals are known to local and federal authorities.
The incident would have been filed as an unsolved (drug-related) murder if a confidential informant in the local P.D. hadn't alerted Wallace to the discovery of the remains of a *third* body in the wreckage.
We determined the source of the explosion to be human in origin — though highly sophisticated and extremely effective. The individual responsible for the blast (see below) was obviously a professional.
It is doubtful that any of the physical evidence collected at the scene will add to our existing body of knowledge — except to positively identify the third entity killed in the explosion as the Primary Target of this investigation.

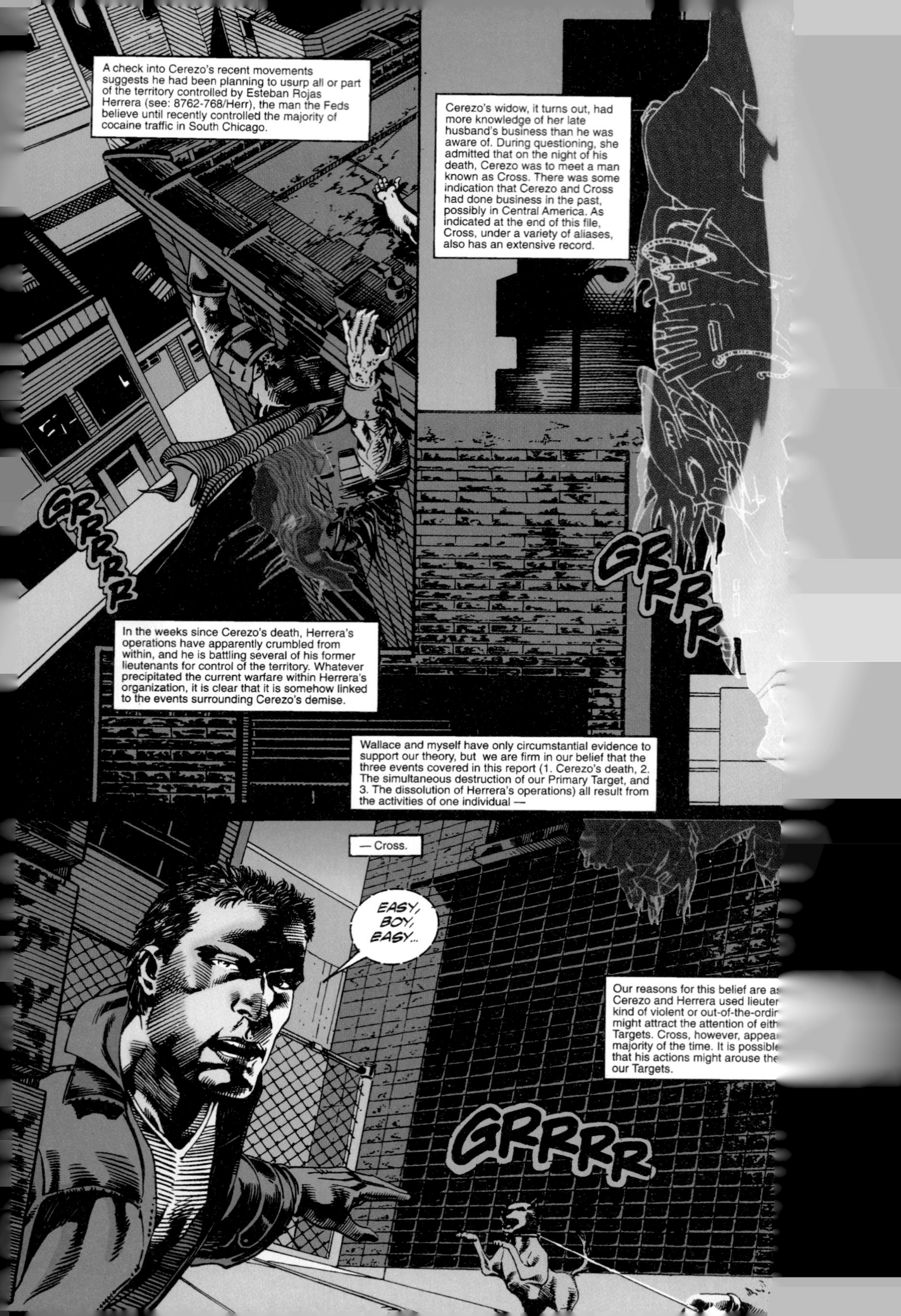
A check into Cerezo's recent movements suggests he had been planning to usurp all or part of the territory controlled by Esteban Rojas Herrera (see: 8762-768/Herr), the man the Feds believe until recently controlled the majority of cocaine traffic in South Chicago.
Cerezo's widow, it turns out, had more knowledge of her late husband's business than he was aware of. During questioning, she admitted that on the night of his death, Cerezo was to meet a man known as Cross. There was some indication that Cerezo and Cross had done business in the past, possibly in Central America. As indicated at the end of this file, Cross, under a variety of aliases, also has an extensive record.
GRRRRR
GRRRR
In the weeks since Cerezo's death, Herrera's operations have apparently crumbled from within, and he is battling several of his former lieutenants for control of the territory. Whatever precipitated the current warfare within Herrera's organization, it is clear that it is somehow linked to the events surrounding Cerezo's demise.
Wallace and myself have only circumstantial evidence to support our theory, but we are firm in our belief that the three events covered in this report (1. Cerezo's death, 2. The simultaneous destruction of our Primary Target, and 3. The dissolution of Herrera's operations) all result from the activities of one individual —
— Cross.
EASY, BOY, EASY...
Our reasons for this belief are as Cerezo and Herrera used lieuter kind of violent or out-of-the-ordir might attract the attention of eith Targets. Cross, however, appear majority of the time. It is possible that his actions might arouse the our Targets.
GRRRRR

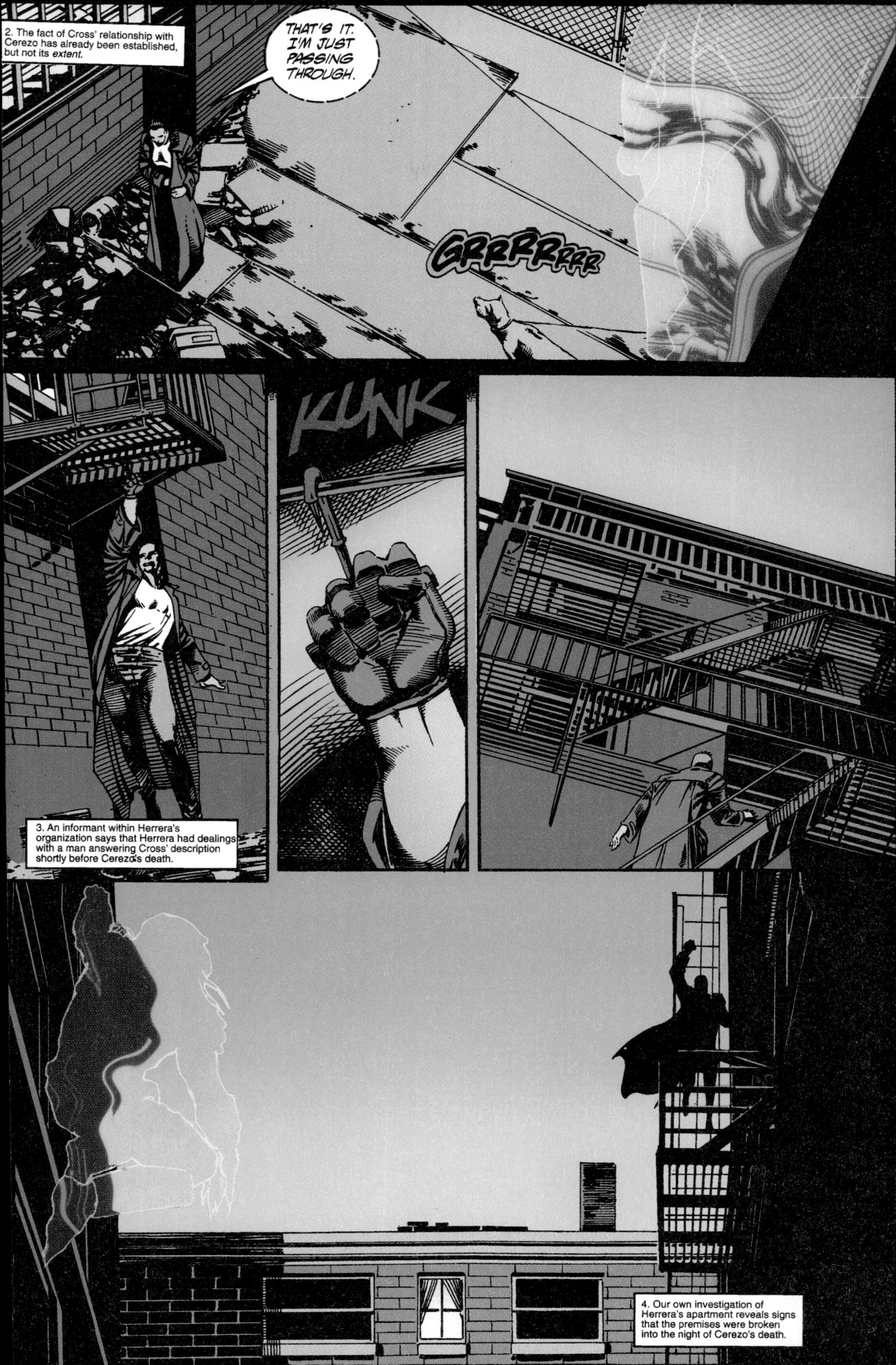
2. The fact of Cross' relationship with Cerezo has already been established, but not its *extent*.
THAT'S IT. I'M JUST PASSING THROUGH.
GRRRRRRR
3. An informant within Herrera's organization says that Herrera had dealings with a man answering Cross' description shortly before Cerezo's death.
KUNK
4. Our own investigation of Herrera's apartment reveals signs that the premises were broken into the night of Cerezo's death.

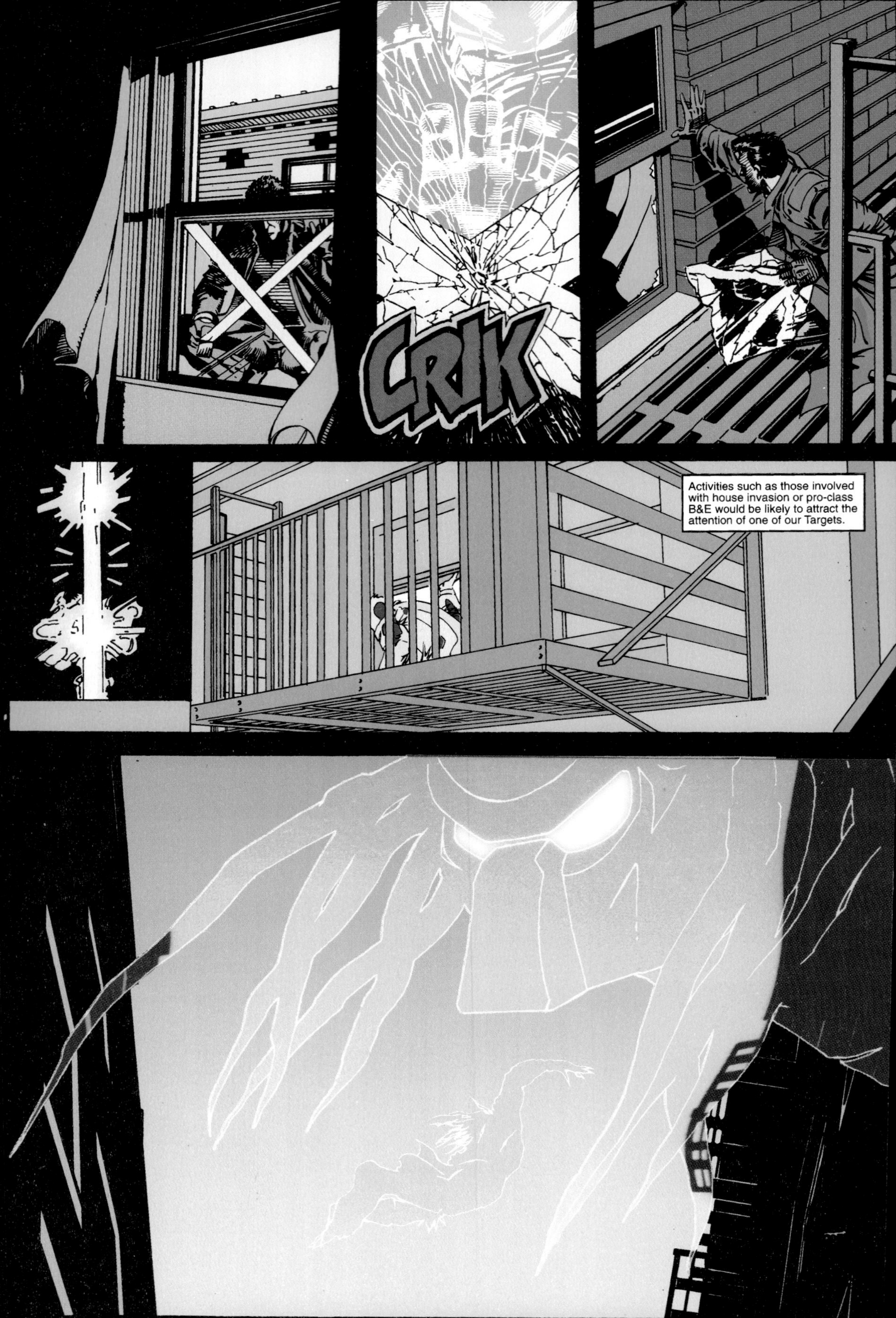
CRIK
Activities such as those involved with house invasion or pro-class B&E would be likely to attract the attention of one of our Targets.

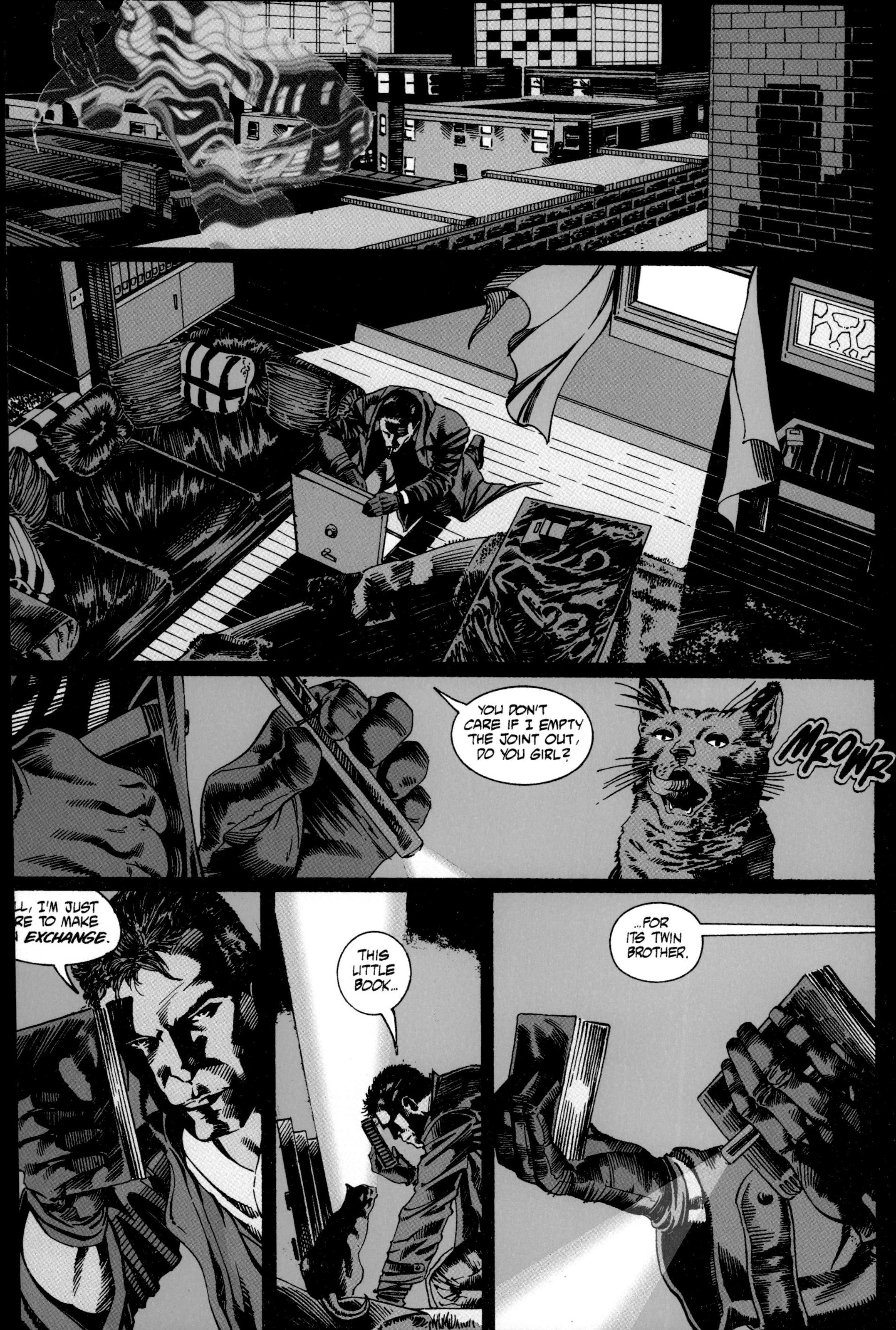
YOU DON'T CARE IF I EMPTY THE JOINT OUT, DO YOU GIRL?
MROWR
LL, I'M JUST RE TO MAKE N EXCHANGE.
THIS LITTLE BOOK...
...FOR ITS TWIN BROTHER.

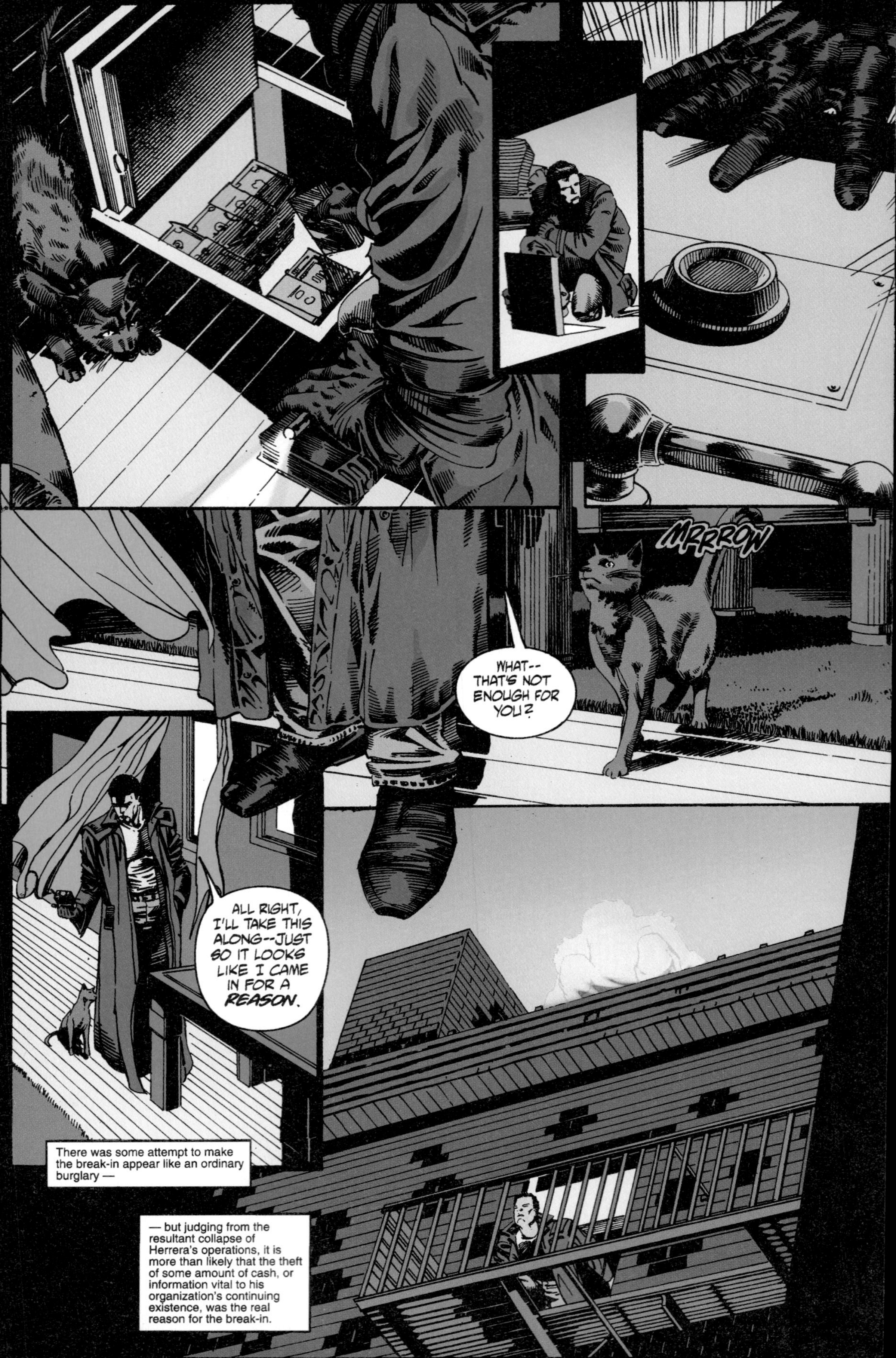
MRRROW
WHAT-- THAT'S NOT ENOUGH FOR YOU?
ALL RIGHT, I'LL TAKE THIS ALONG--JUST SO IT LOOKS LIKE I CAME IN FOR A REASON.
There was some attempt to make the break-in appear like an ordinary burglary —
— but judging from the resultant collapse of Herrera's operations, it is more than likely that the theft of some amount of cash, or information vital to his organization's continuing existence, was the real reason for the break-in.

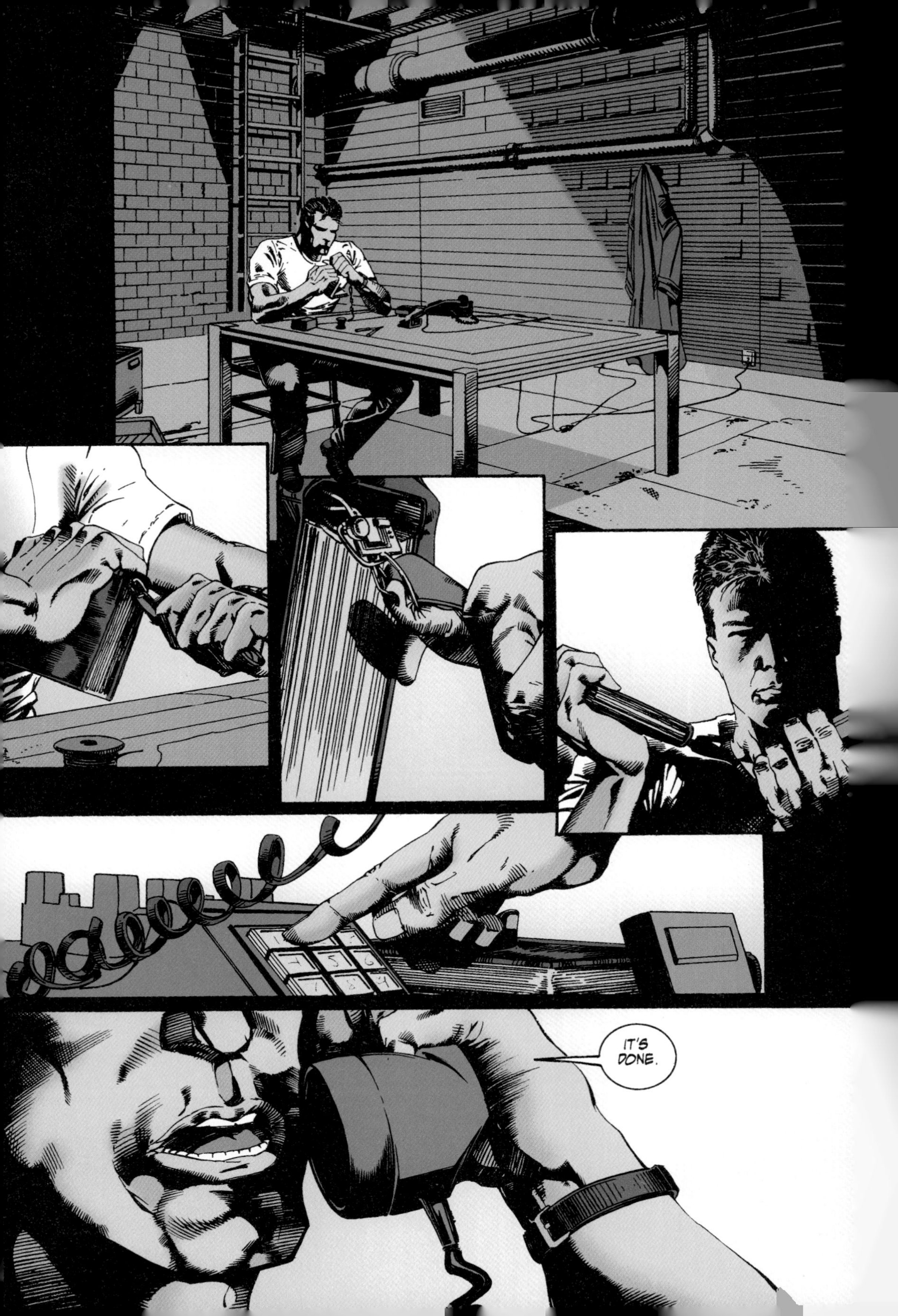
IT'S DONE.

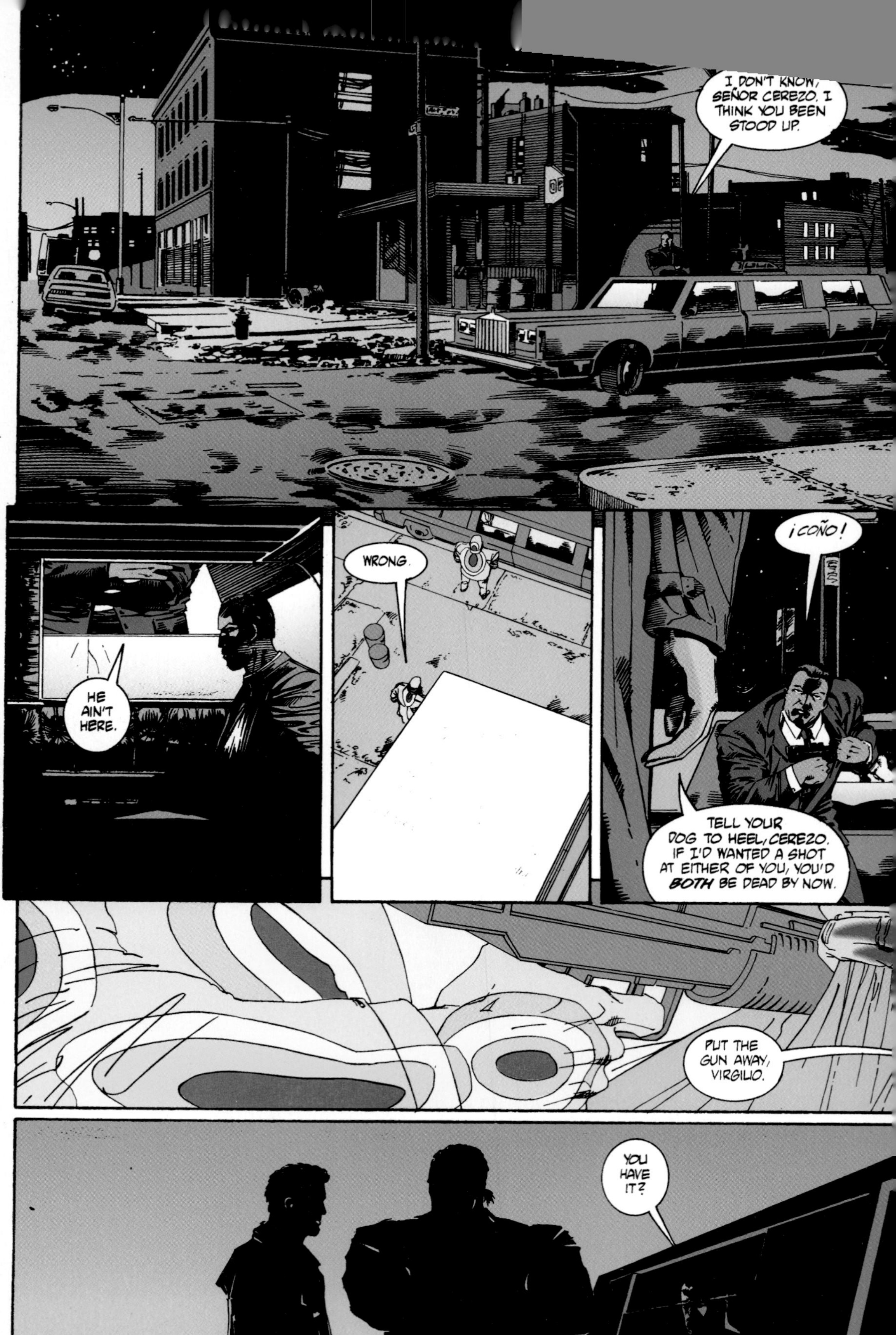

I DON'T KNOW, SEÑOR CEREZO. I THINK YOU BEEN STOOD UP.
HE AIN'T HERE.
WRONG.
¡COÑO!
TELL YOUR DOG TO HEEL, CEREZO. IF I'D WANTED A SHOT AT EITHER OF YOU, YOU'D BOTH BE DEAD BY NOW.
PUT THE GUN AWAY, VIRGILIO.
YOU HAVE IT?

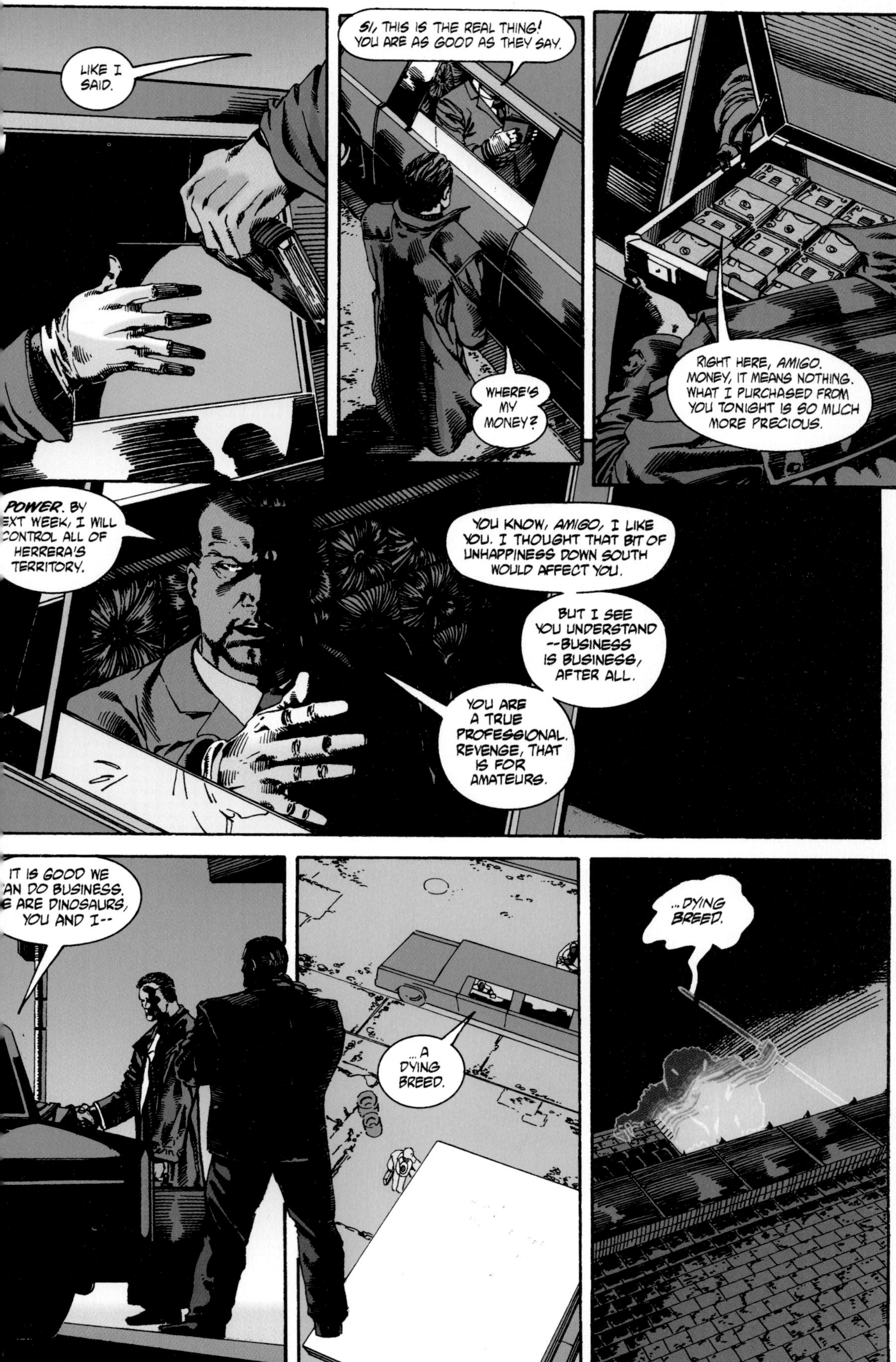
LIKE I SAID.
SI, THIS IS THE REAL THING! YOU ARE AS GOOD AS THEY SAY.
WHERE'S MY MONEY?
RIGHT HERE, AMIGO. MONEY, IT MEANS NOTHING. WHAT I PURCHASED FROM YOU TONIGHT IS SO MUCH MORE PRECIOUS.
POWER. BY EXT WEEK, I WILL CONTROL ALL OF HERRERA'S TERRITORY.
YOU KNOW, AMIGO, I LIKE YOU. I THOUGHT THAT BIT OF UNHAPPINESS DOWN SOUTH WOULD AFFECT YOU.
BUT I SEE YOU UNDERSTAND --BUSINESS IS BUSINESS, AFTER ALL.
YOU ARE A TRUE PROFESSIONAL. REVENGE, THAT IS FOR AMATEURS.
IT IS GOOD WE AN DO BUSINESS. E ARE DINOSAURS, YOU AND I--
...A DYING BREED.
...DYING BREED.

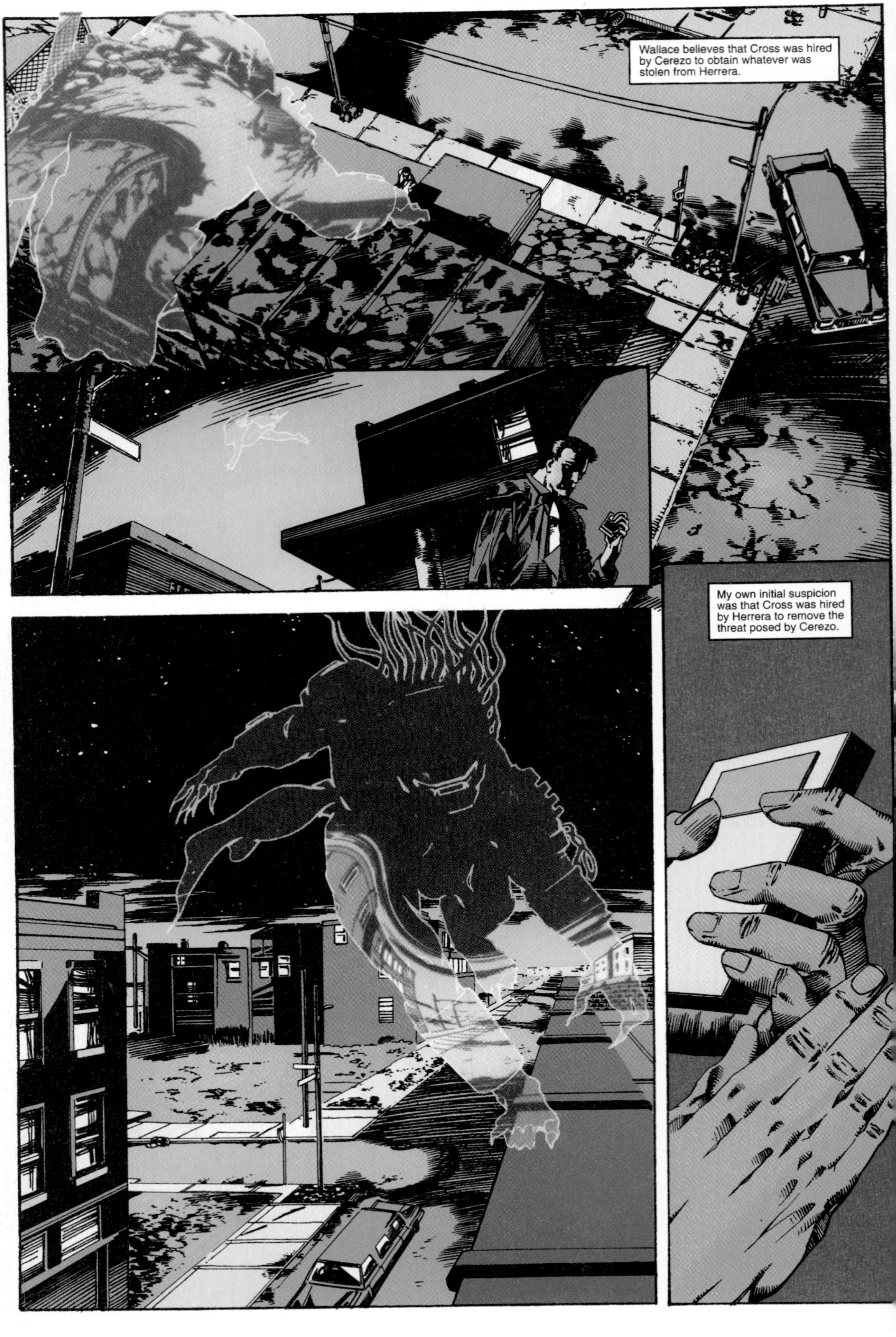
Wallace believes that Cross was hired by Cerezo to obtain whatever was stolen from Herrera.
My own initial suspicion was that Cross was hired by Herrera to remove the threat posed by Cerezo.

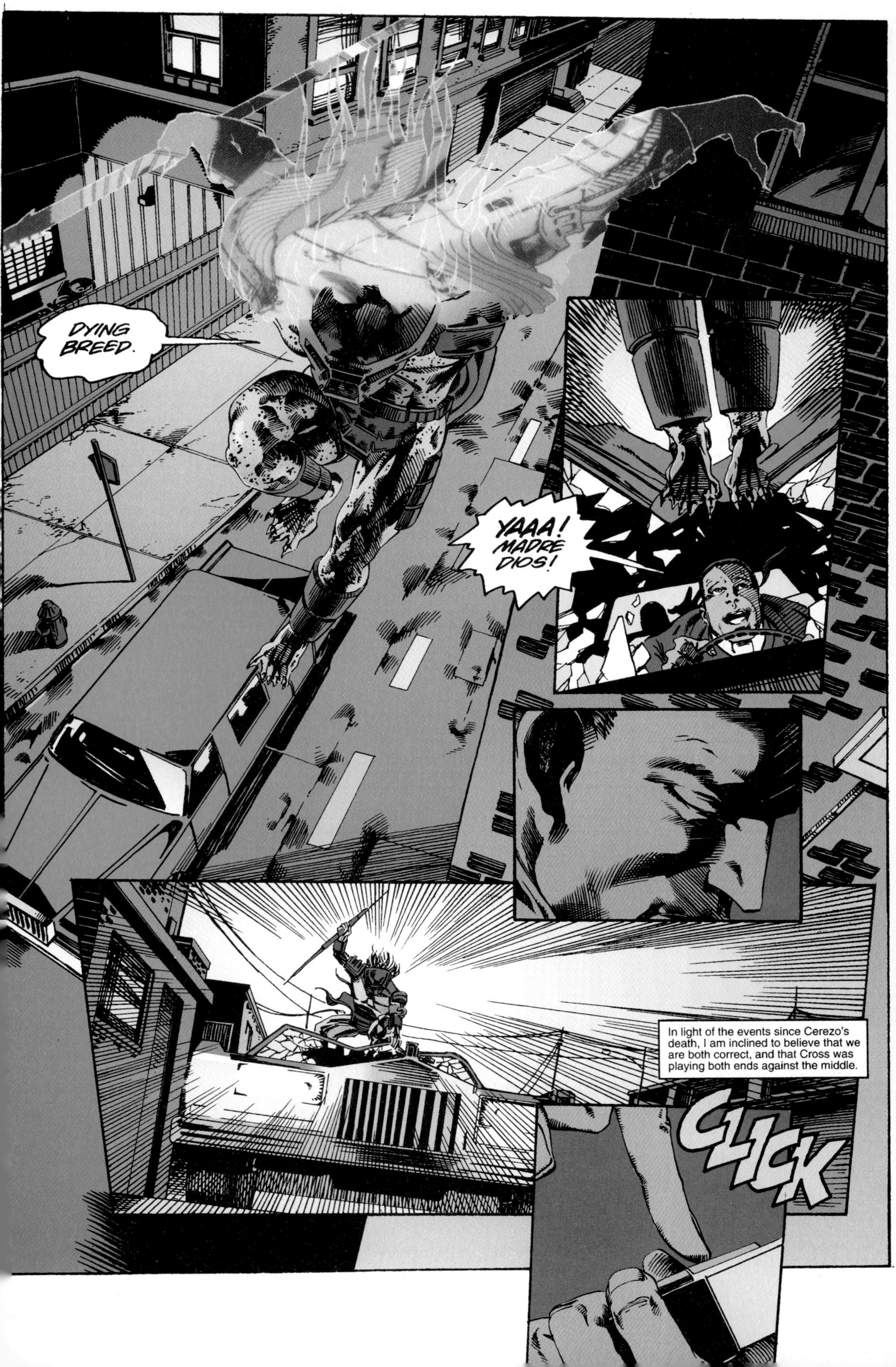
DYING BREED.
YAAA! MADRE DIOS!
In light of the events since Cerezo's death, I am inclined to believe that we are both correct, and that Cross was playing both ends against the middle.
CLICK

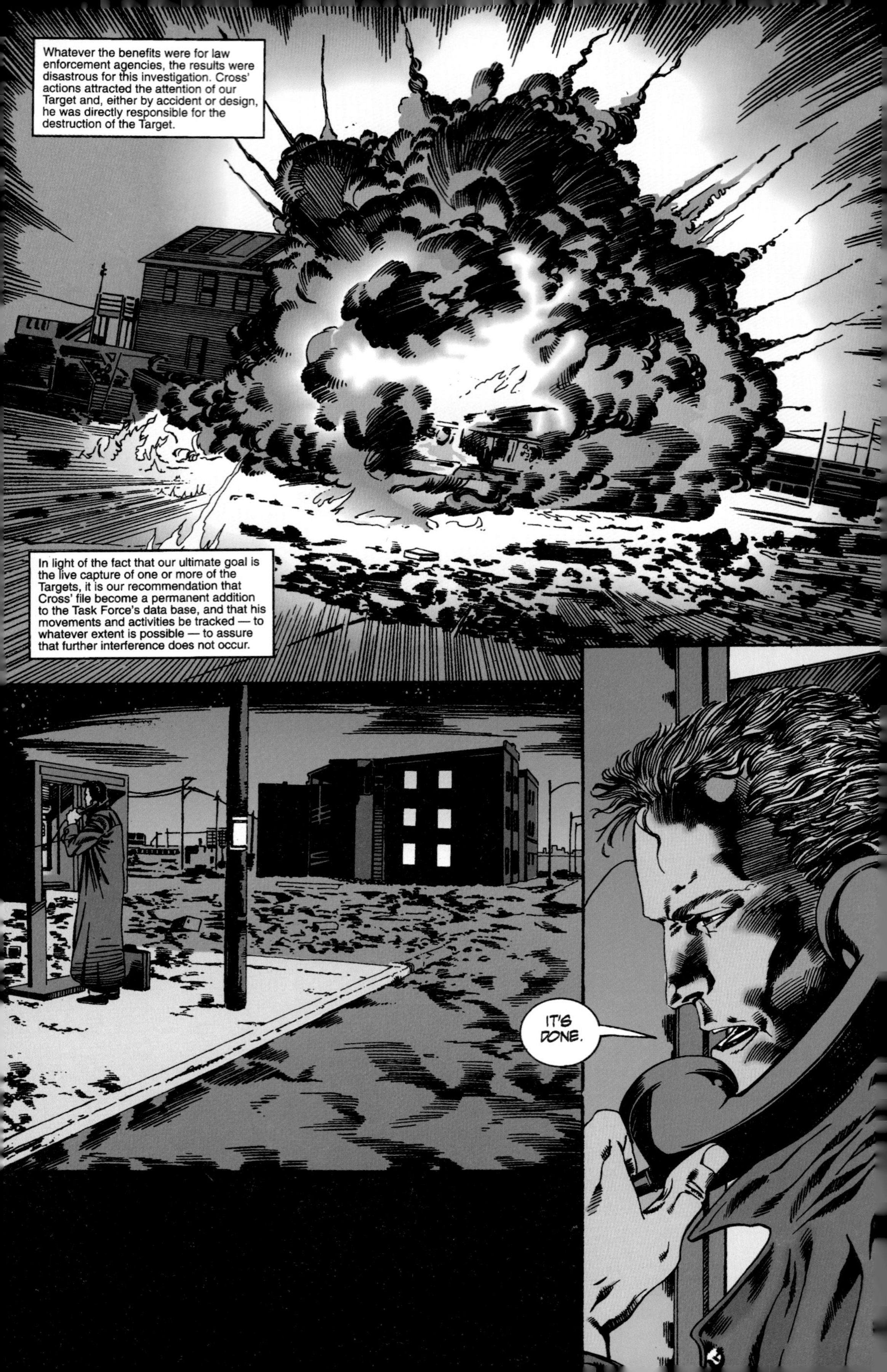
Whatever the benefits were for law enforcement agencies, the results were disastrous for this investigation. Cross' actions attracted the attention of our Target and, either by accident or design, he was directly responsible for the destruction of the Target.
In light of the fact that our ultimate goal is the live capture of one or more of the Targets, it is our recommendation that Cross' file become a permanent addition to the Task Force's data base, and that his movements and activities be tracked — to whatever extent is possible — to assure that further interference does not occur.
IT'S DONE.

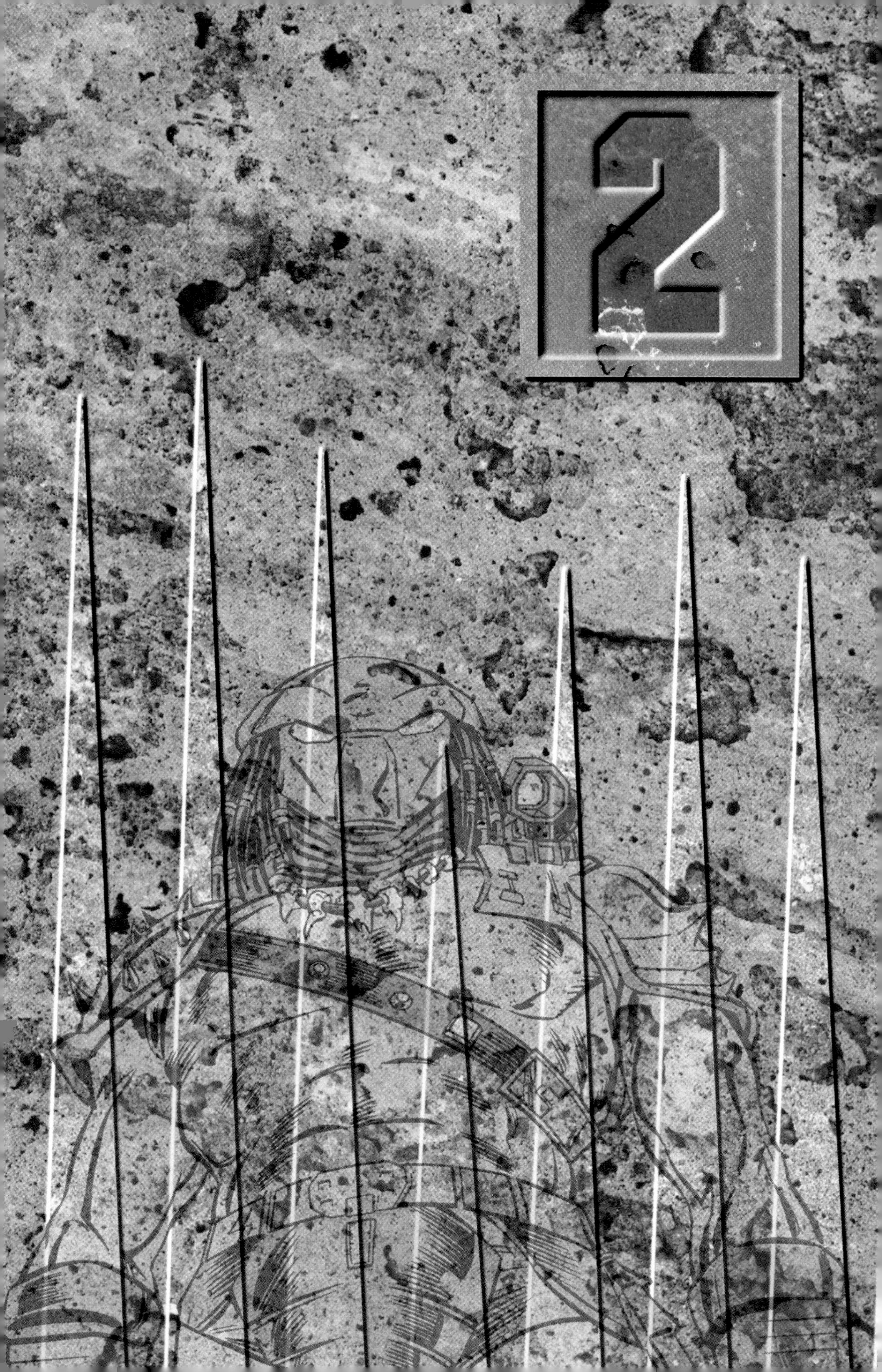
2

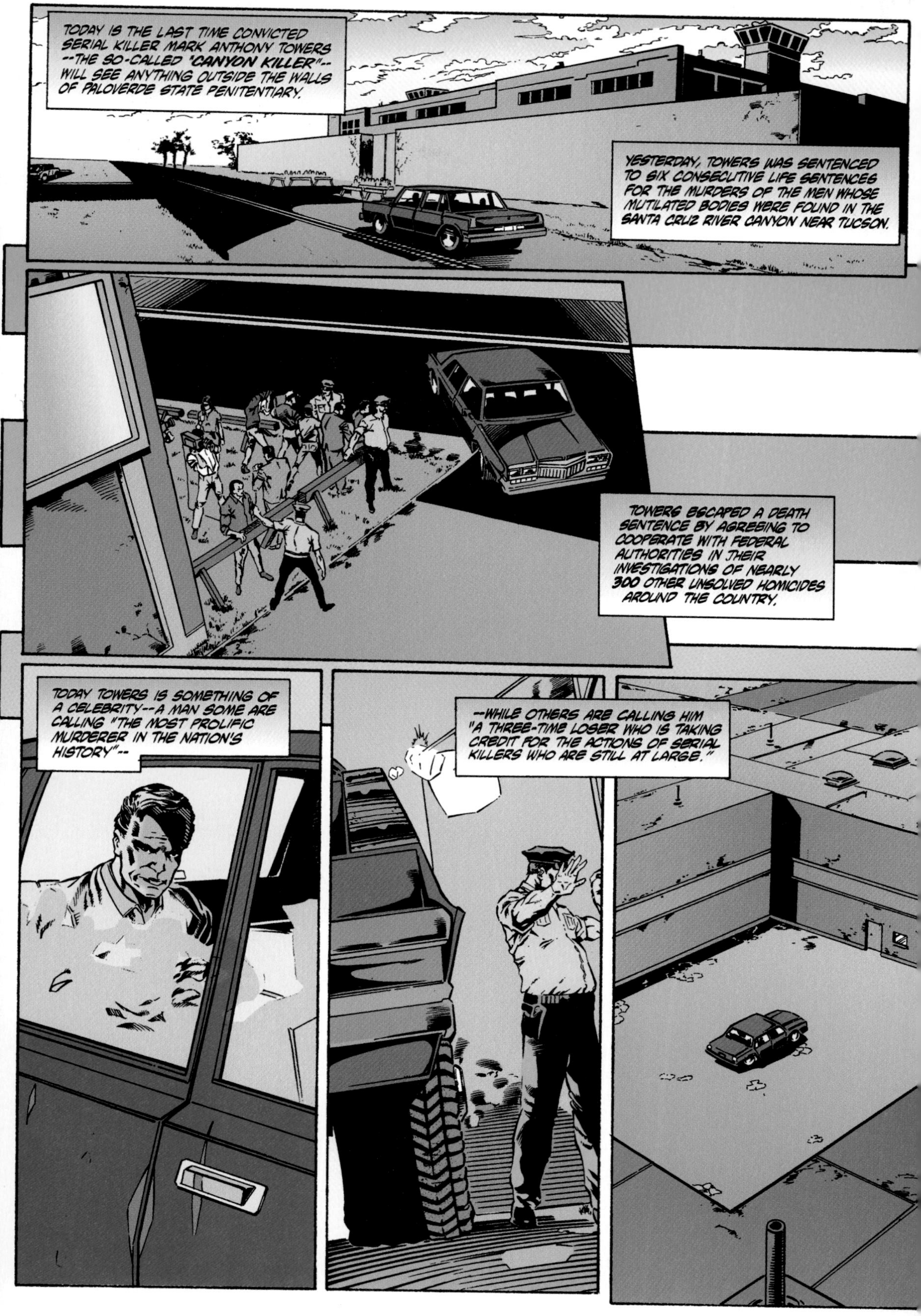
TODAY IS THE LAST TIME CONVICTED SERIAL KILLER MARK ANTHONY TOWERS --THE SO-CALLED "CANYON KILLER"-- WILL SEE ANYTHING OUTSIDE THE WALLS OF PALOVERDE STATE PENITENTIARY.
YESTERDAY, TOWERS WAS SENTENCED TO SIX CONSECUTIVE LIFE SENTENCES FOR THE MURDERS OF THE MEN WHOSE MUTILATED BODIES WERE FOUND IN THE SANTA CRUZ RIVER CANYON NEAR TUCSON.
TOWERS ESCAPED A DEATH SENTENCE BY AGREEING TO COOPERATE WITH FEDERAL AUTHORITIES IN THEIR INVESTIGATIONS OF NEARLY 300 OTHER UNSOLVED HOMICIDES AROUND THE COUNTRY.
TODAY TOWERS IS SOMETHING OF A CELEBRITY--A MAN SOME ARE CALLING "THE MOST PROLIFIC MURDERER IN THE NATION'S HISTORY"--
--WHILE OTHERS ARE CALLING HIM "A THREE-TIME LOSER WHO IS TAKING CREDIT FOR THE ACTIONS OF SERIAL KILLERS WHO ARE STILL AT LARGE."

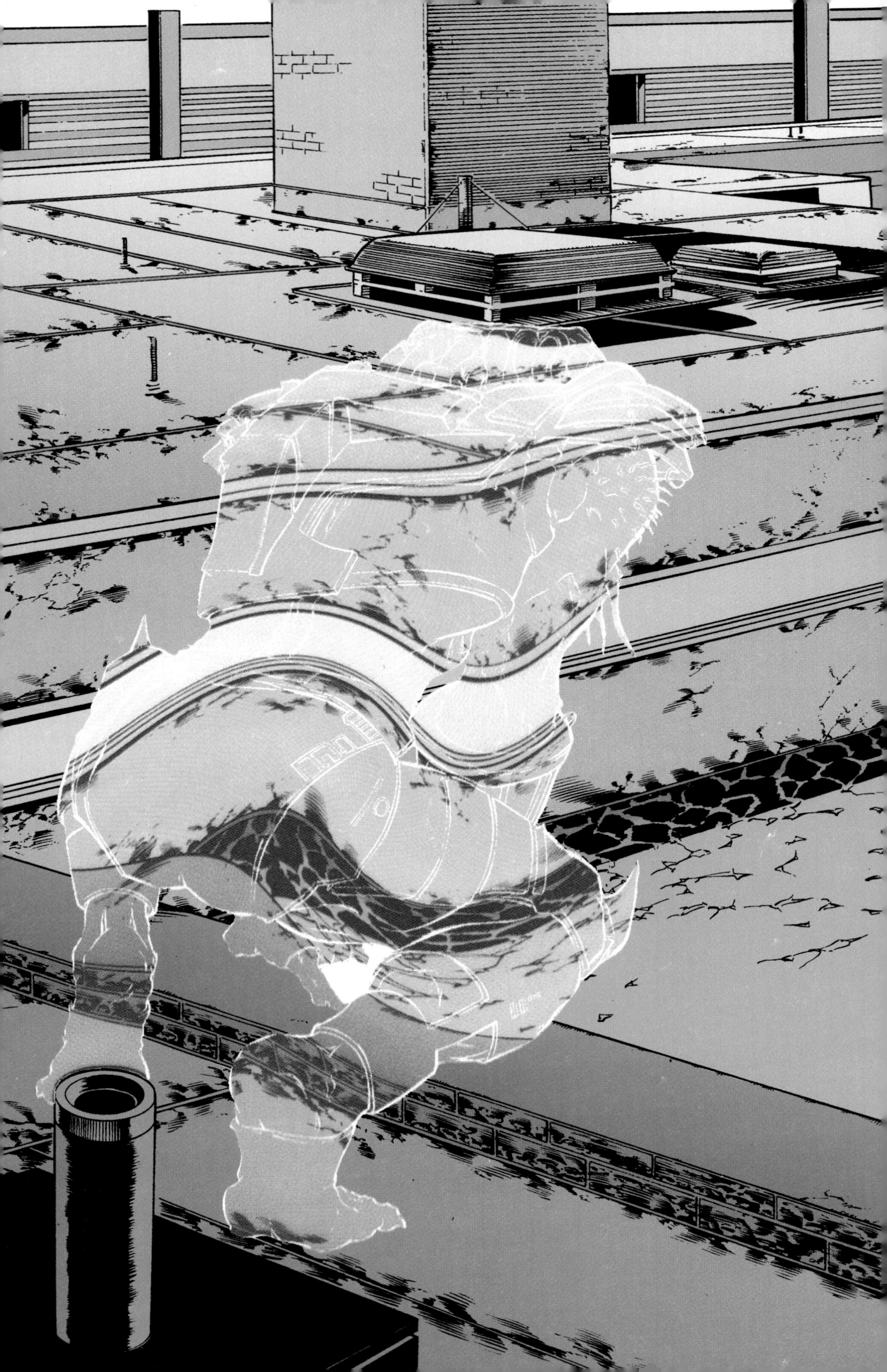

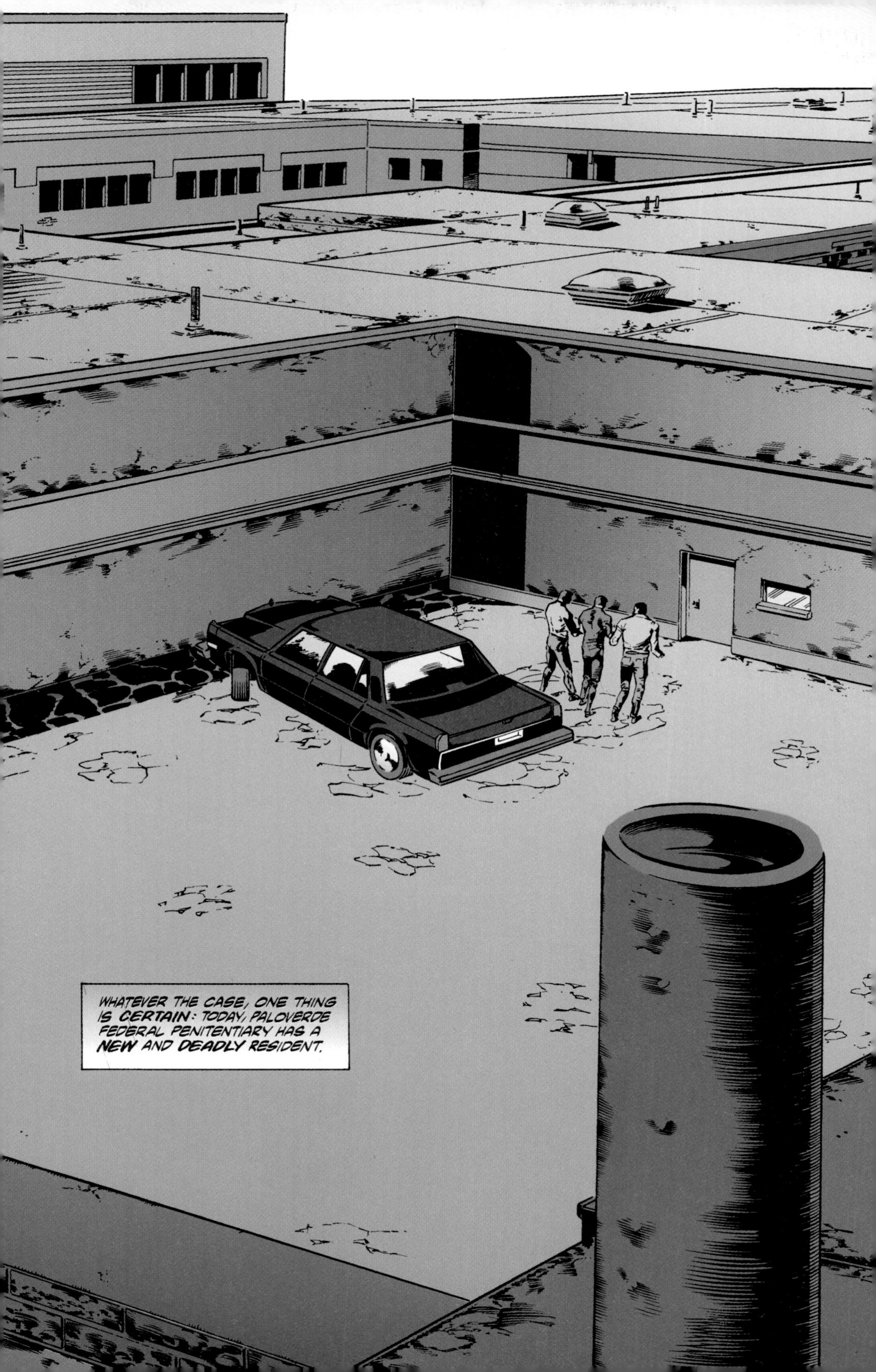
WHATEVER THE CASE, ONE THING IS CERTAIN: TODAY, PALOVERDE FEDERAL PENITENTIARY HAS A NEW AND DEADLY RESIDENT.

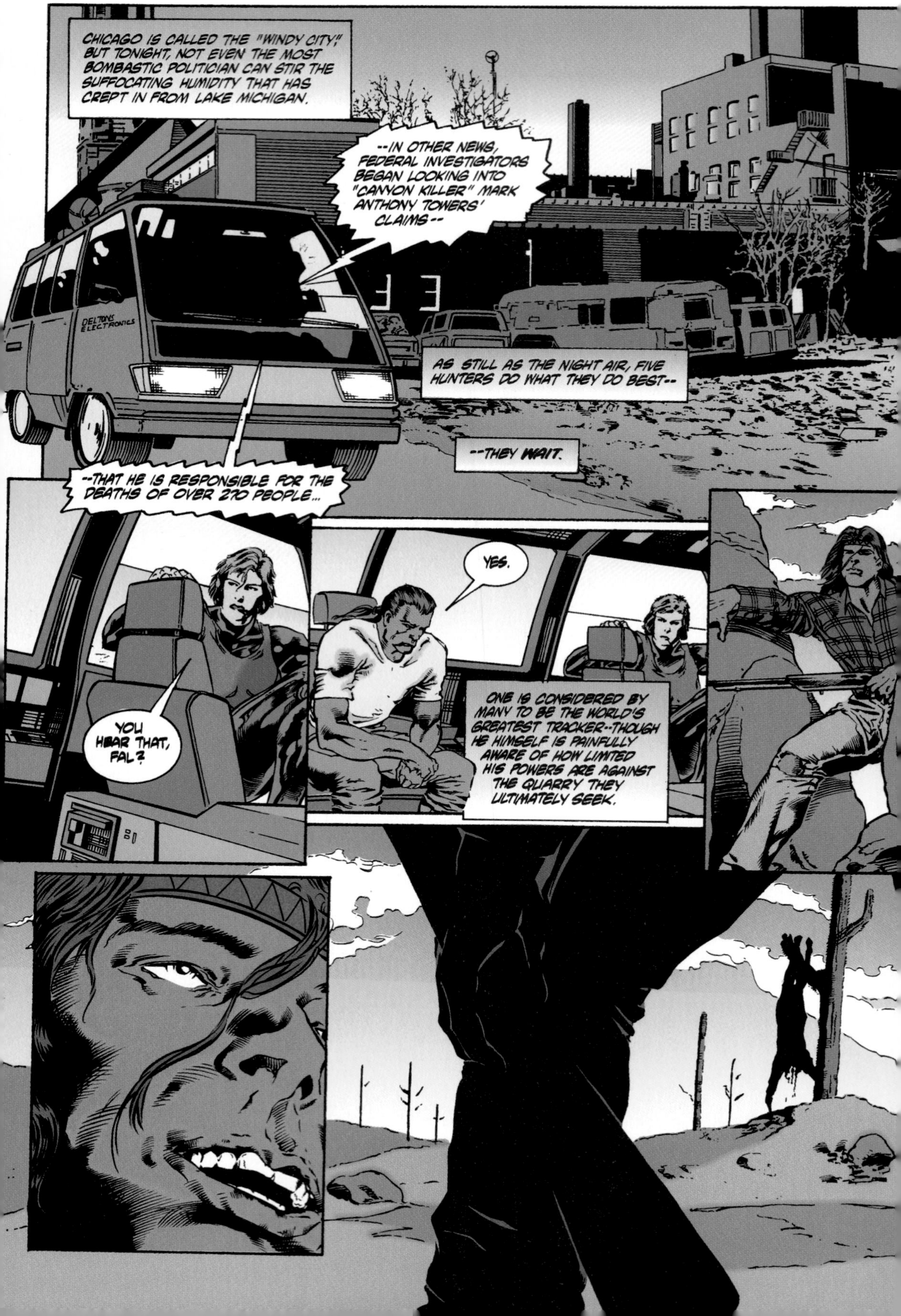
CHICAGO IS CALLED THE "WINDY CITY," BUT TONIGHT, NOT EVEN THE MOST BOMBASTIC POLITICIAN CAN STIR THE SUFFOCATING HUMIDITY THAT HAS CREPT IN FROM LAKE MICHIGAN.
--IN OTHER NEWS, FEDERAL INVESTIGATORS BEGAN LOOKING INTO "CANYON KILLER" MARK ANTHONY TOWERS' CLAIMS--
DELTONS ELECTRONICS
AS STILL AS THE NIGHT AIR, FIVE HUNTERS DO WHAT THEY DO BEST--
--THEY WAIT.
--THAT HE IS RESPONSIBLE FOR THE DEATHS OF OVER 270 PEOPLE...
YOU HEAR THAT, FAL?
YES.
ONE IS CONSIDERED BY MANY TO BE THE WORLD'S GREATEST TRACKER--THOUGH HE HIMSELF IS PAINFULLY AWARE OF HOW LIMITED HIS POWERS ARE AGAINST THE QUARRY THEY ULTIMATELY SEEK.

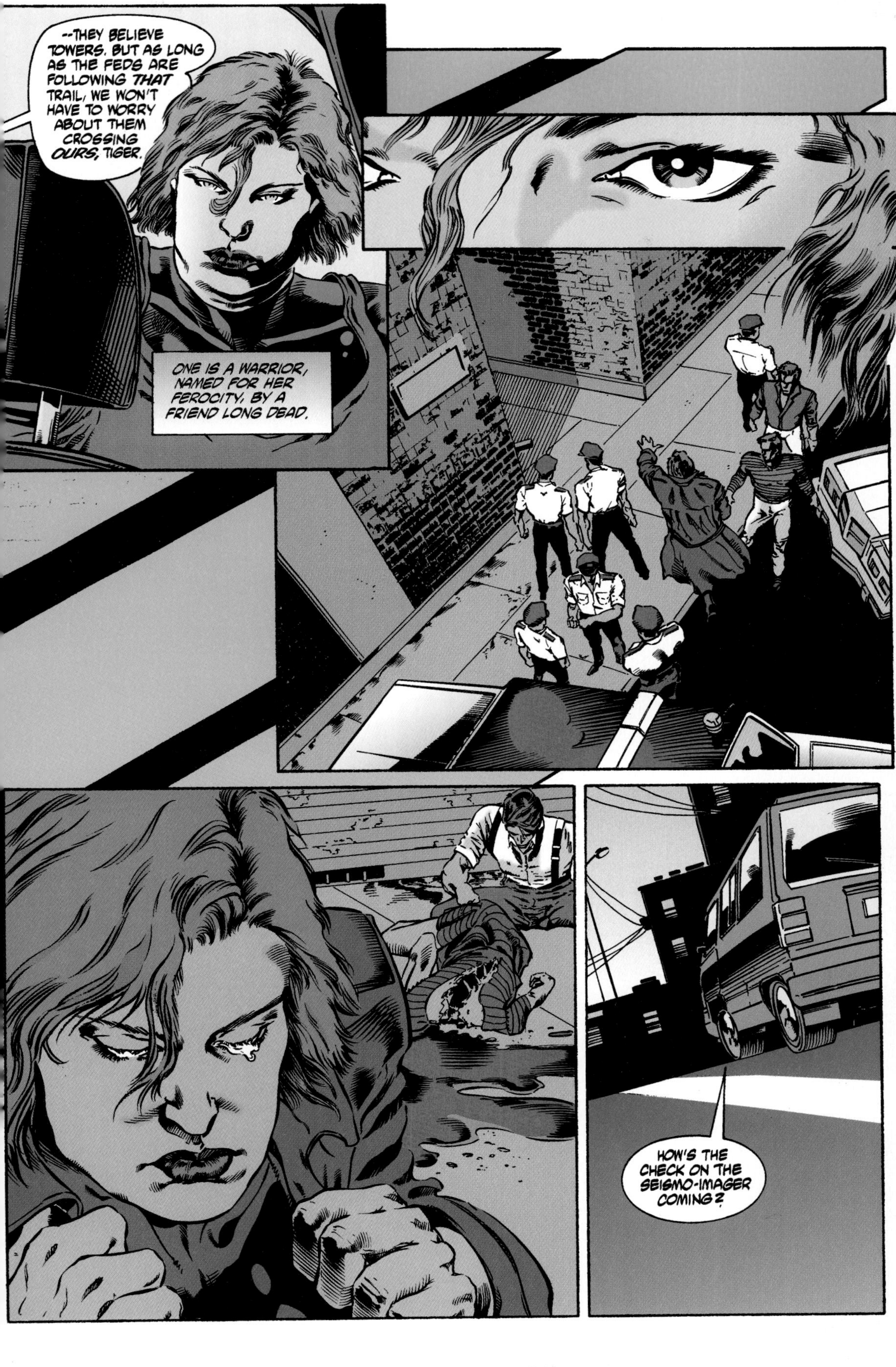
--THEY BELIEVE TOWERS. BUT AS LONG AS THE FEDS ARE FOLLOWING *THAT* TRAIL, WE WON'T HAVE TO WORRY ABOUT THEM CROSSING *OURS*, TIGER.
ONE IS A WARRIOR, NAMED FOR HER FEROCITY, BY A FRIEND LONG DEAD.
HOW'S THE CHECK ON THE SEISMO-IMAGER COMING?

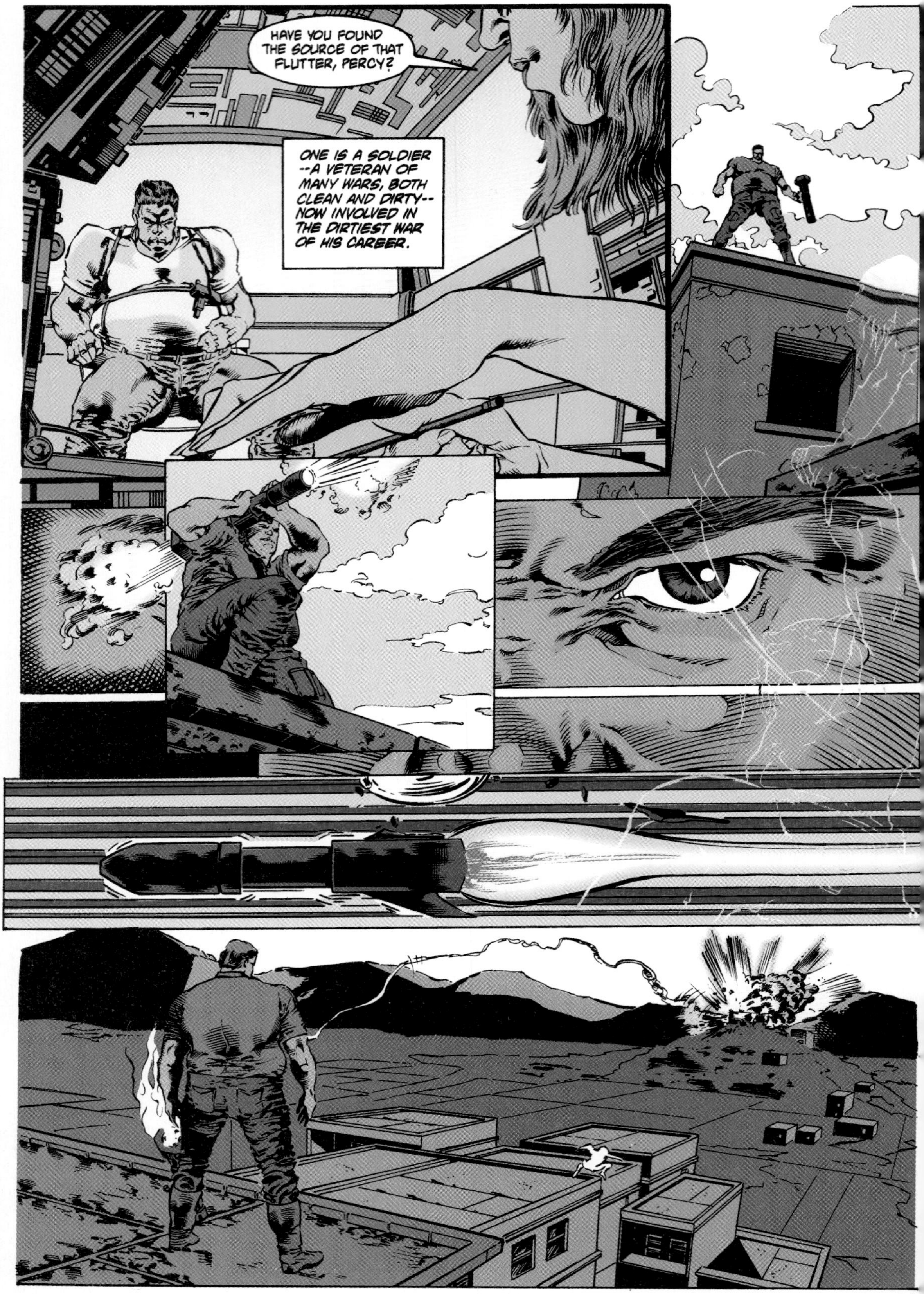
HAVE YOU FOUND THE SOURCE OF THAT FLUTTER, PERCY?
ONE IS A SOLDIER --A VETERAN OF MANY WARS, BOTH CLEAN AND DIRTY-- NOW INVOLVED IN THE DIRTIEST WAR OF HIS CAREER.

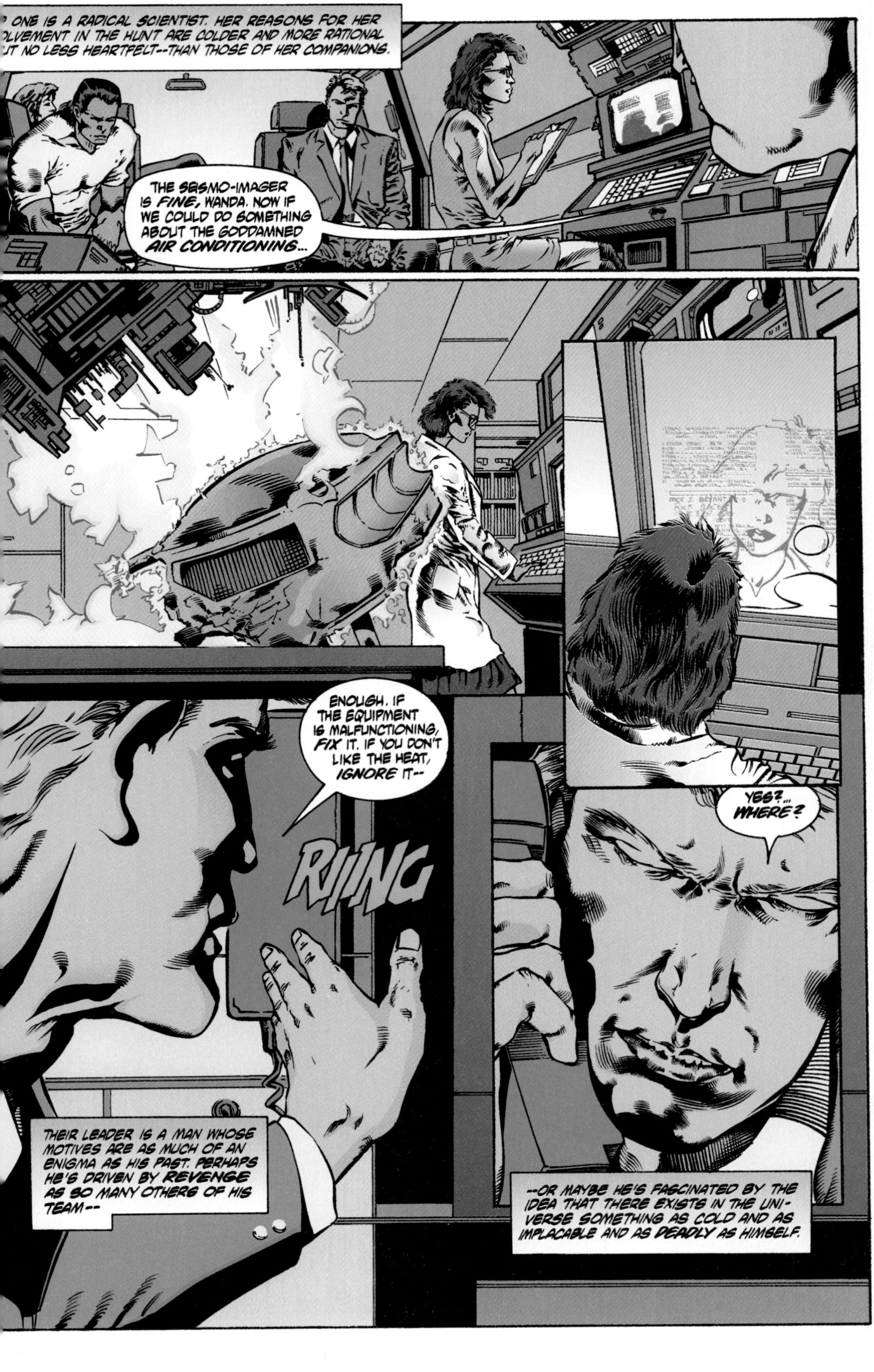
ONE IS A RADICAL SCIENTIST. HER REASONS FOR HER
OLVEMENT IN THE HUNT ARE COLDER AND MORE RATIONAL
T NO LESS HEARTFELT--THAN THOSE OF HER COMPANIONS.
THE SEISMO-IMAGER IS FINE, WANDA. NOW IF WE COULD DO SOMETHING ABOUT THE GODDAMNED AIR CONDITIONING...
ENOUGH. IF THE EQUIPMENT IS MALFUNCTIONING, FIX IT. IF YOU DON'T LIKE THE HEAT, IGNORE IT--
RIIING
YES?... WHERE?
THEIR LEADER IS A MAN WHOSE MOTIVES ARE AS MUCH OF AN ENIGMA AS HIS PAST. PERHAPS HE'S DRIVEN BY REVENGE AS SO MANY OTHERS OF HIS TEAM--
--OR MAYBE HE'S FASCINATED BY THE IDEA THAT THERE EXISTS IN THE UNIVERSE SOMETHING AS COLD AND AS IMPLACABLE AND AS DEADLY AS HIMSELF.

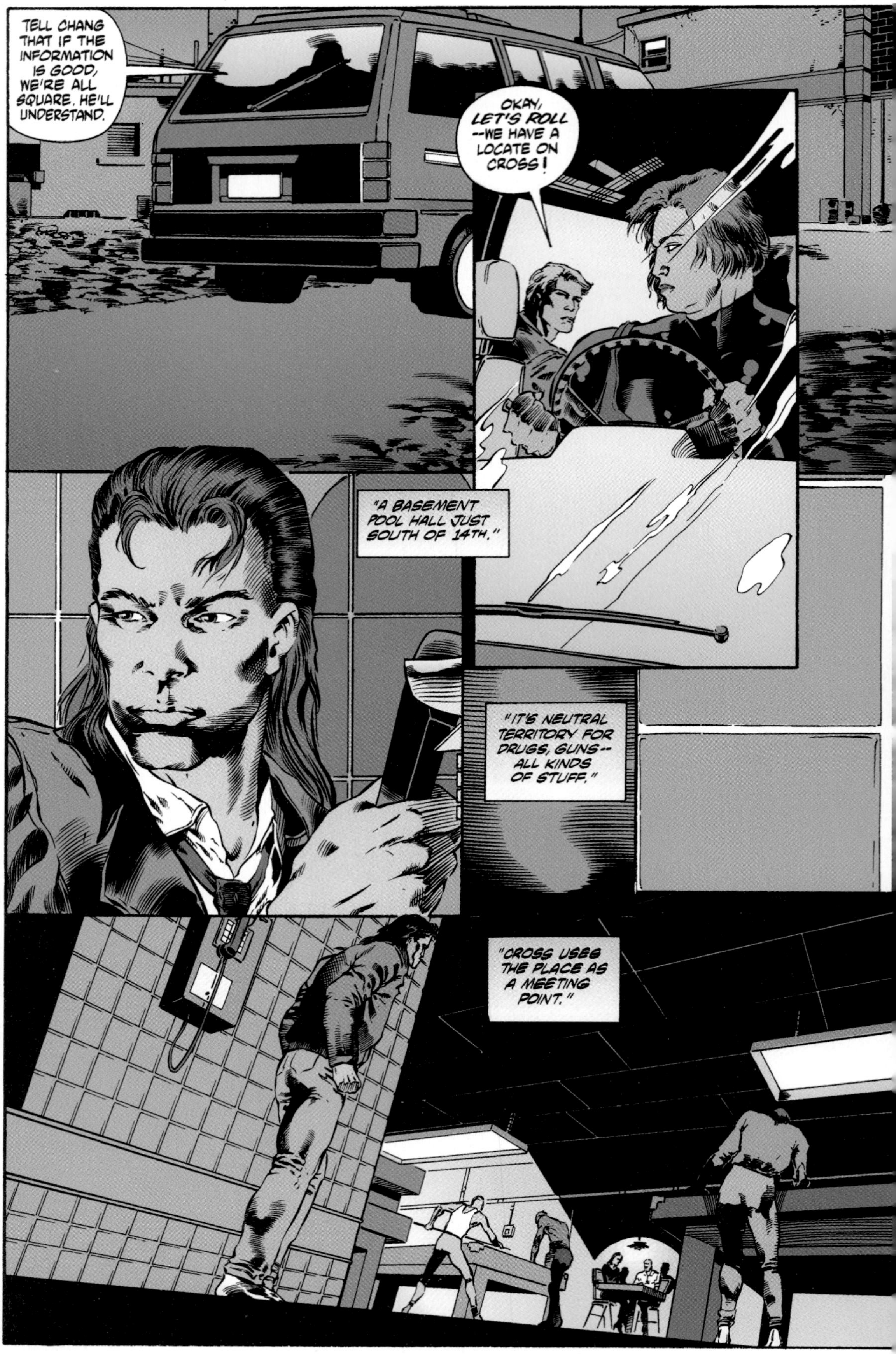
TELL CHANG THAT IF THE INFORMATION IS GOOD, WE'RE ALL SQUARE. HE'LL UNDERSTAND.
OKAY, LET'S ROLL --WE HAVE A LOCATE ON CROSS!
"A BASEMENT POOL HALL JUST SOUTH OF 14TH."
"IT'S NEUTRAL TERRITORY FOR DRUGS, GUNS-- ALL KINDS OF STUFF."
"CROSS USES THE PLACE AS A MEETING POINT."

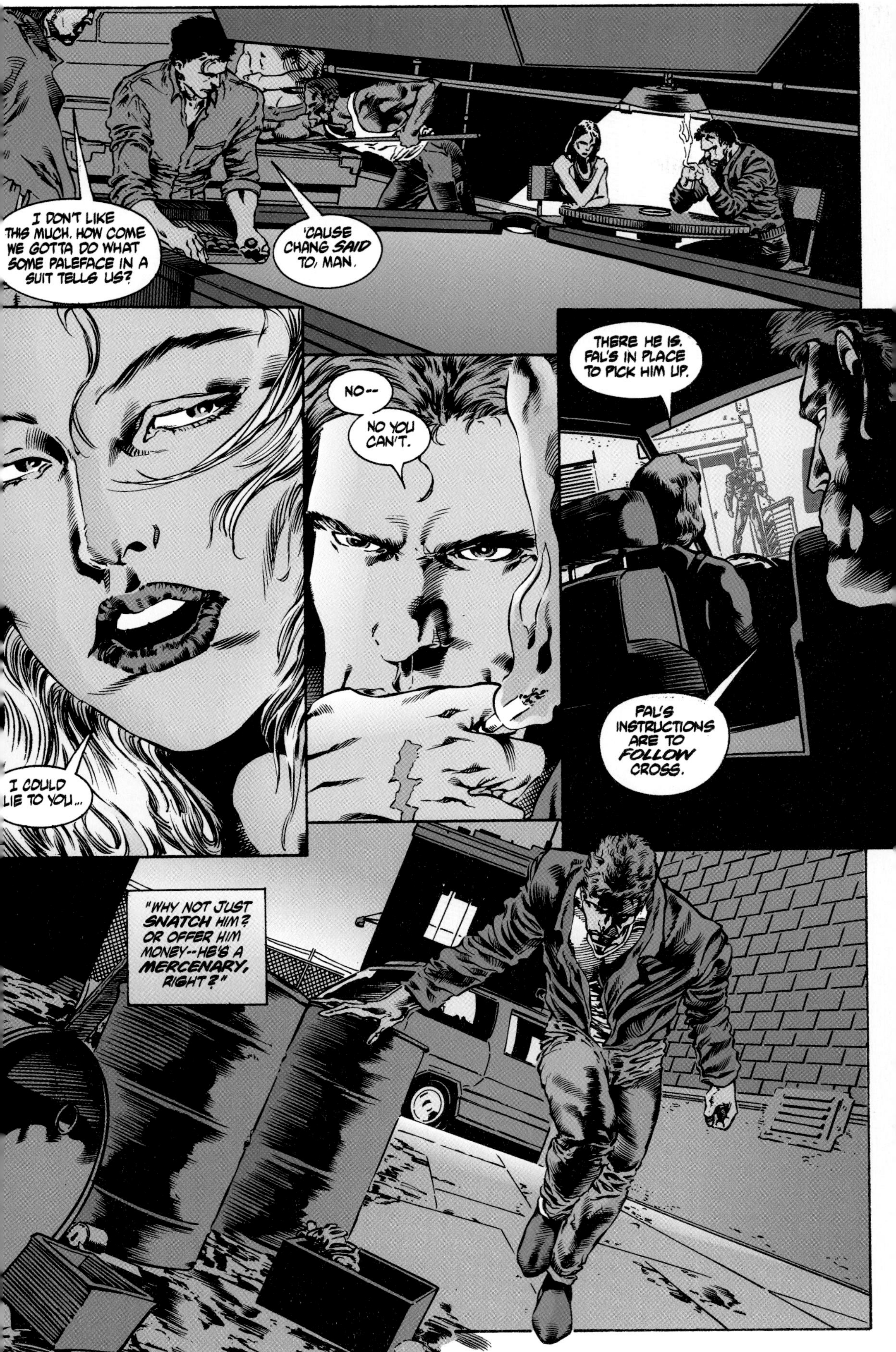
I DON'T LIKE THIS MUCH. HOW COME WE GOTTA DO WHAT SOME PALEFACE IN A SUIT TELLS US?
'CAUSE CHANG SAID TO, MAN.
I COULD LIE TO YOU...
NO--
NO YOU CAN'T.
THERE HE IS. FAL'S IN PLACE TO PICK HIM UP.
FAL'S INSTRUCTIONS ARE TO FOLLOW CROSS.
"WHY NOT JUST SNATCH HIM? OR OFFER HIM MONEY--HE'S A MERCENARY, RIGHT?"

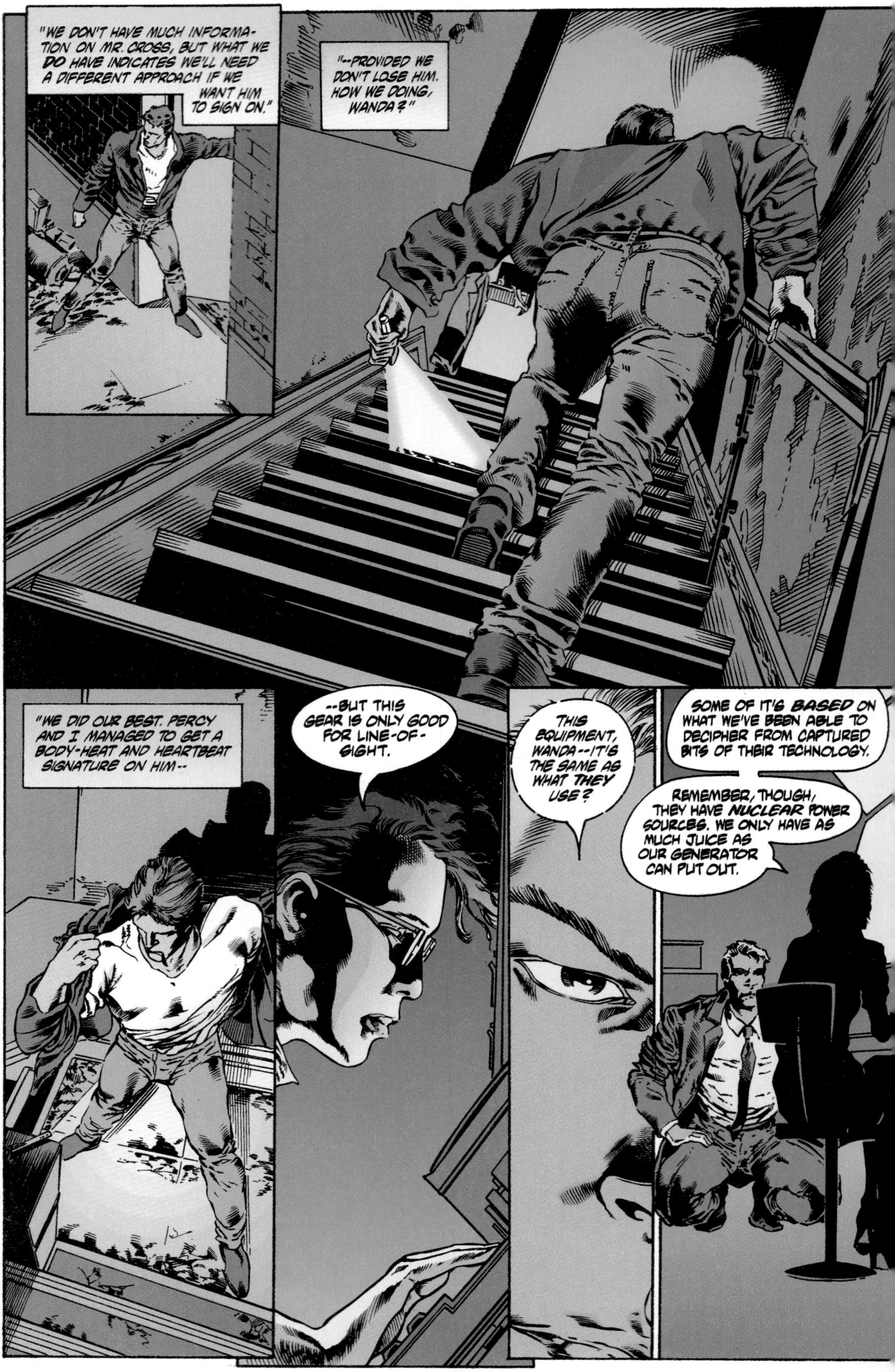
"WE DON'T HAVE MUCH INFORMATION ON MR. CROSS, BUT WHAT WE DO HAVE INDICATES WE'LL NEED A DIFFERENT APPROACH IF WE WANT HIM TO SIGN ON."
"--PROVIDED WE DON'T LOSE HIM. HOW WE DOING, WANDA?"
"WE DID OUR BEST. PERCY AND I MANAGED TO GET A BODY-HEAT AND HEARTBEAT SIGNATURE ON HIM--
--BUT THIS GEAR IS ONLY GOOD FOR LINE-OF-SIGHT.
THIS EQUIPMENT, WANDA--IT'S THE SAME AS WHAT THEY USE?
SOME OF IT'S BASED ON WHAT WE'VE BEEN ABLE TO DECIPHER FROM CAPTURED BITS OF THEIR TECHNOLOGY.
REMEMBER, THOUGH, THEY HAVE NUCLEAR POWER SOURCES. WE ONLY HAVE AS MUCH JUICE AS OUR GENERATOR CAN PUT OUT.

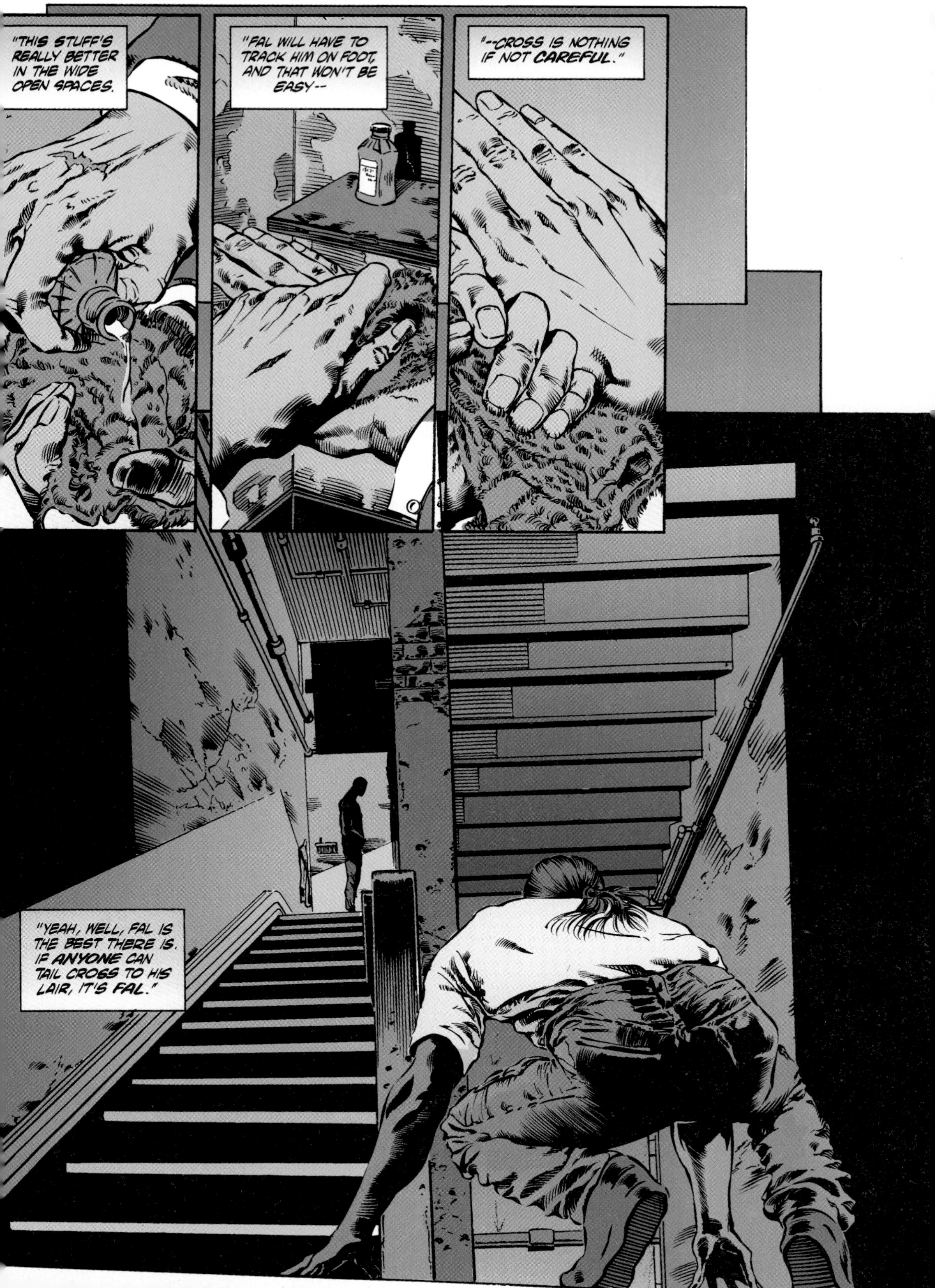
"THIS STUFF'S REALLY BETTER IN THE WIDE OPEN SPACES.
"FAL WILL HAVE TO TRACK HIM ON FOOT, AND THAT WON'T BE EASY--
"--CROSS IS NOTHING IF NOT CAREFUL."
"YEAH, WELL, FAL IS THE BEST THERE IS. IF ANYONE CAN TAIL CROSS TO HIS LAIR, IT'S FAL."

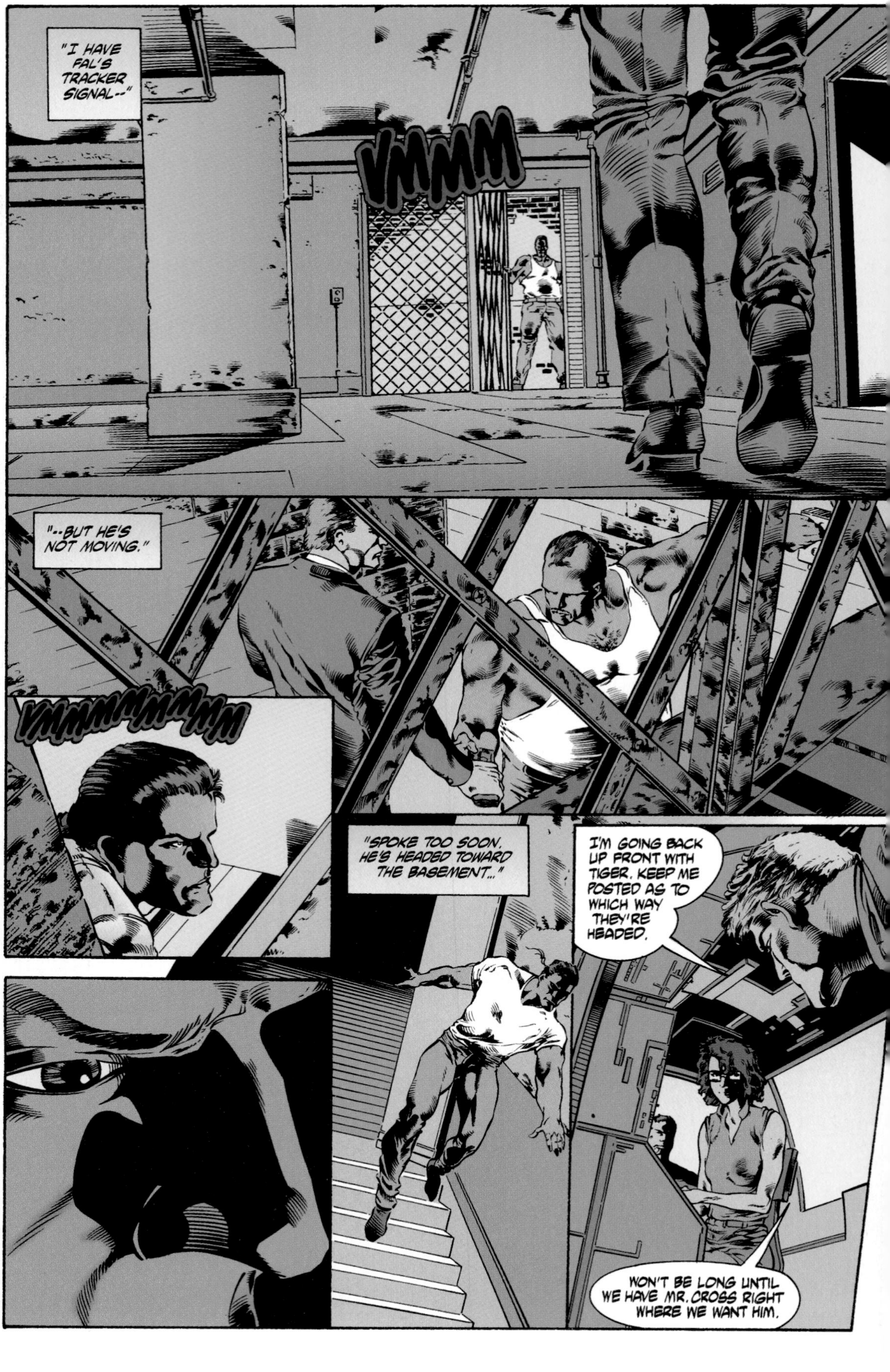
"I HAVE FAL'S TRACKER SIGNAL--"
VMMM
"--BUT HE'S NOT MOVING."
VMMMMMMMMM
"SPOKE TOO SOON. HE'S HEADED TOWARD THE BASEMENT..."
I'M GOING BACK UP FRONT WITH TIGER. KEEP ME POSTED AS TO WHICH WAY THEY'RE HEADED.
WON'T BE LONG UNTIL WE HAVE MR. CROSS RIGHT WHERE WE WANT HIM.

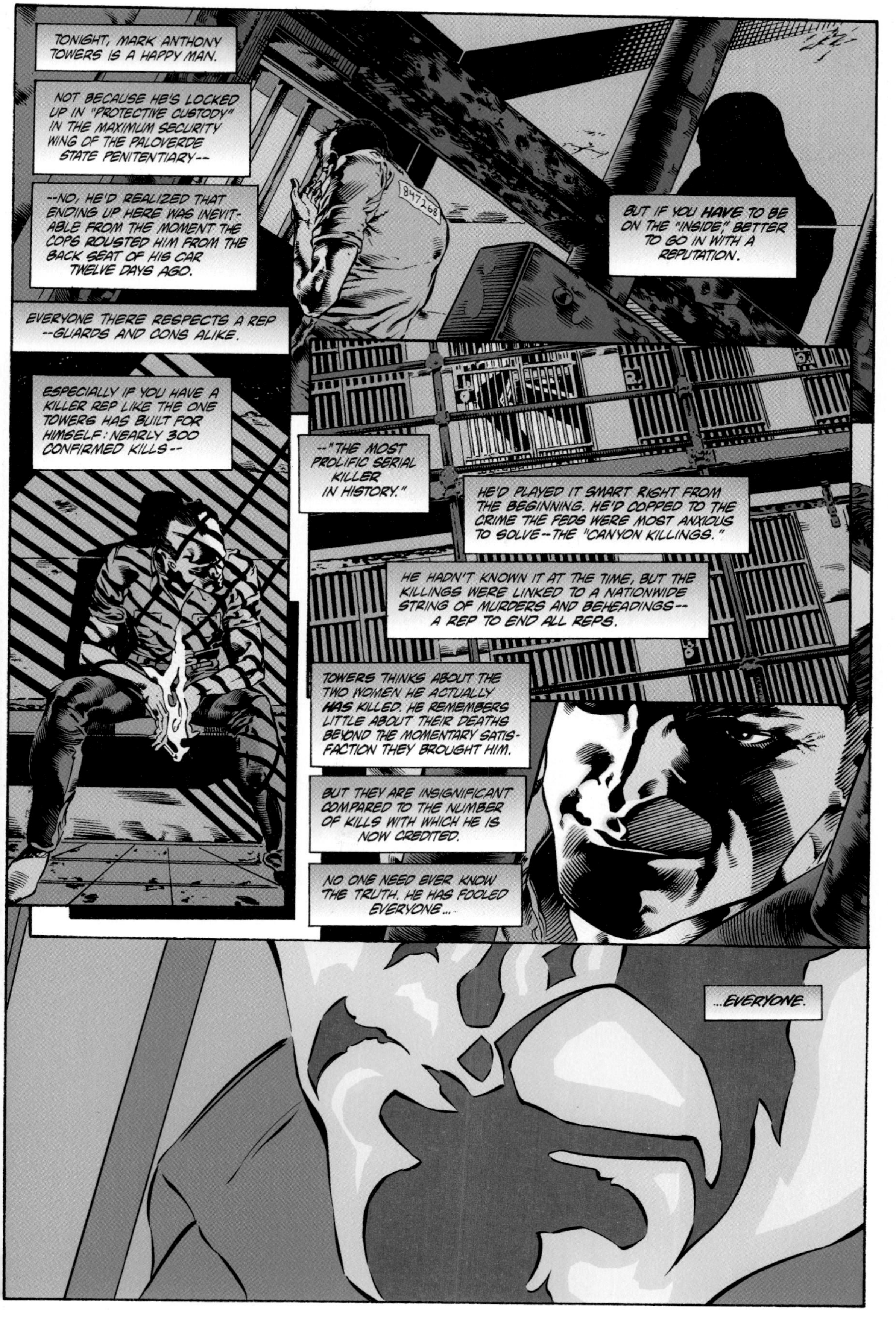
TONIGHT, MARK ANTHONY TOWERS IS A HAPPY MAN.
NOT BECAUSE HE'S LOCKED UP IN "PROTECTIVE CUSTODY" IN THE MAXIMUM SECURITY WING OF THE PALOVERDE STATE PENITENTIARY--
--NO, HE'D REALIZED THAT ENDING UP HERE WAS INEVITABLE FROM THE MOMENT THE COPS ROUSTED HIM FROM THE BACK SEAT OF HIS CAR TWELVE DAYS AGO.
847268
BUT IF YOU HAVE TO BE ON THE "INSIDE," BETTER TO GO IN WITH A REPUTATION.
EVERYONE THERE RESPECTS A REP --GUARDS AND CONS ALIKE.
ESPECIALLY IF YOU HAVE A KILLER REP LIKE THE ONE TOWERS HAS BUILT FOR HIMSELF: NEARLY 300 CONFIRMED KILLS--
--"THE MOST PROLIFIC SERIAL KILLER IN HISTORY."
HE'D PLAYED IT SMART RIGHT FROM THE BEGINNING. HE'D COPPED TO THE CRIME THE FEDS WERE MOST ANXIOUS TO SOLVE--THE "CANYON KILLINGS."
HE HADN'T KNOWN IT AT THE TIME, BUT THE KILLINGS WERE LINKED TO A NATIONWIDE STRING OF MURDERS AND BEHEADINGS-- A REP TO END ALL REPS.
TOWERS THINKS ABOUT THE TWO WOMEN HE ACTUALLY HAS KILLED. HE REMEMBERS LITTLE ABOUT THEIR DEATHS BEYOND THE MOMENTARY SATISFACTION THEY BROUGHT HIM.
BUT THEY ARE INSIGNIFICANT COMPARED TO THE NUMBER OF KILLS WITH WHICH HE IS NOW CREDITED.
NO ONE NEED EVER KNOW THE TRUTH. HE HAS FOOLED EVERYONE...
...EVERYONE.

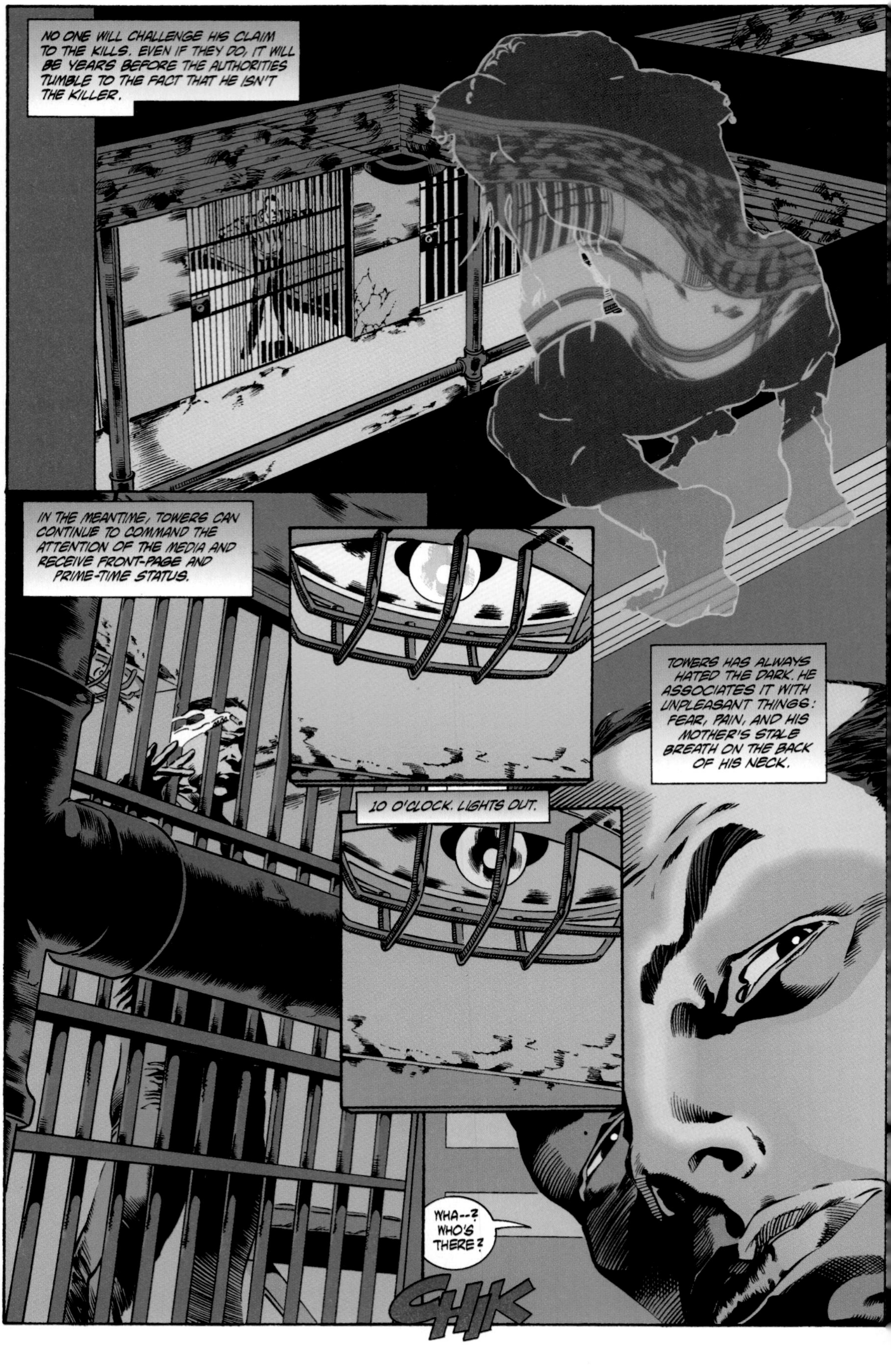
NO ONE WILL CHALLENGE HIS CLAIM TO THE KILLS. EVEN IF THEY DO, IT WILL BE YEARS BEFORE THE AUTHORITIES TUMBLE TO THE FACT THAT HE ISN'T THE KILLER.
IN THE MEANTIME, TOWERS CAN CONTINUE TO COMMAND THE ATTENTION OF THE MEDIA AND RECEIVE FRONT-PAGE AND PRIME-TIME STATUS.
TOWERS HAS ALWAYS HATED THE DARK. HE ASSOCIATES IT WITH UNPLEASANT THINGS: FEAR, PAIN, AND HIS MOTHER'S STALE BREATH ON THE BACK OF HIS NECK.
10 O'CLOCK. LIGHTS OUT.
WHA--? WHO'S THERE?
CHK

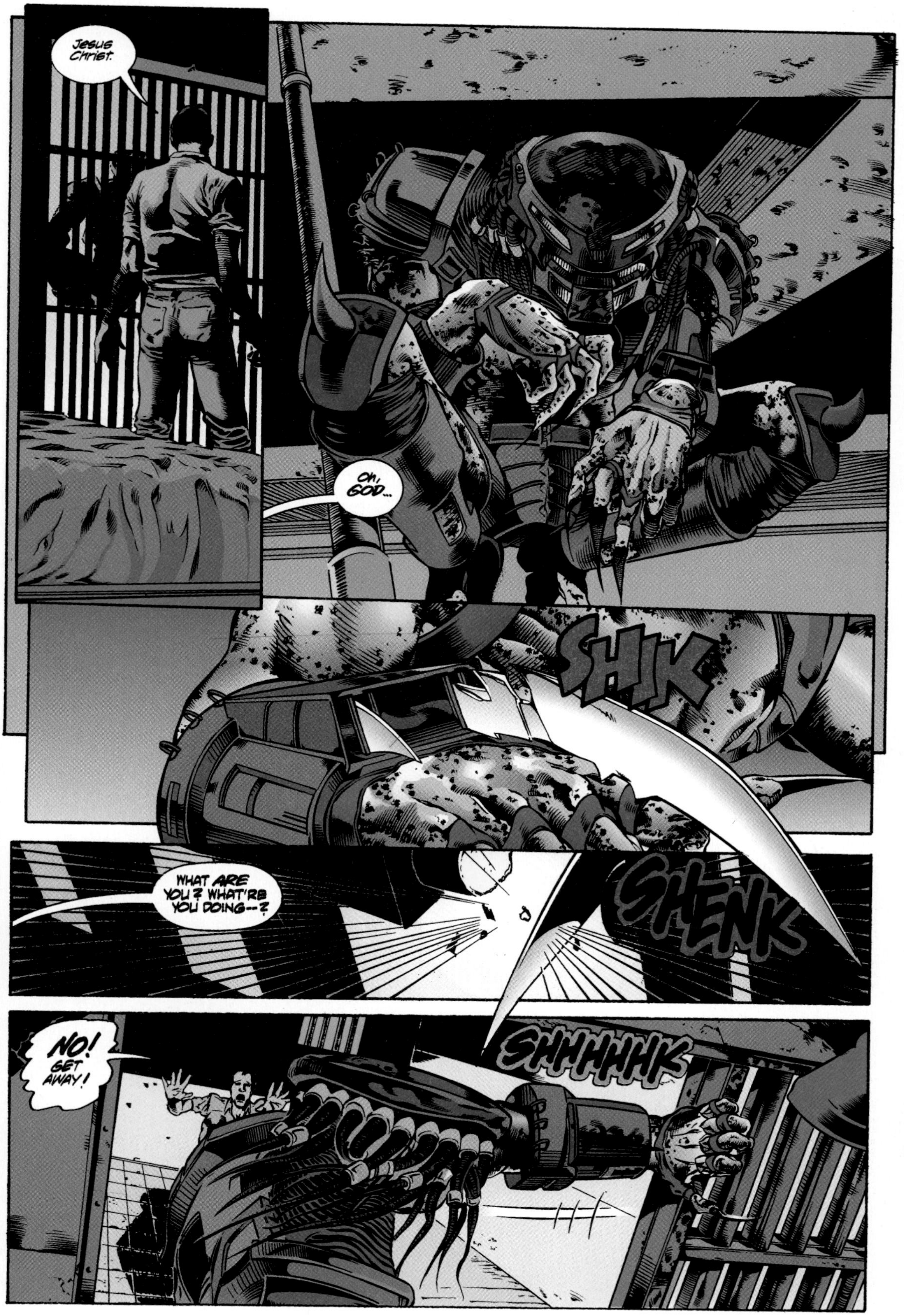
Jesus Christ.
Oh, GOD...
SHIK
WHAT ARE YOU? WHAT'RE YOU DOING--?
SHENK
NO! GET AWAY!
SHHHHHK

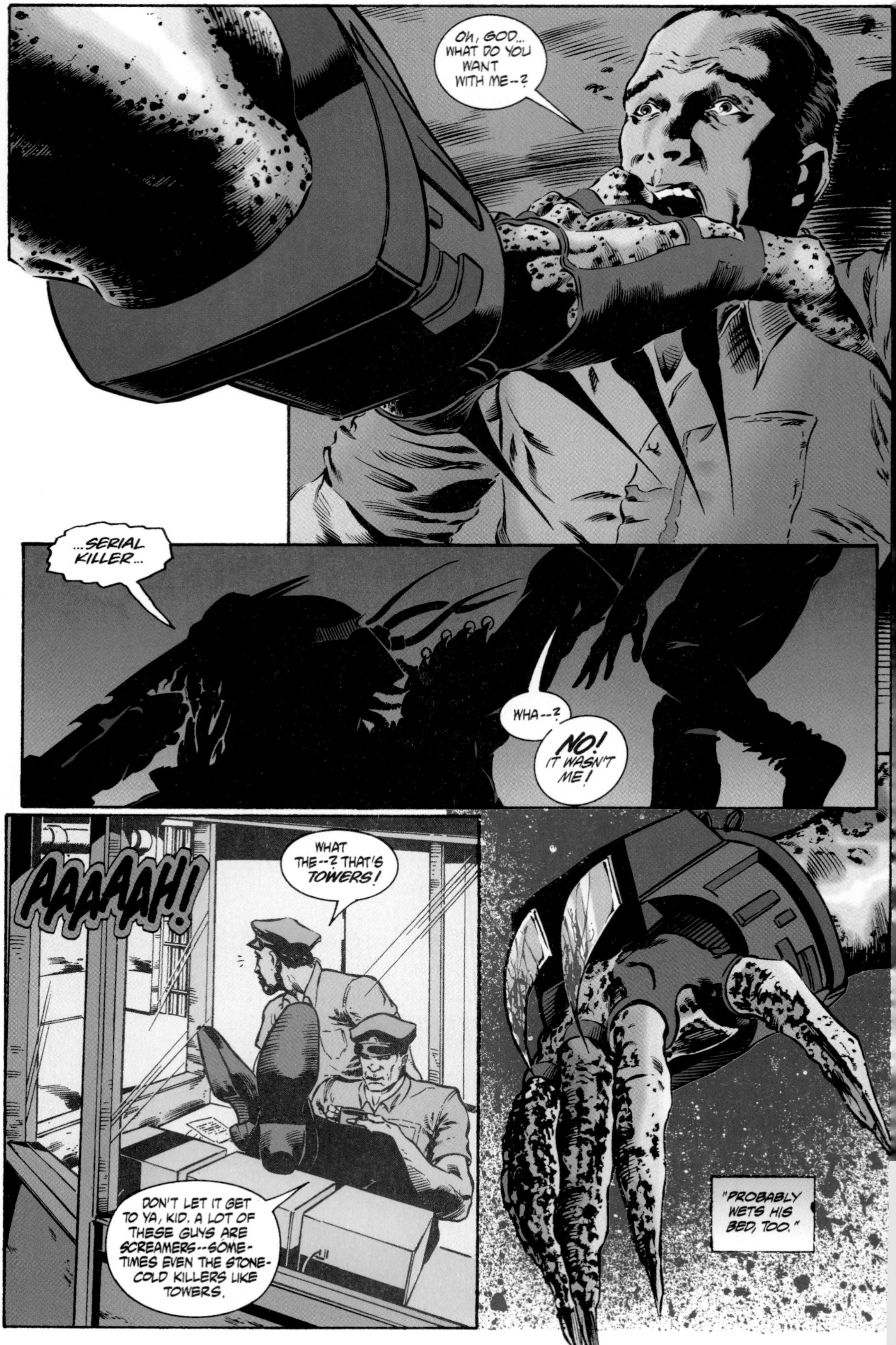
OH, GOD...
WHAT DO YOU WANT WITH ME--?
...SERIAL KILLER...
WHA--?
NO! IT WASN'T ME!
AAAAAH!
WHAT THE--? THAT'S TOWERS!
DON'T LET IT GET TO YA, KID. A LOT OF THESE GUYS ARE SCREAMERS--SOMETIMES EVEN THE STONE-COLD KILLERS LIKE TOWERS.
"PROBABLY WETS HIS BED, TOO."

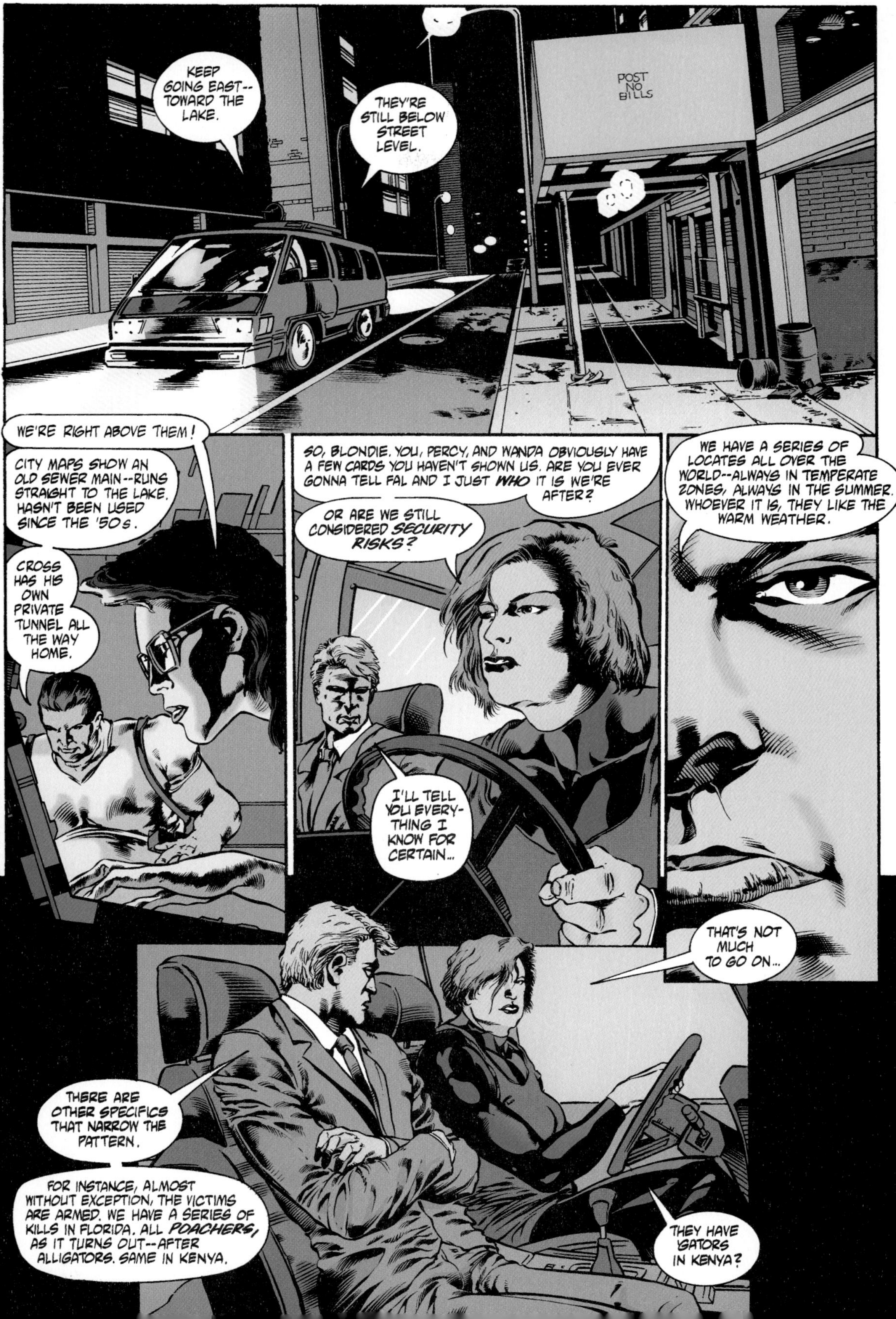
KEEP GOING EAST-- TOWARD THE LAKE.
THEY'RE STILL BELOW STREET LEVEL.
POST NO BILLS
WE'RE RIGHT ABOVE THEM!
CITY MAPS SHOW AN OLD SEWER MAIN--RUNS STRAIGHT TO THE LAKE. HASN'T BEEN USED SINCE THE '50s.
CROSS HAS HIS OWN PRIVATE TUNNEL ALL THE WAY HOME.
SO, BLONDIE. YOU, PERCY, AND WANDA OBVIOUSLY HAVE A FEW CARDS YOU HAVEN'T SHOWN US. ARE YOU EVER GONNA TELL FAL AND I JUST WHO IT IS WE'RE AFTER?
OR ARE WE STILL CONSIDERED SECURITY RISKS?
I'LL TELL YOU EVERY-THING I KNOW FOR CERTAIN...
WE HAVE A SERIES OF LOCATES ALL OVER THE WORLD--ALWAYS IN TEMPERATE ZONES, ALWAYS IN THE SUMMER. WHOEVER IT IS, THEY LIKE THE WARM WEATHER.
THAT'S NOT MUCH TO GO ON...
THERE ARE OTHER SPECIFICS THAT NARROW THE PATTERN.
FOR INSTANCE, ALMOST WITHOUT EXCEPTION, THE VICTIMS ARE ARMED. WE HAVE A SERIES OF KILLS IN FLORIDA. ALL POACHERS, AS IT TURNS OUT--AFTER ALLIGATORS. SAME IN KENYA.
THEY HAVE 'GATORS IN KENYA?

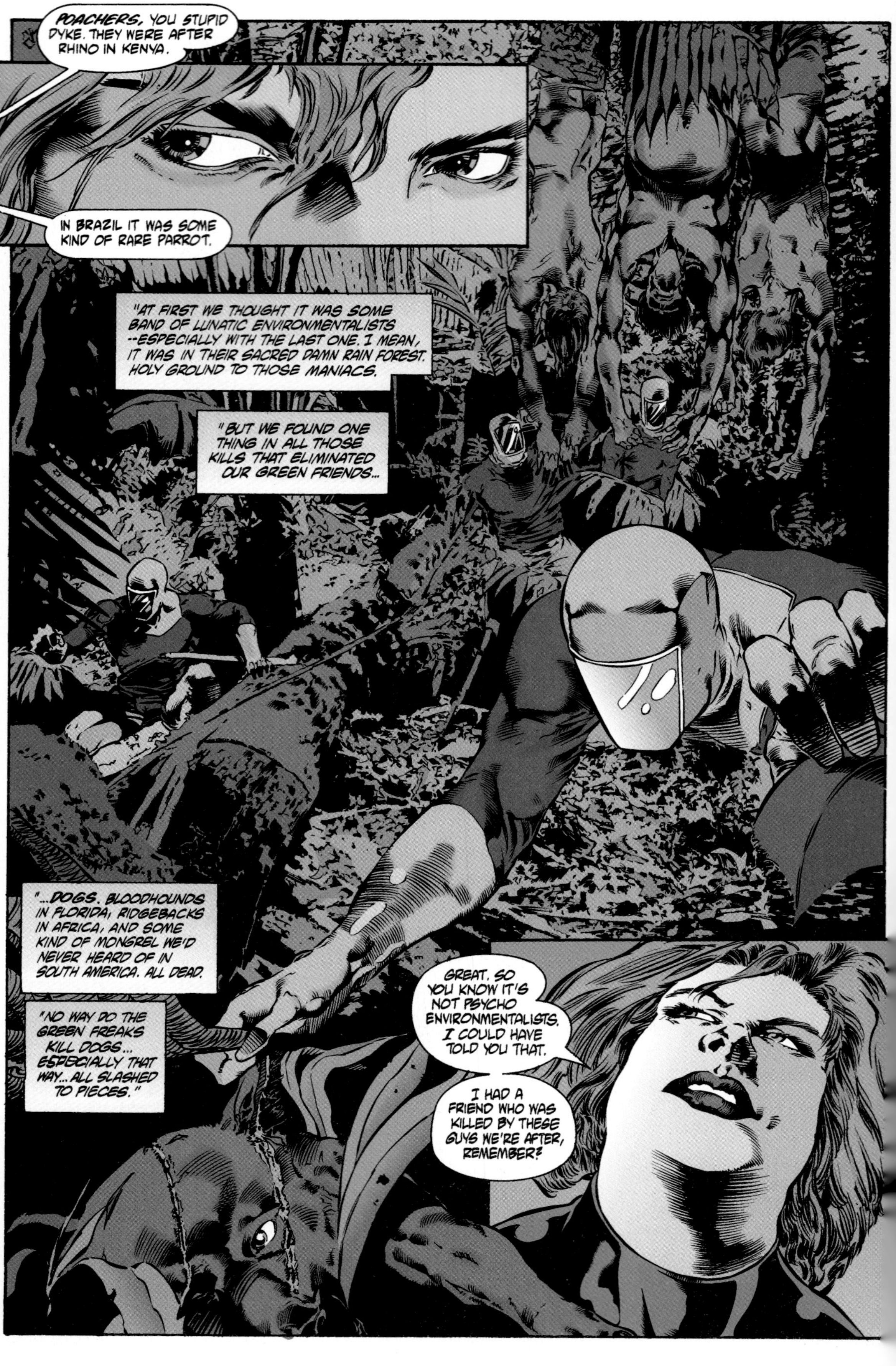
POACHERS, YOU STUPID DYKE. THEY WERE AFTER RHINO IN KENYA.
IN BRAZIL IT WAS SOME KIND OF RARE PARROT.
"AT FIRST WE THOUGHT IT WAS SOME BAND OF LUNATIC ENVIRONMENTALISTS --ESPECIALLY WITH THE LAST ONE. I MEAN, IT WAS IN THEIR SACRED DAMN RAIN FOREST. HOLY GROUND TO THOSE MANIACS.
"BUT WE FOUND ONE THING IN ALL THOSE KILLS THAT ELIMINATED OUR GREEN FRIENDS...
"...DOGS. BLOODHOUNDS IN FLORIDA, RIDGEBACKS IN AFRICA, AND SOME KIND OF MONGREL WE'D NEVER HEARD OF IN SOUTH AMERICA. ALL DEAD.
"NO WAY DO THE GREEN FREAKS KILL DOGS... ESPECIALLY THAT WAY... ALL SLASHED TO PIECES."
GREAT. SO YOU KNOW IT'S NOT PSYCHO ENVIRONMENTALISTS. I COULD HAVE TOLD YOU THAT.
I HAD A FRIEND WHO WAS KILLED BY THESE GUYS WE'RE AFTER, REMEMBER?

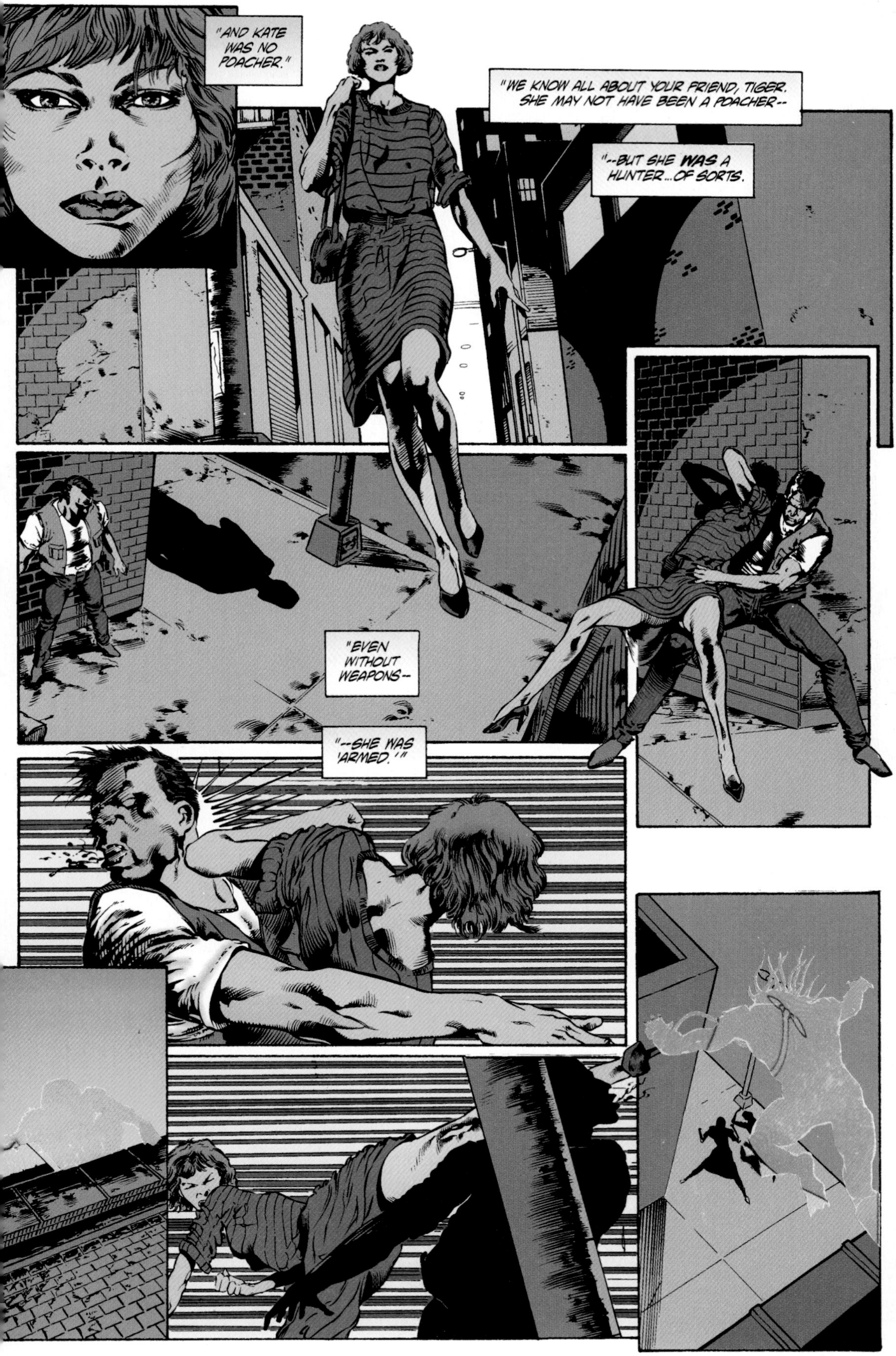
"AND KATE WAS NO POACHER."
"WE KNOW ALL ABOUT YOUR FRIEND, TIGER. SHE MAY NOT HAVE BEEN A POACHER--
"--BUT SHE WAS A HUNTER...OF SORTS.
"EVEN WITHOUT WEAPONS--
"--SHE WAS 'ARMED.'"

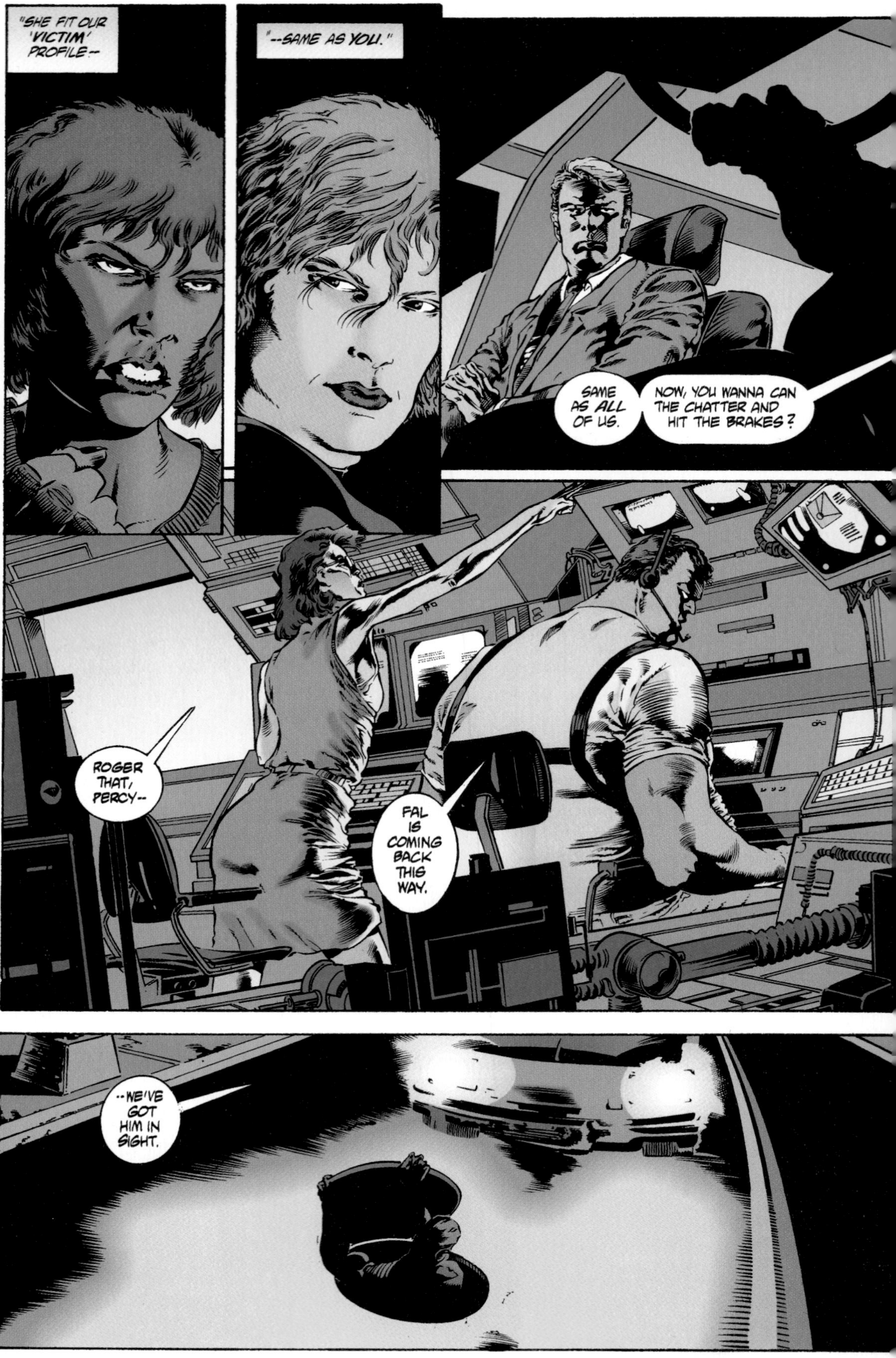
"SHE FIT OUR 'VICTIM' PROFILE--
"--SAME AS YOU."
SAME AS ALL OF US.
NOW, YOU WANNA CAN THE CHATTER AND HIT THE BRAKES?
ROGER THAT, PERCY--
FAL IS COMING BACK THIS WAY.
--WE'VE GOT HIM IN SIGHT.

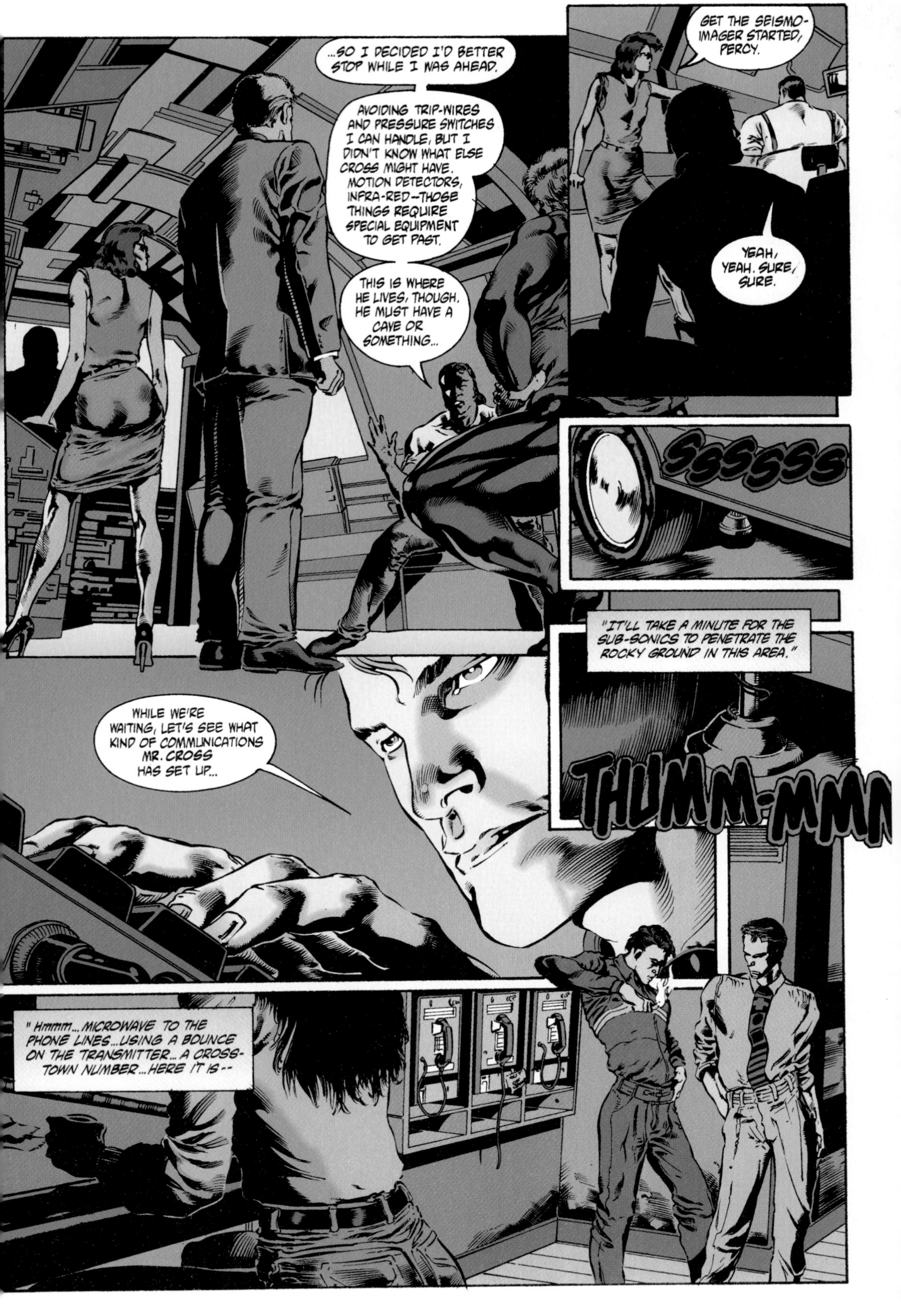
...SO I DECIDED I'D BETTER STOP WHILE I WAS AHEAD.
AVOIDING TRIP-WIRES AND PRESSURE SWITCHES I CAN HANDLE, BUT I DIDN'T KNOW WHAT ELSE CROSS MIGHT HAVE. MOTION DETECTORS, INFRA-RED--THOSE THINGS REQUIRE SPECIAL EQUIPMENT TO GET PAST.
THIS IS WHERE HE LIVES, THOUGH. HE MUST HAVE A CAVE OR SOMETHING...
GET THE SEISMO-IMAGER STARTED, PERCY.
YEAH, YEAH. SURE, SURE.
SSSSSS
"IT'LL TAKE A MINUTE FOR THE SUB-SONICS TO PENETRATE THE ROCKY GROUND IN THIS AREA."
THUMM-MMM
WHILE WE'RE WAITING, LET'S SEE WHAT KIND OF COMMUNICATIONS MR. CROSS HAS SET UP...
"Hmmm... MICROWAVE TO THE PHONE LINES...USING A BOUNCE ON THE TRANSMITTER... A CROSS-TOWN NUMBER...HERE IT IS--

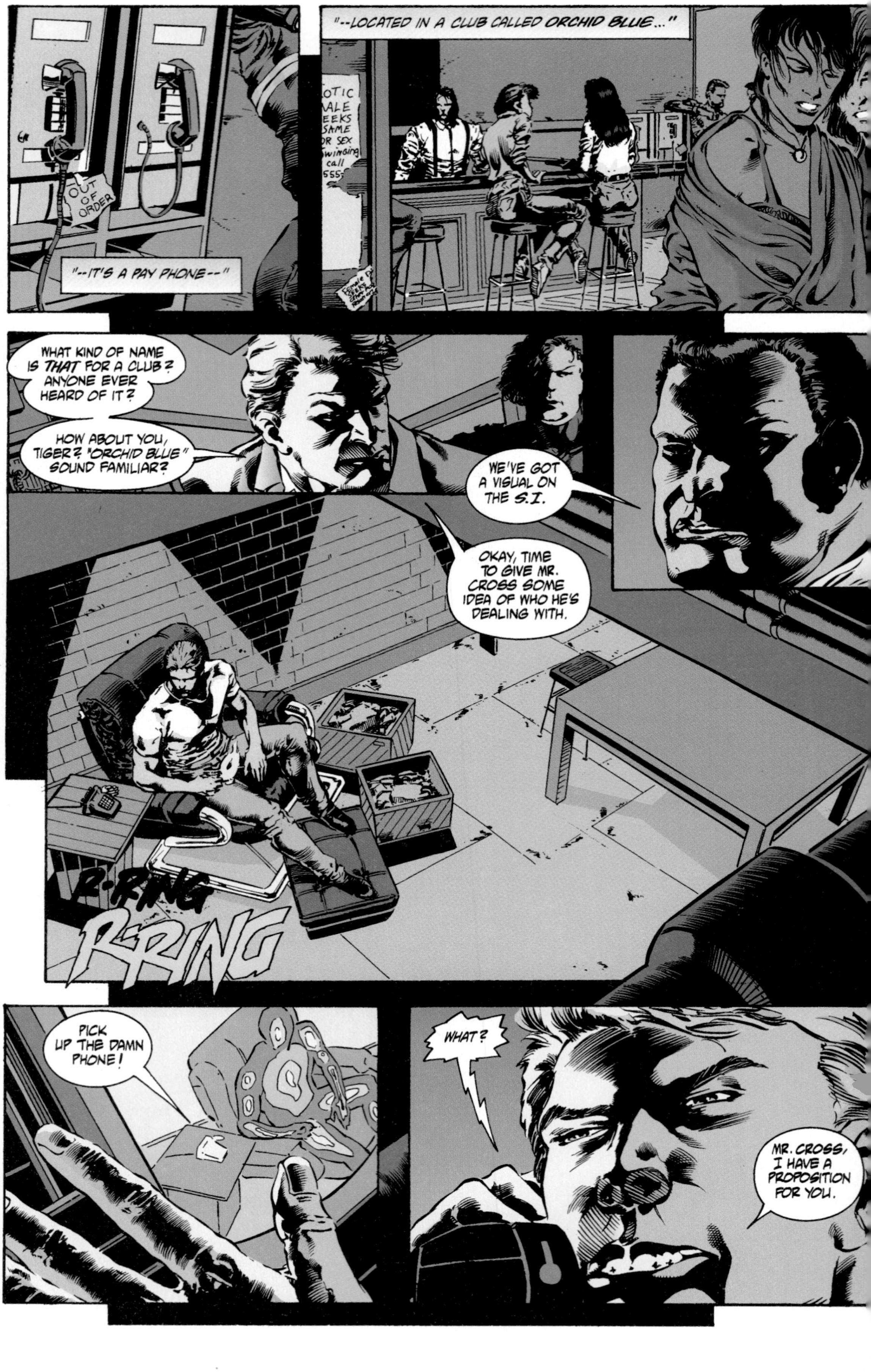
"--IT'S A PAY PHONE--"
OUT OF ORDER
"--LOCATED IN A CLUB CALLED ORCHID BLUE..."
WHAT KIND OF NAME IS THAT FOR A CLUB? ANYONE EVER HEARD OF IT?
HOW ABOUT YOU, TIGER? "ORCHID BLUE" SOUND FAMILIAR?
WE'VE GOT A VISUAL ON THE S.I.
OKAY, TIME TO GIVE MR. CROSS SOME IDEA OF WHO HE'S DEALING WITH.
R-RING
R-RING
PICK UP THE DAMN PHONE!
WHAT?
MR. CROSS, I HAVE A PROPOSITION FOR YOU.

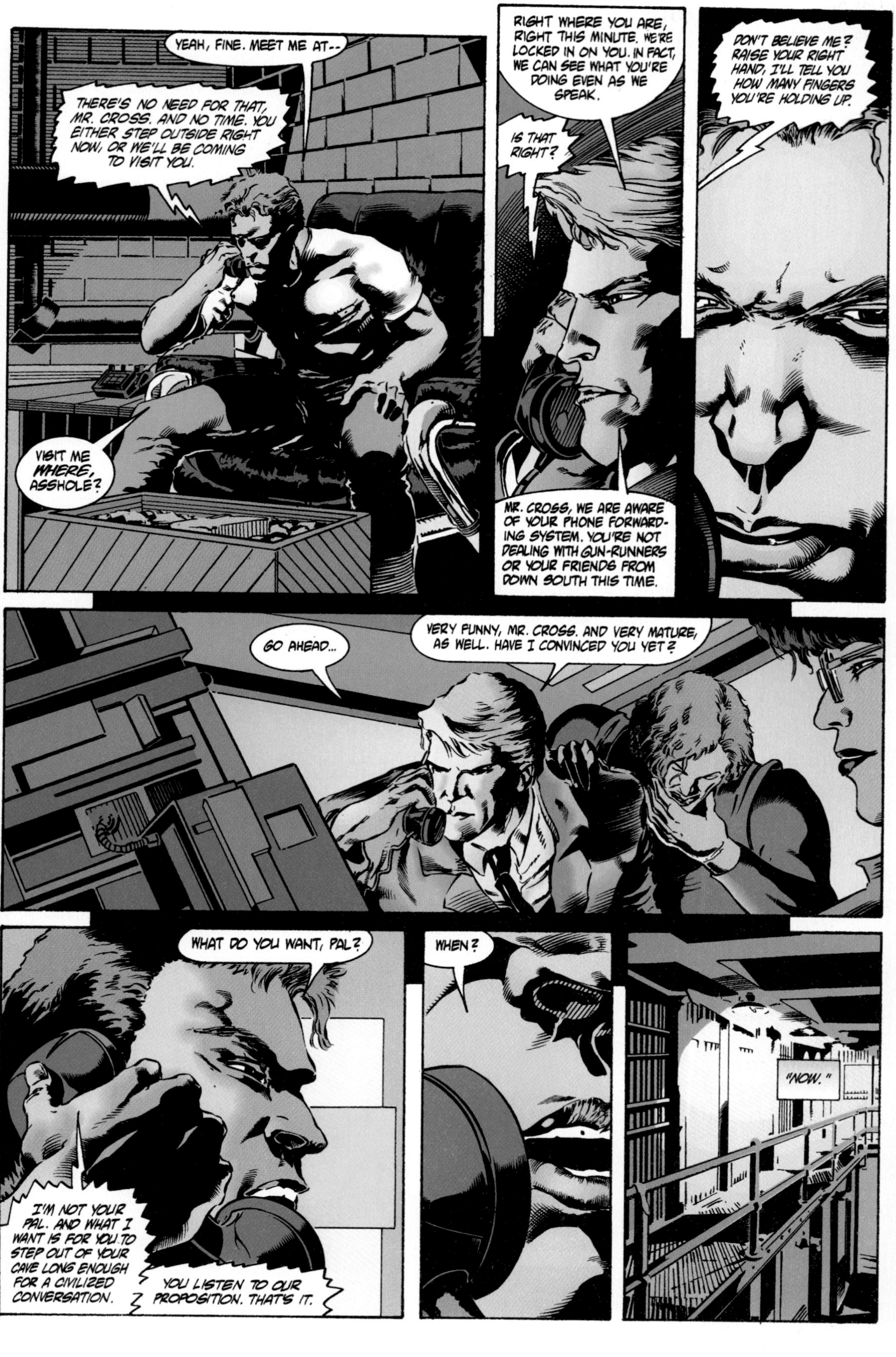
YEAH, FINE. MEET ME AT--
THERE'S NO NEED FOR THAT, MR. CROSS. AND NO TIME. YOU EITHER STEP OUTSIDE RIGHT NOW, OR WE'LL BE COMING TO VISIT YOU.
VISIT ME WHERE, ASSHOLE?
RIGHT WHERE YOU ARE, RIGHT THIS MINUTE. WE'RE LOCKED IN ON YOU. IN FACT, WE CAN SEE WHAT YOU'RE DOING EVEN AS WE SPEAK.
IS THAT RIGHT?
MR. CROSS, WE ARE AWARE OF YOUR PHONE FORWARDING SYSTEM. YOU'RE NOT DEALING WITH GUN-RUNNERS OR YOUR FRIENDS FROM DOWN SOUTH THIS TIME.
DON'T BELIEVE ME? RAISE YOUR RIGHT HAND, I'LL TELL YOU HOW MANY FINGERS YOU'RE HOLDING UP.
GO AHEAD...
VERY FUNNY, MR. CROSS. AND VERY MATURE, AS WELL. HAVE I CONVINCED YOU YET?
WHAT DO YOU WANT, PAL?
I'M NOT YOUR PAL. AND WHAT I WANT IS FOR YOU TO STEP OUT OF YOUR CAVE LONG ENOUGH FOR A CIVILIZED CONVERSATION.
YOU LISTEN TO OUR PROPOSITION. THAT'S IT.
WHEN?
"NOW."

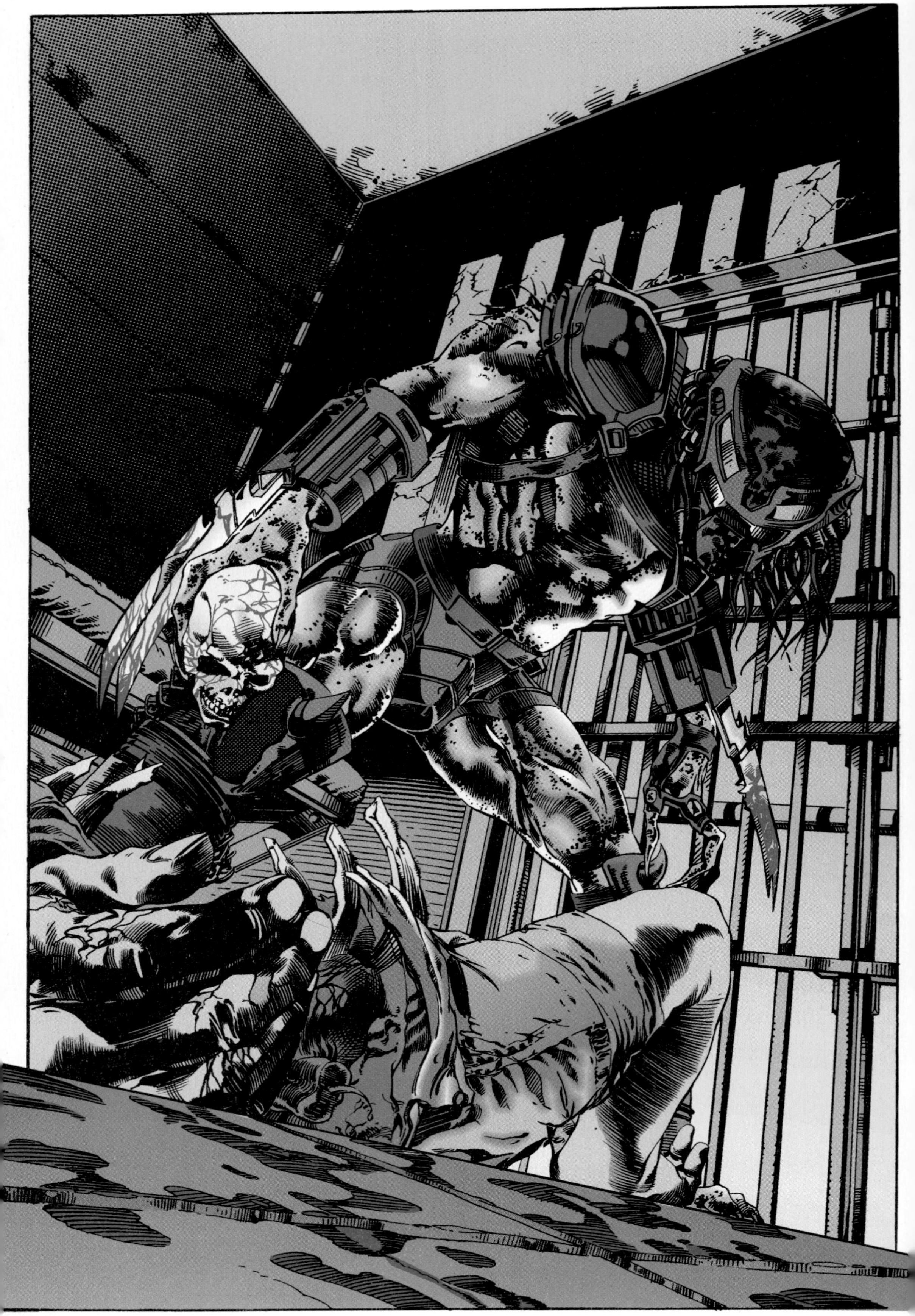

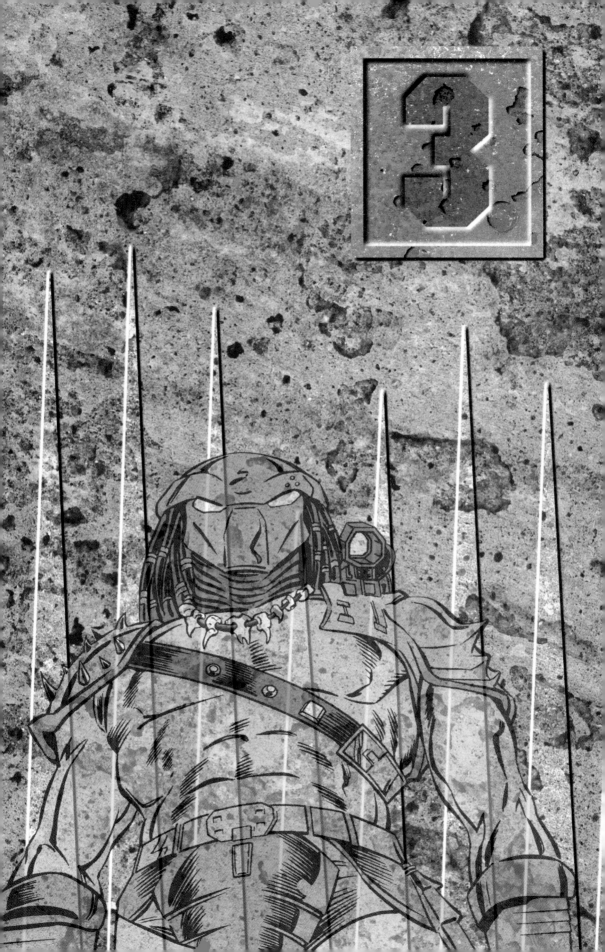

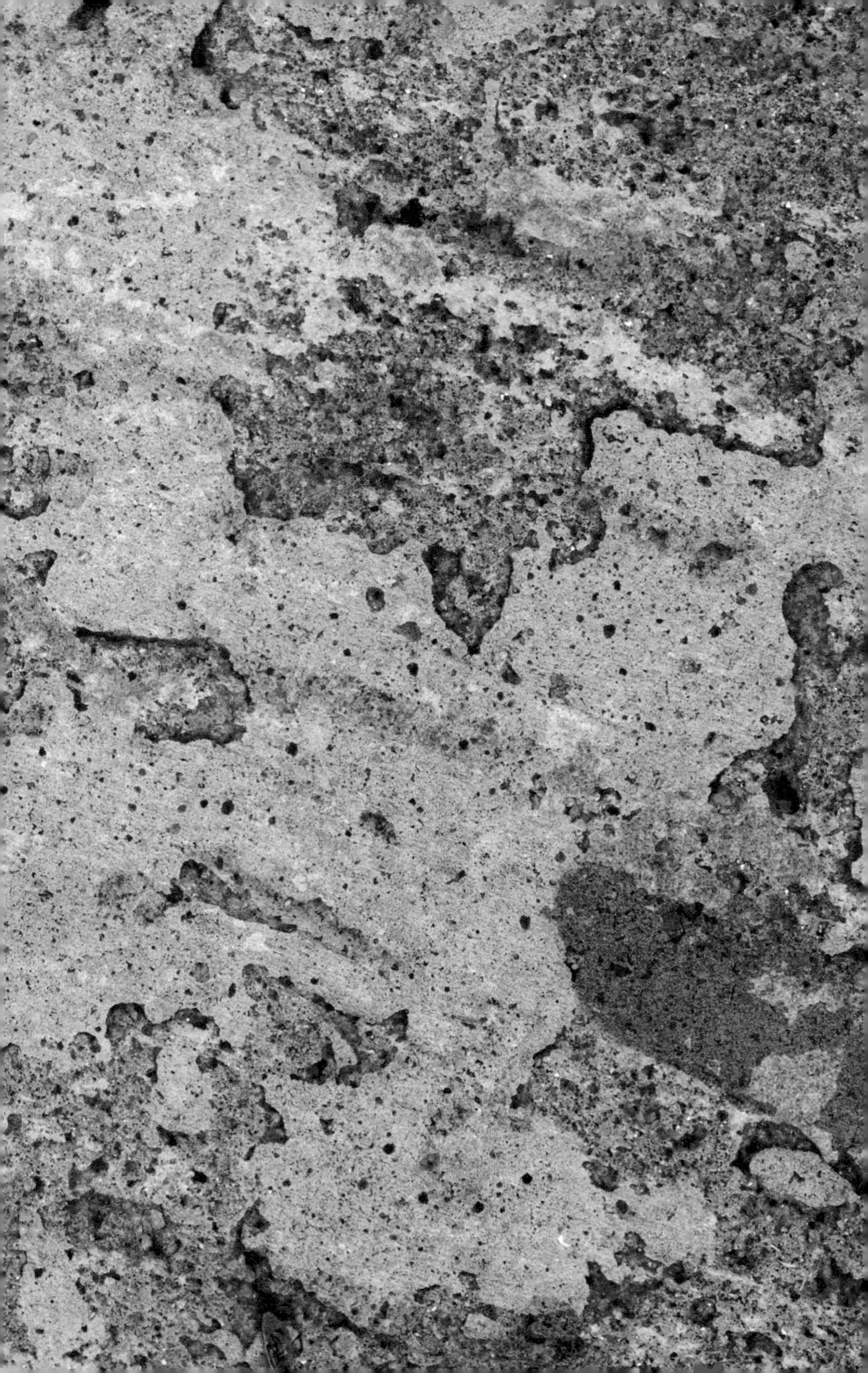

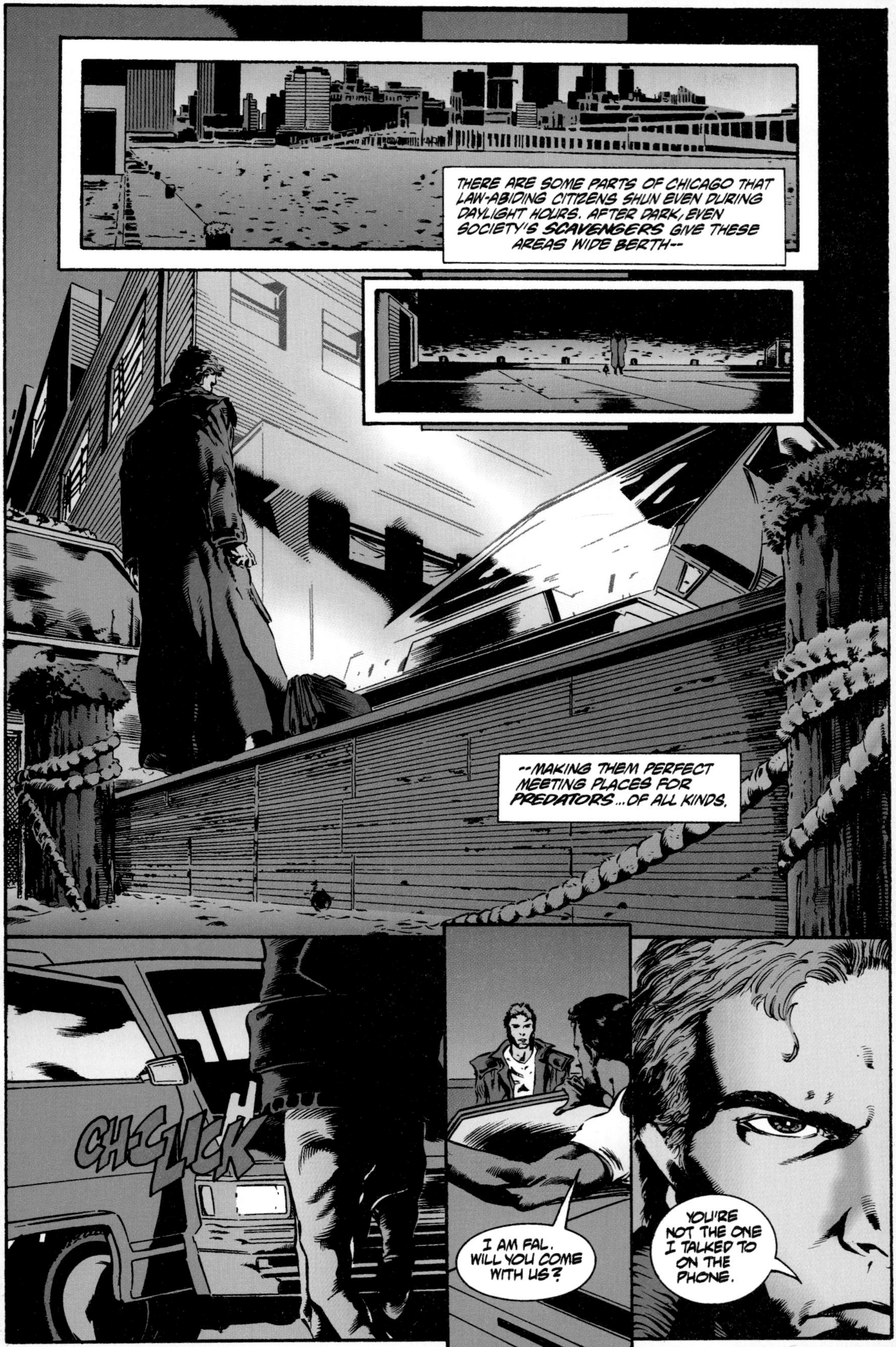
THERE ARE SOME PARTS OF CHICAGO THAT LAW-ABIDING CITIZENS SHUN EVEN DURING DAYLIGHT HOURS. AFTER DARK, EVEN SOCIETY'S SCAVENGERS GIVE THESE AREAS WIDE BERTH--
--MAKING THEM PERFECT MEETING PLACES FOR PREDATORS...OF ALL KINDS.
CH-CLICK
I AM FAL. WILL YOU COME WITH US?
YOU'RE NOT THE ONE I TALKED TO ON THE PHONE.

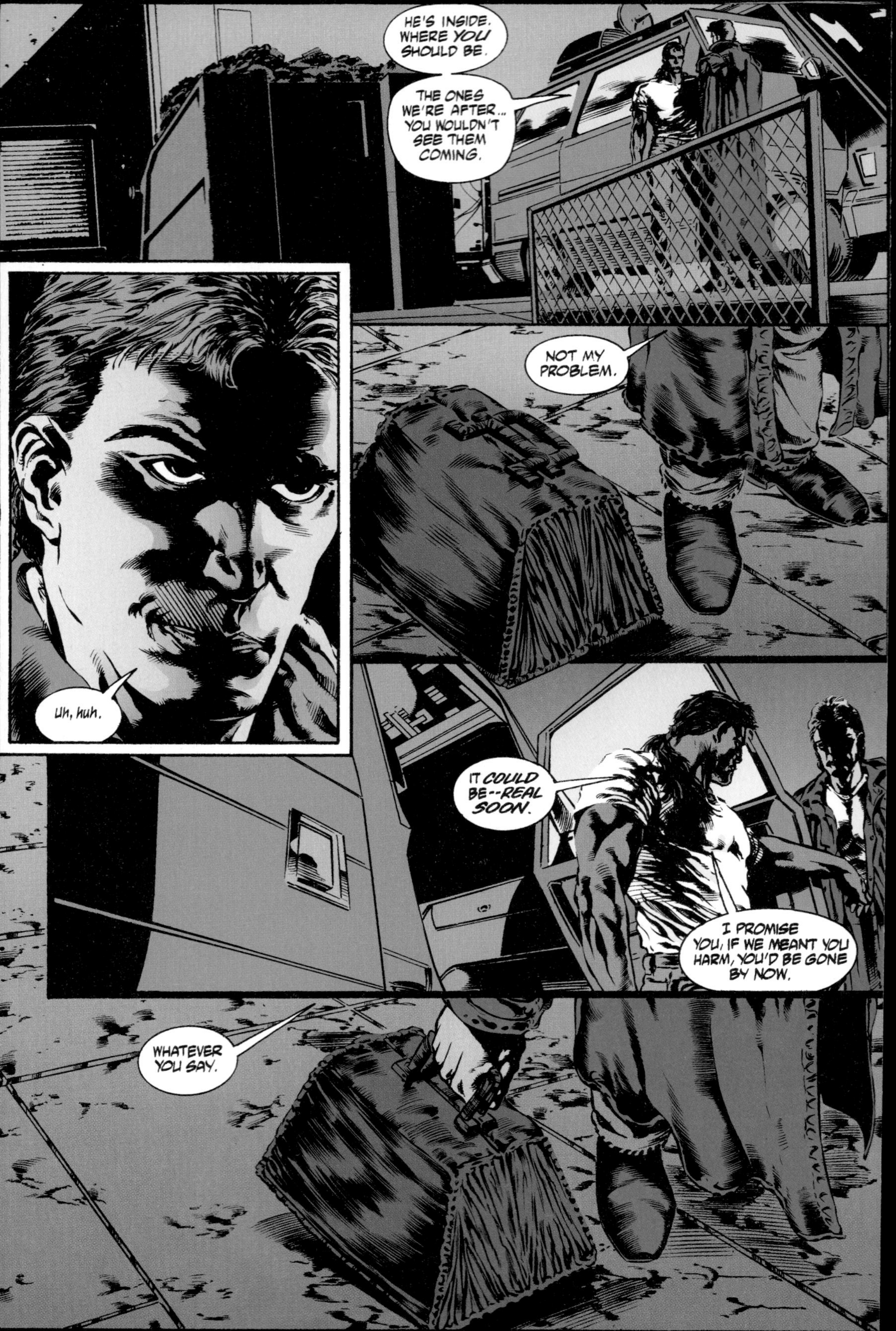
HE'S INSIDE. WHERE YOU SHOULD BE.
THE ONES WE'RE AFTER... YOU WOULDN'T SEE THEM COMING.
NOT MY PROBLEM.
UH, HUH.
IT COULD BE--REAL SOON.
I PROMISE YOU, IF WE MEANT YOU HARM, YOU'D BE GONE BY NOW.
WHATEVER YOU SAY.

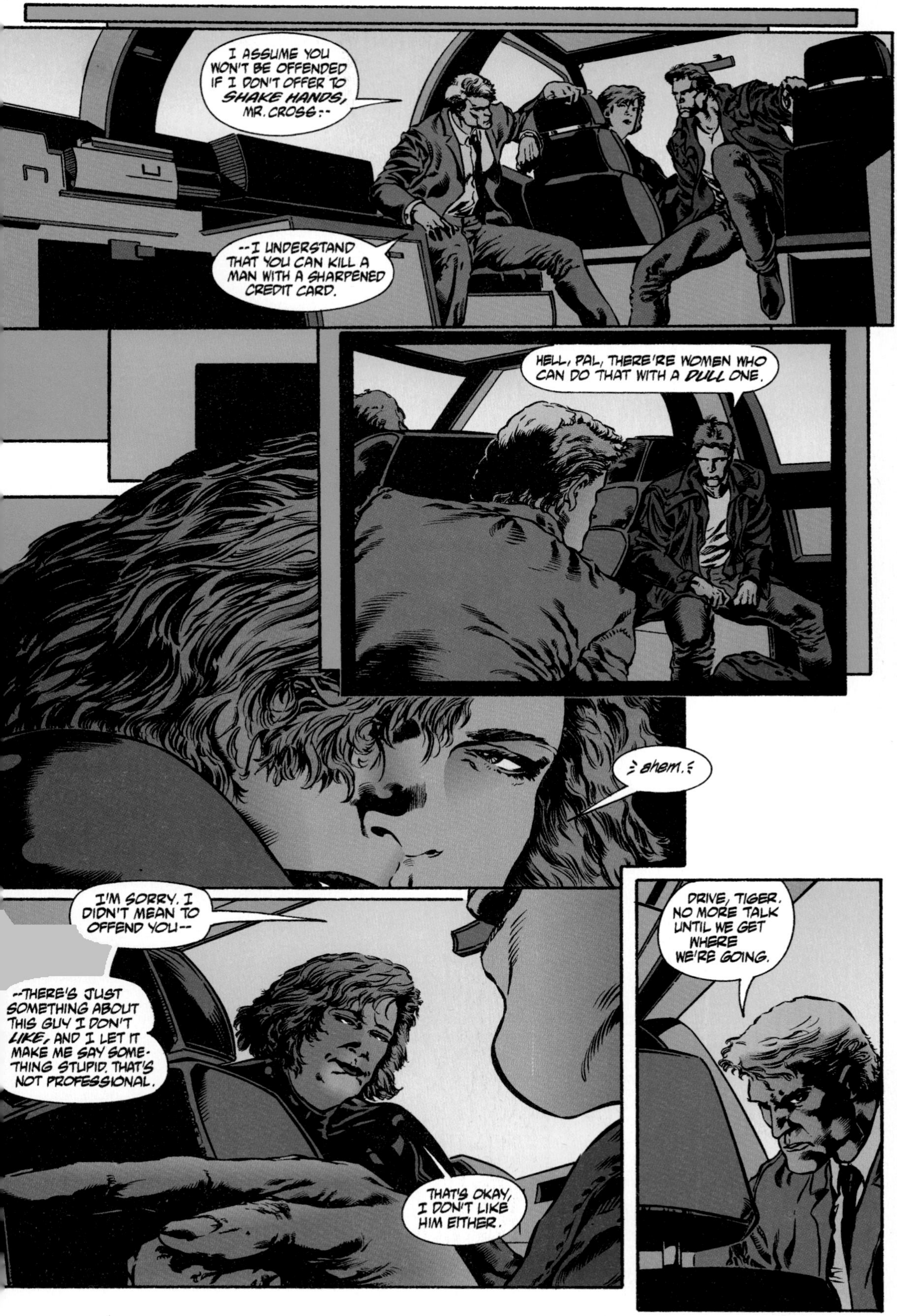
I ASSUME YOU WON'T BE OFFENDED IF I DON'T OFFER TO SHAKE HANDS, MR. CROSS:-
--I UNDERSTAND THAT YOU CAN KILL A MAN WITH A SHARPENED CREDIT CARD.
HELL, PAL, THERE'RE WOMEN WHO CAN DO THAT WITH A DULL ONE.
ahem.
I'M SORRY. I DIDN'T MEAN TO OFFEND YOU--
--THERE'S JUST SOMETHING ABOUT THIS GUY I DON'T LIKE, AND I LET IT MAKE ME SAY SOMETHING STUPID. THAT'S NOT PROFESSIONAL.
THAT'S OKAY, I DON'T LIKE HIM EITHER.
DRIVE, TIGER. NO MORE TALK UNTIL WE GET WHERE WE'RE GOING.

PALOVERDE STATE PENITENTIARY, ARIZONA

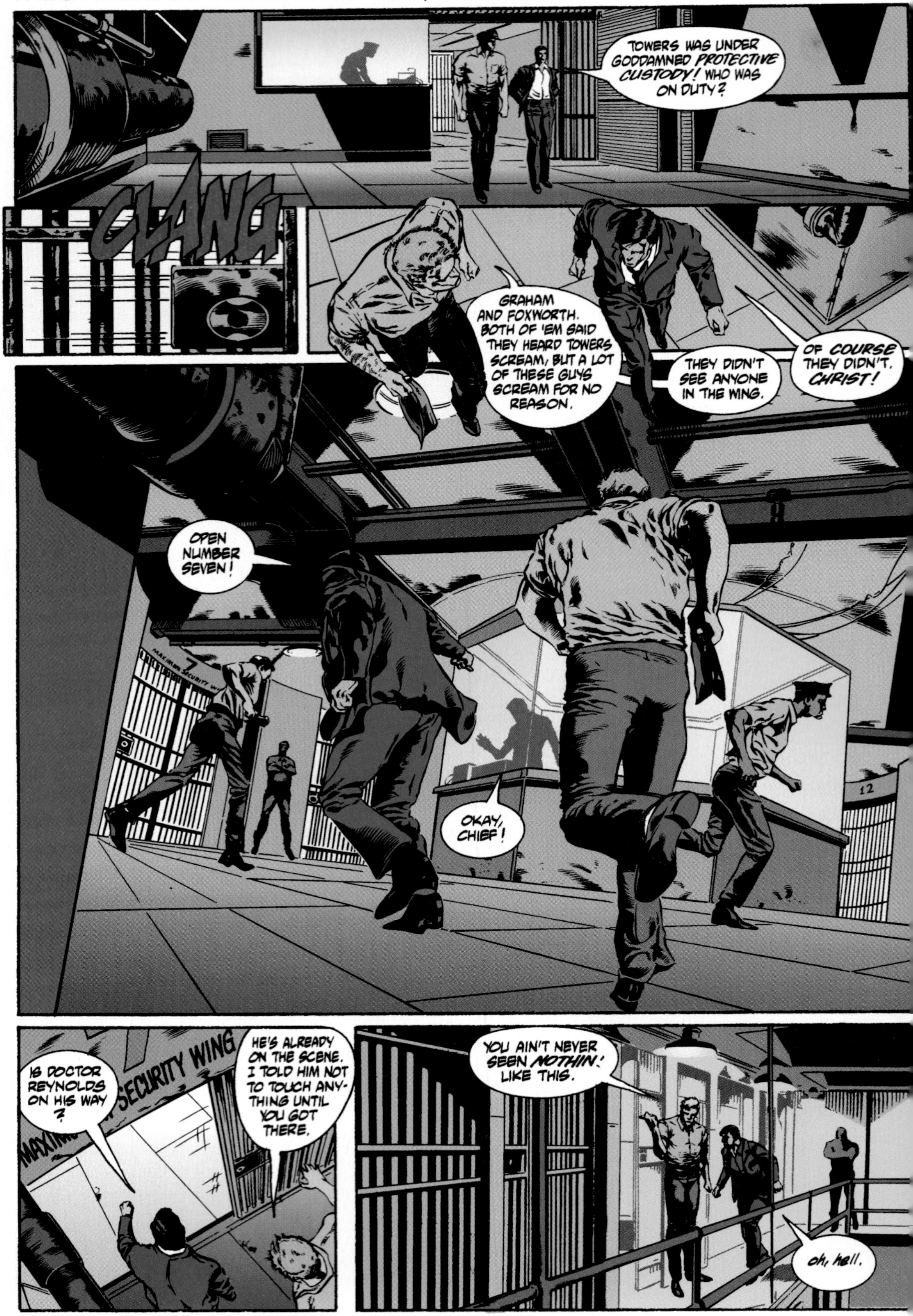
TOWERS WAS UNDER GODDAMNED PROTECTIVE CUSTODY! WHO WAS ON DUTY?
CLANG
GRAHAM AND FOXWORTH. BOTH OF 'EM SAID THEY HEARD TOWERS SCREAM, BUT A LOT OF THESE GUYS SCREAM FOR NO REASON.
THEY DIDN'T SEE ANYONE IN THE WING.
OF COURSE THEY DIDN'T. CHRIST!
OPEN NUMBER SEVEN!
OKAY, CHIEF!
IS DOCTOR REYNOLDS ON HIS WAY?
HE'S ALREADY ON THE SCENE. I TOLD HIM NOT TO TOUCH ANYTHING UNTIL YOU GOT THERE.
SECURITY WING
YOU AIN'T NEVER SEEN NOTHIN' LIKE THIS.
oh, hell.

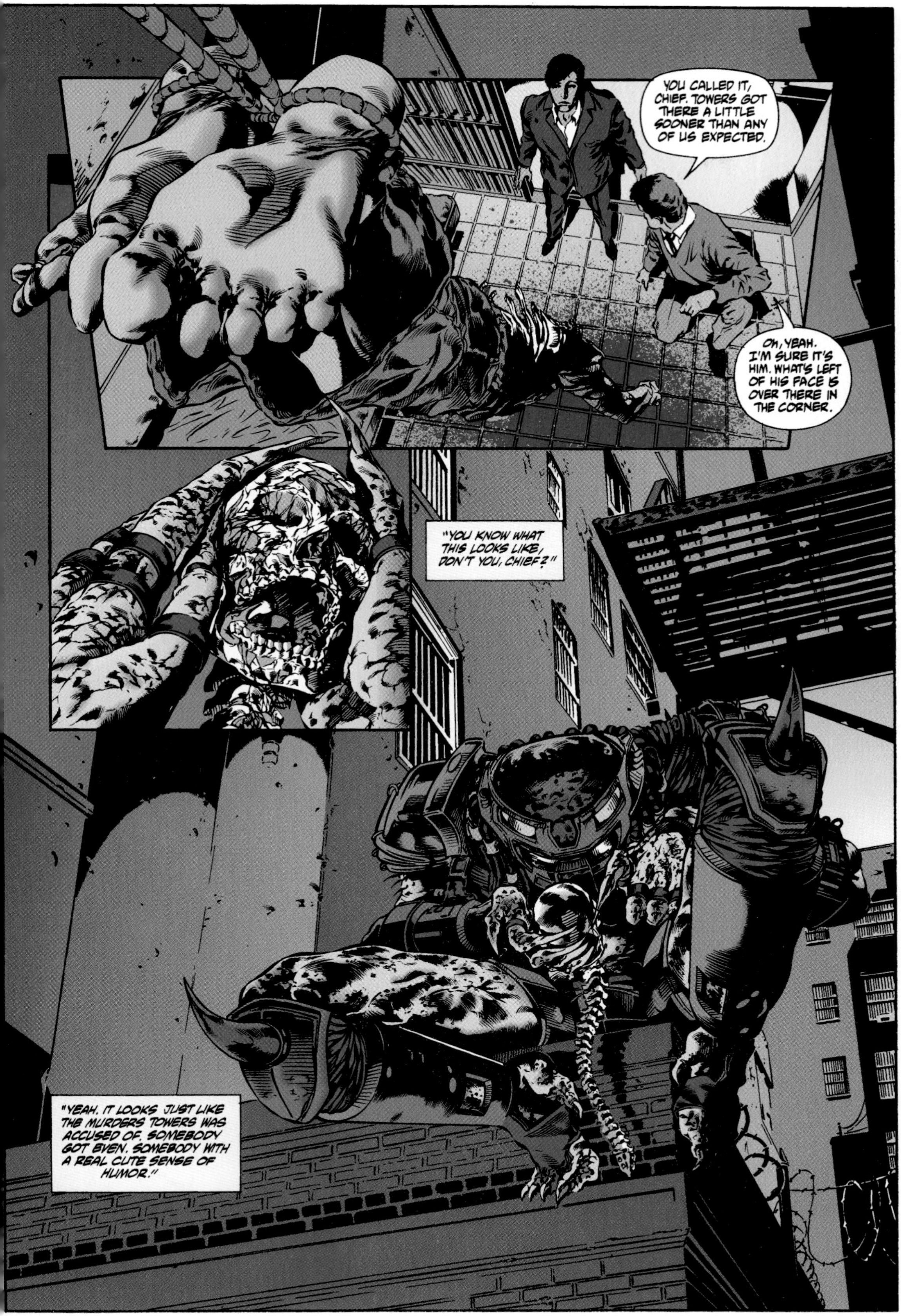
YOU CALLED IT, CHIEF. TOWERS GOT THERE A LITTLE SOONER THAN ANY OF US EXPECTED.
OH, YEAH. I'M SURE IT'S HIM. WHAT'S LEFT OF HIS FACE IS OVER THERE IN THE CORNER.
"YOU KNOW WHAT THIS LOOKS LIKE, DON'T YOU, CHIEF?"
"YEAH. IT LOOKS JUST LIKE THE MURDERS TOWERS WAS ACCUSED OF. SOMEBODY GOT EVEN. SOMEBODY WITH A REAL CUTE SENSE OF HUMOR."

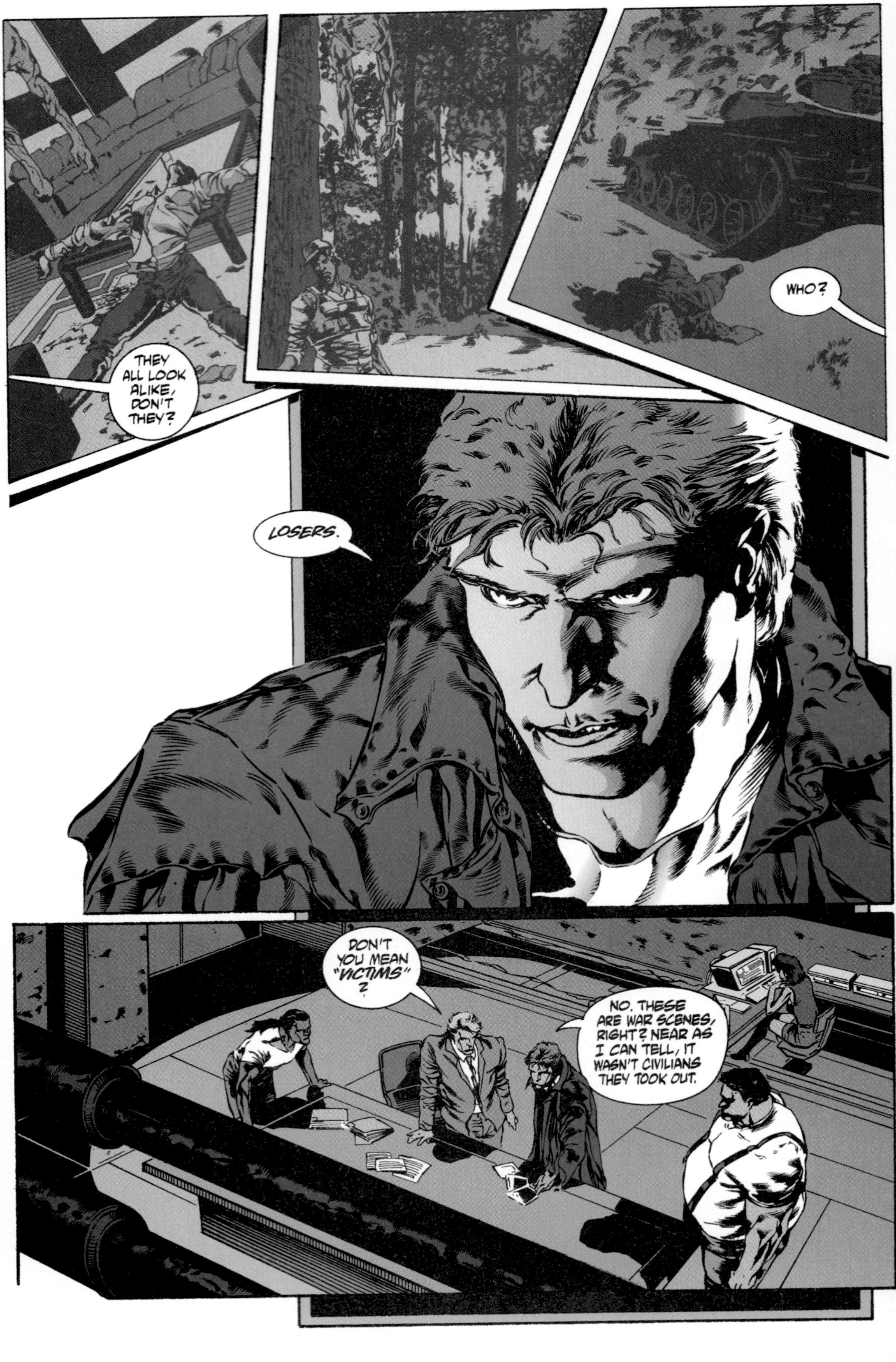
THEY ALL LOOK ALIKE, DON'T THEY?
WHO?
LOSERS.
DON'T YOU MEAN "VICTIMS"?
NO. THESE ARE WAR SCENES, RIGHT? NEAR AS I CAN TELL, IT WASN'T CIVILIANS THEY TOOK OUT.

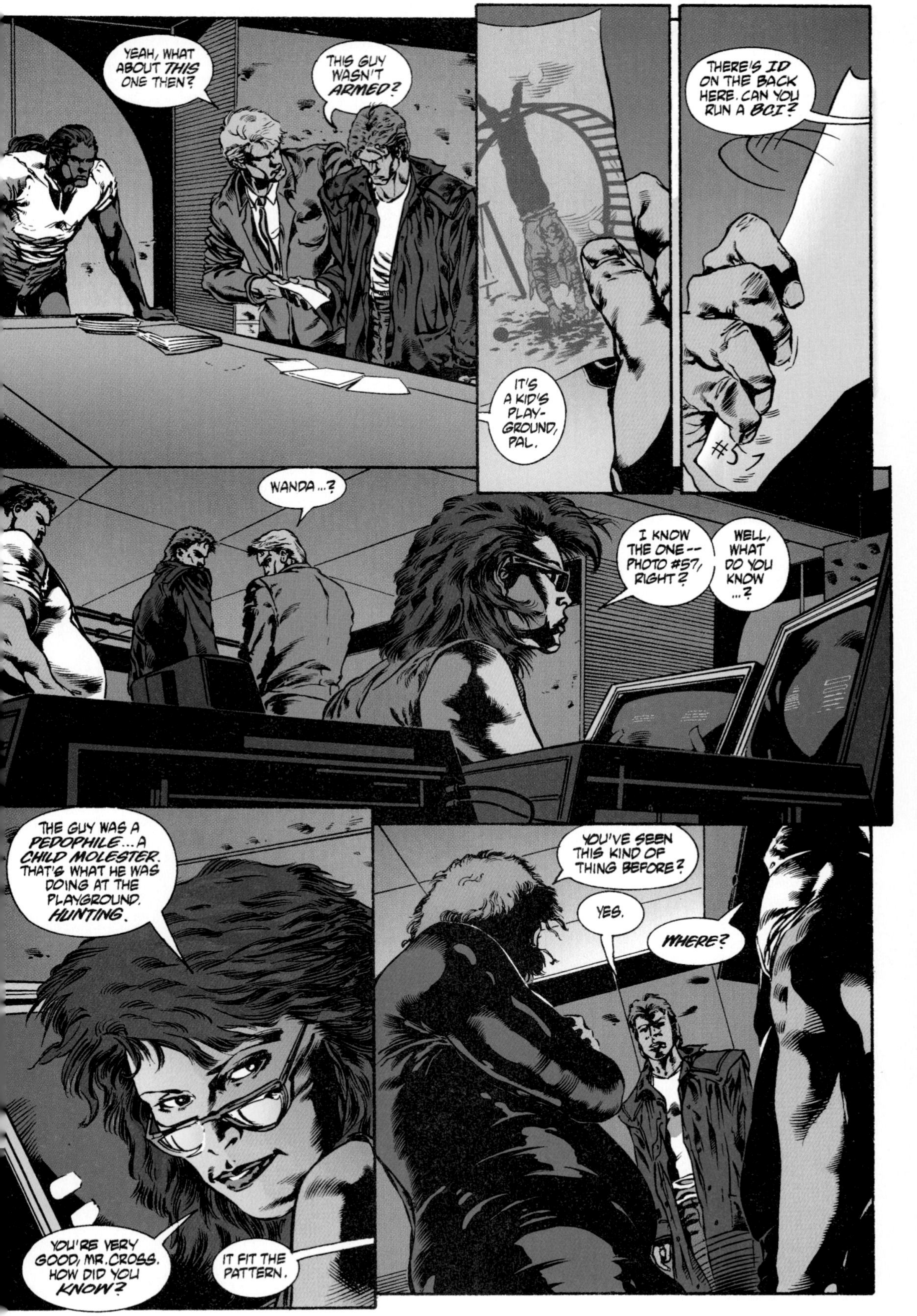
YEAH, WHAT ABOUT *THIS* ONE THEN?
THIS GUY WASN'T *ARMED*?
IT'S A KID'S PLAY-GROUND, PAL.
THERE'S *ID* ON THE BACK HERE. CAN YOU RUN A *BCI*?
#57
WANDA...?
I KNOW THE ONE-- PHOTO #57, RIGHT?
WELL, WHAT DO YOU KNOW...?
THE GUY WAS A *PEDOPHILE*...A *CHILD MOLESTER*. THAT'S WHAT HE WAS DOING AT THE PLAYGROUND. *HUNTING*.
YOU'RE VERY GOOD, MR. CROSS. HOW DID YOU *KNOW*?
IT FIT THE PATTERN.
YOU'VE SEEN THIS KIND OF THING BEFORE?
YES.
WHERE?

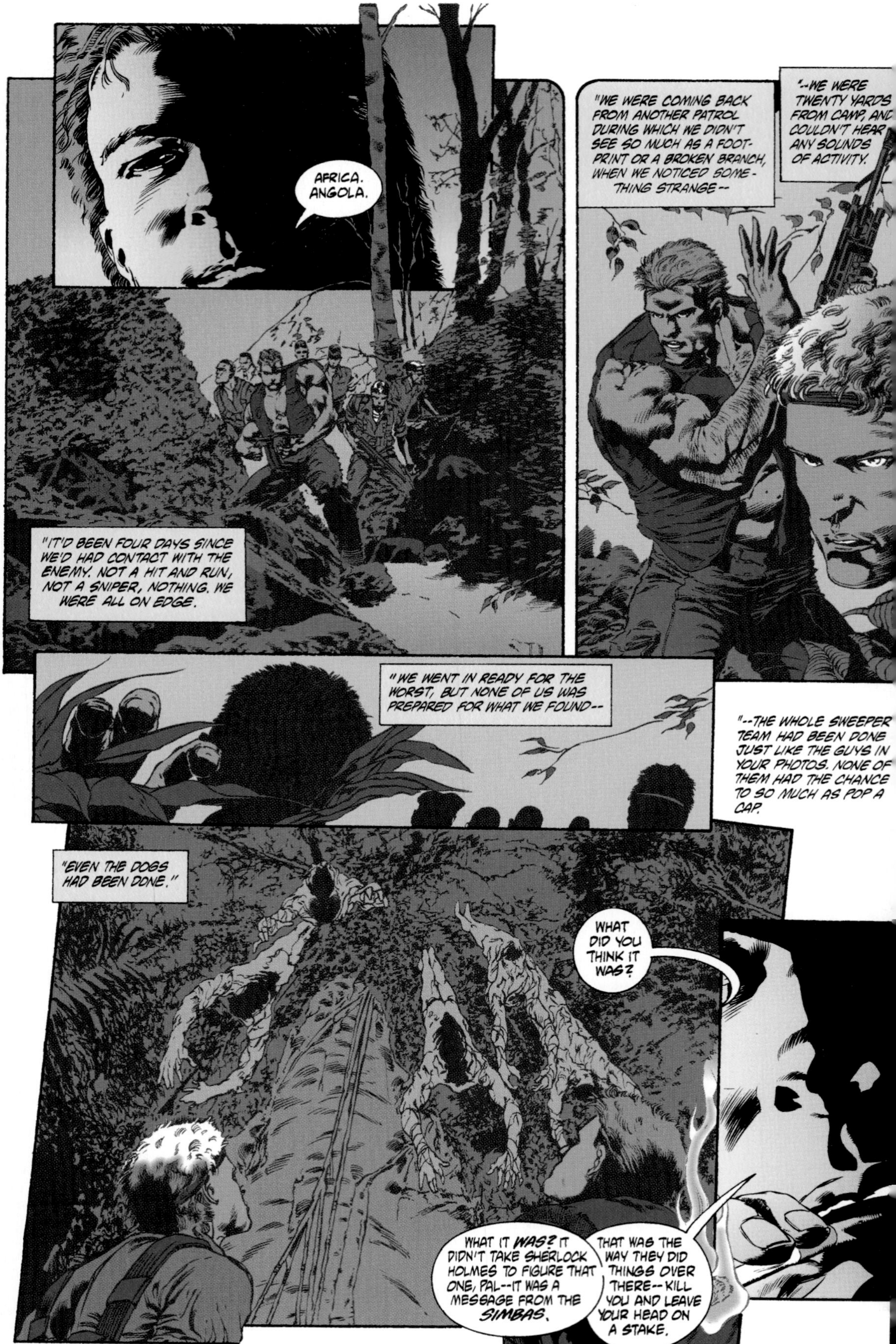

AFRICA. ANGOLA.
"IT'D BEEN FOUR DAYS SINCE WE'D HAD CONTACT WITH THE ENEMY. NOT A HIT AND RUN, NOT A SNIPER, NOTHING. WE WERE ALL ON EDGE.
"WE WERE COMING BACK FROM ANOTHER PATROL DURING WHICH WE DIDN'T SEE SO MUCH AS A FOOT-PRINT OR A BROKEN BRANCH, WHEN WE NOTICED SOME-THING STRANGE--
"--WE WERE TWENTY YARDS FROM CAMP, AND COULDN'T HEAR ANY SOUNDS OF ACTIVITY.
"WE WENT IN READY FOR THE WORST, BUT NONE OF US WAS PREPARED FOR WHAT WE FOUND--
"--THE WHOLE SWEEPER TEAM HAD BEEN DONE JUST LIKE THE GUYS IN YOUR PHOTOS. NONE OF THEM HAD THE CHANCE TO SO MUCH AS POP A CAP.
"EVEN THE DOGS HAD BEEN DONE."
WHAT DID YOU THINK IT WAS?
WHAT IT *WAS?* IT DIDN'T TAKE SHERLOCK HOLMES TO FIGURE THAT ONE, PAL--IT WAS A MESSAGE FROM THE *SIMBAS*.
THAT WAS THE WAY THEY DID THINGS OVER THERE--KILL YOU AND LEAVE YOUR HEAD ON A STAKE.

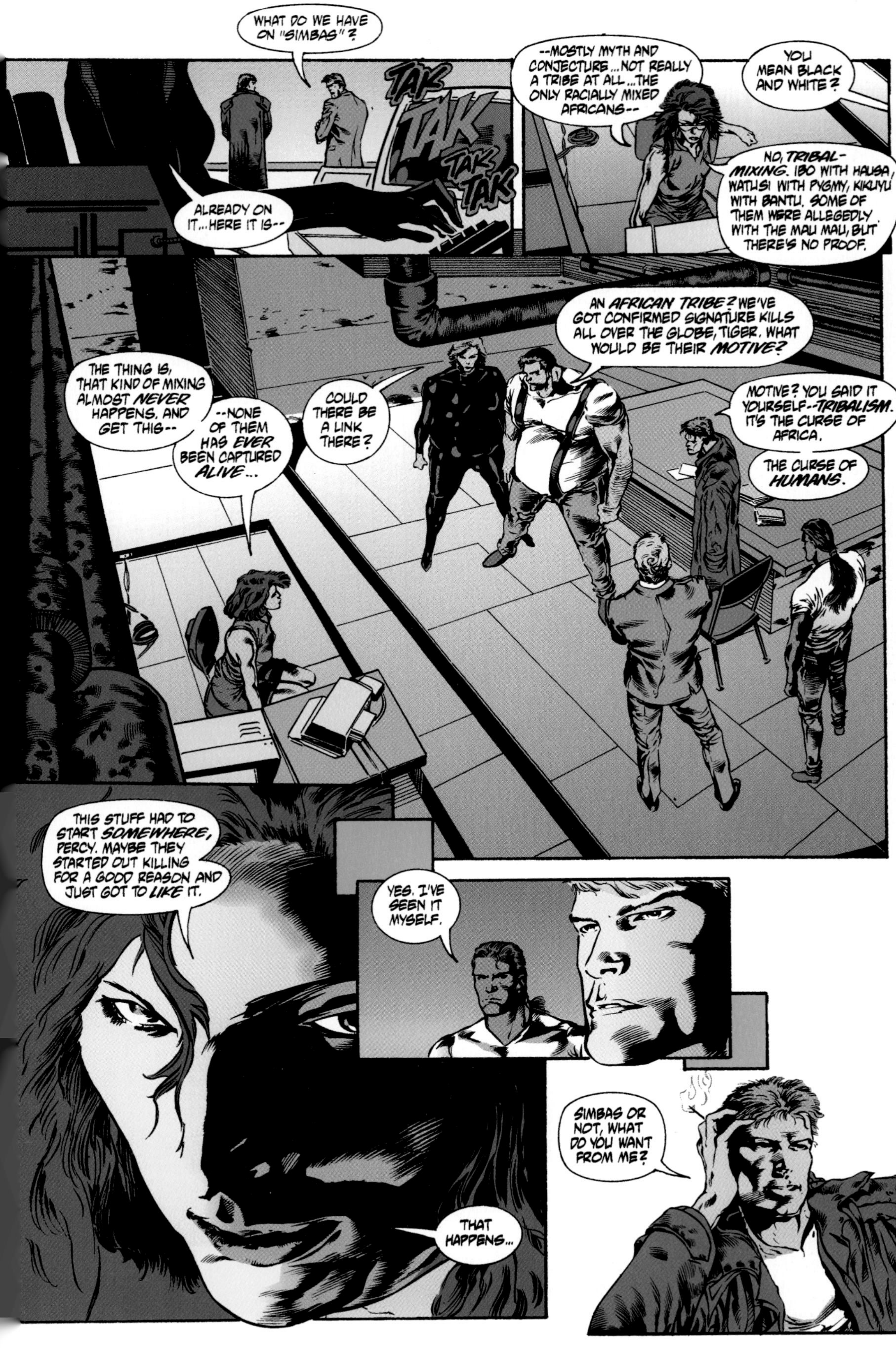
WHAT DO WE HAVE ON "SIMBAS"?
TAK TAK TAK TAK
ALREADY ON IT...HERE IT IS--
--MOSTLY MYTH AND CONJECTURE...NOT REALLY A TRIBE AT ALL...THE ONLY RACIALLY MIXED AFRICANS--
YOU MEAN BLACK AND WHITE?
NO, TRIBAL-MIXING. IBO WITH HAUSA, WATUSI WITH PYGMY, KIKUYU WITH BANTU. SOME OF THEM WERE ALLEGEDLY WITH THE MAU MAU, BUT THERE'S NO PROOF.
THE THING IS, THAT KIND OF MIXING ALMOST NEVER HAPPENS. AND GET THIS--
--NONE OF THEM HAS EVER BEEN CAPTURED ALIVE...
COULD THERE BE A LINK THERE?
AN AFRICAN TRIBE? WE'VE GOT CONFIRMED SIGNATURE KILLS ALL OVER THE GLOBE, TIGER. WHAT WOULD BE THEIR MOTIVE?
MOTIVE? YOU SAID IT YOURSELF--TRIBALISM. IT'S THE CURSE OF AFRICA.
THE CURSE OF HUMANS.
THIS STUFF HAD TO START SOMEWHERE, PERCY. MAYBE THEY STARTED OUT KILLING FOR A GOOD REASON AND JUST GOT TO LIKE IT.
YES. I'VE SEEN IT MYSELF.
THAT HAPPENS...
SIMBAS OR NOT, WHAT DO YOU WANT FROM ME?

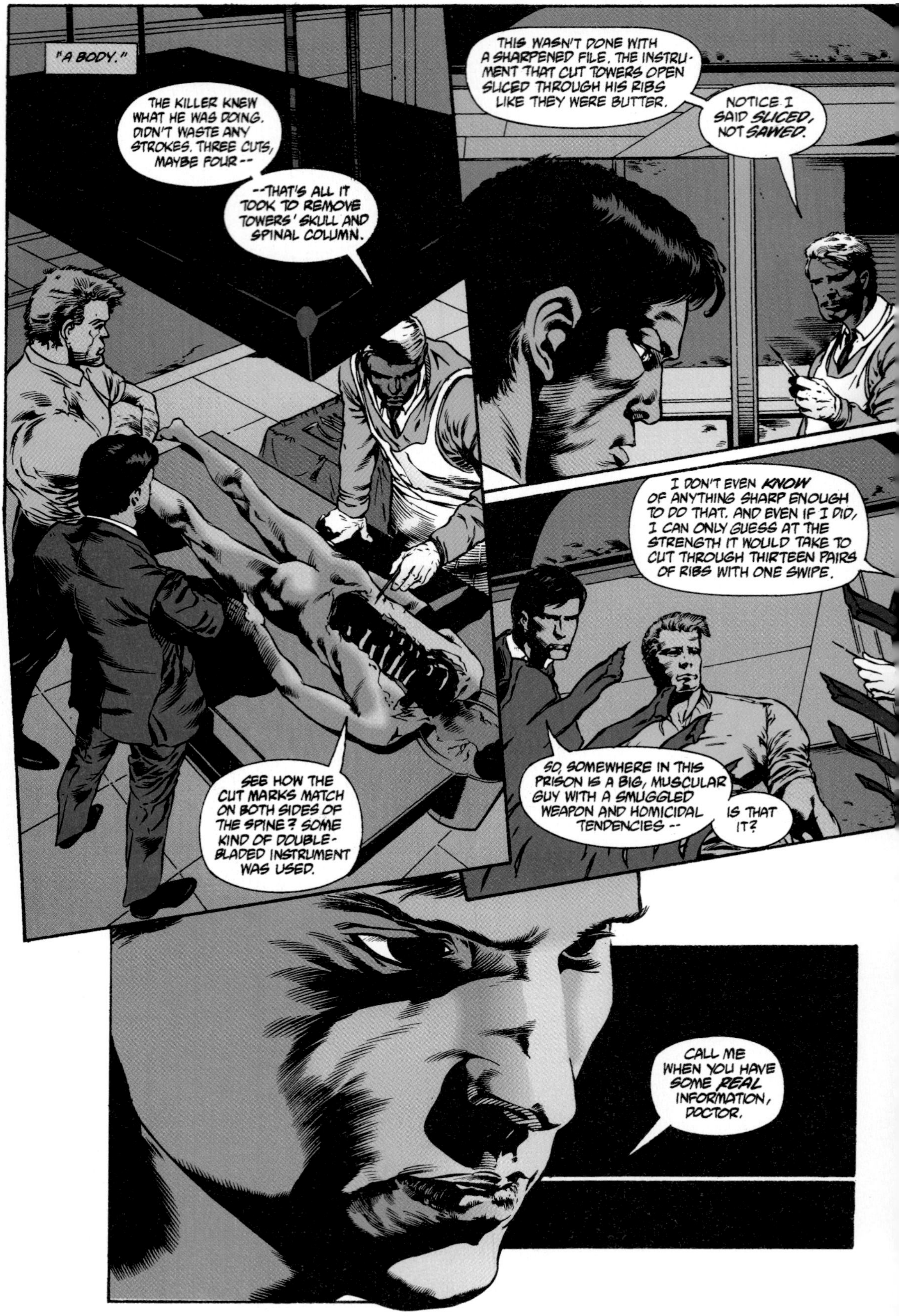
"A BODY."
THE KILLER KNEW WHAT HE WAS DOING. DIDN'T WASTE ANY STROKES. THREE CUTS, MAYBE FOUR --
--THAT'S ALL IT TOOK TO REMOVE TOWERS' SKULL AND SPINAL COLUMN.
SEE HOW THE CUT MARKS MATCH ON BOTH SIDES OF THE SPINE? SOME KIND OF DOUBLE-BLADED INSTRUMENT WAS USED.
THIS WASN'T DONE WITH A SHARPENED FILE. THE INSTRUMENT THAT CUT TOWERS OPEN SLICED THROUGH HIS RIBS LIKE THEY WERE BUTTER.
NOTICE I SAID SLICED, NOT SAWED.
I DON'T EVEN KNOW OF ANYTHING SHARP ENOUGH TO DO THAT. AND EVEN IF I DID, I CAN ONLY GUESS AT THE STRENGTH IT WOULD TAKE TO CUT THROUGH THIRTEEN PAIRS OF RIBS WITH ONE SWIPE.
SO, SOMEWHERE IN THIS PRISON IS A BIG, MUSCULAR GUY WITH A SMUGGLED WEAPON AND HOMICIDAL TENDENCIES --
IS THAT IT?
CALL ME WHEN YOU HAVE SOME REAL INFORMATION, DOCTOR.

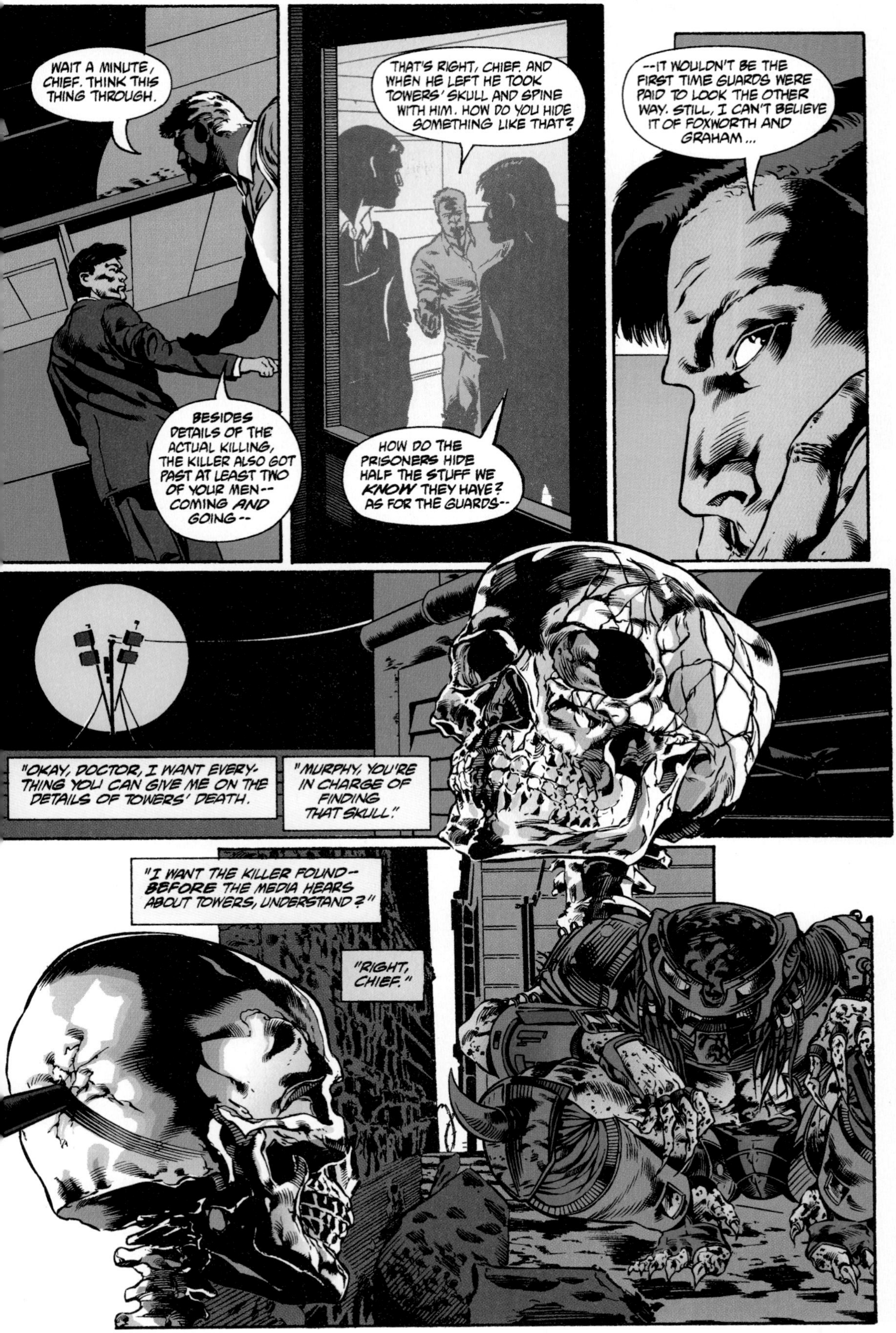
WAIT A MINUTE, CHIEF. THINK THIS THING THROUGH.
BESIDES DETAILS OF THE ACTUAL KILLING, THE KILLER ALSO GOT PAST AT LEAST TWO OF YOUR MEN--COMING AND GOING--
THAT'S RIGHT, CHIEF. AND WHEN HE LEFT HE TOOK TOWERS' SKULL AND SPINE WITH HIM. HOW DO YOU HIDE SOMETHING LIKE THAT?
HOW DO THE PRISONERS HIDE HALF THE STUFF WE KNOW THEY HAVE? AS FOR THE GUARDS--
--IT WOULDN'T BE THE FIRST TIME GUARDS WERE PAID TO LOOK THE OTHER WAY. STILL, I CAN'T BELIEVE IT OF FOXWORTH AND GRAHAM...
"OKAY, DOCTOR, I WANT EVERYTHING YOU CAN GIVE ME ON THE DETAILS OF TOWERS' DEATH.
"MURPHY, YOU'RE IN CHARGE OF FINDING THAT SKULL."
"I WANT THE KILLER FOUND--BEFORE THE MEDIA HEARS ABOUT TOWERS, UNDERSTAND?"
"RIGHT, CHIEF."

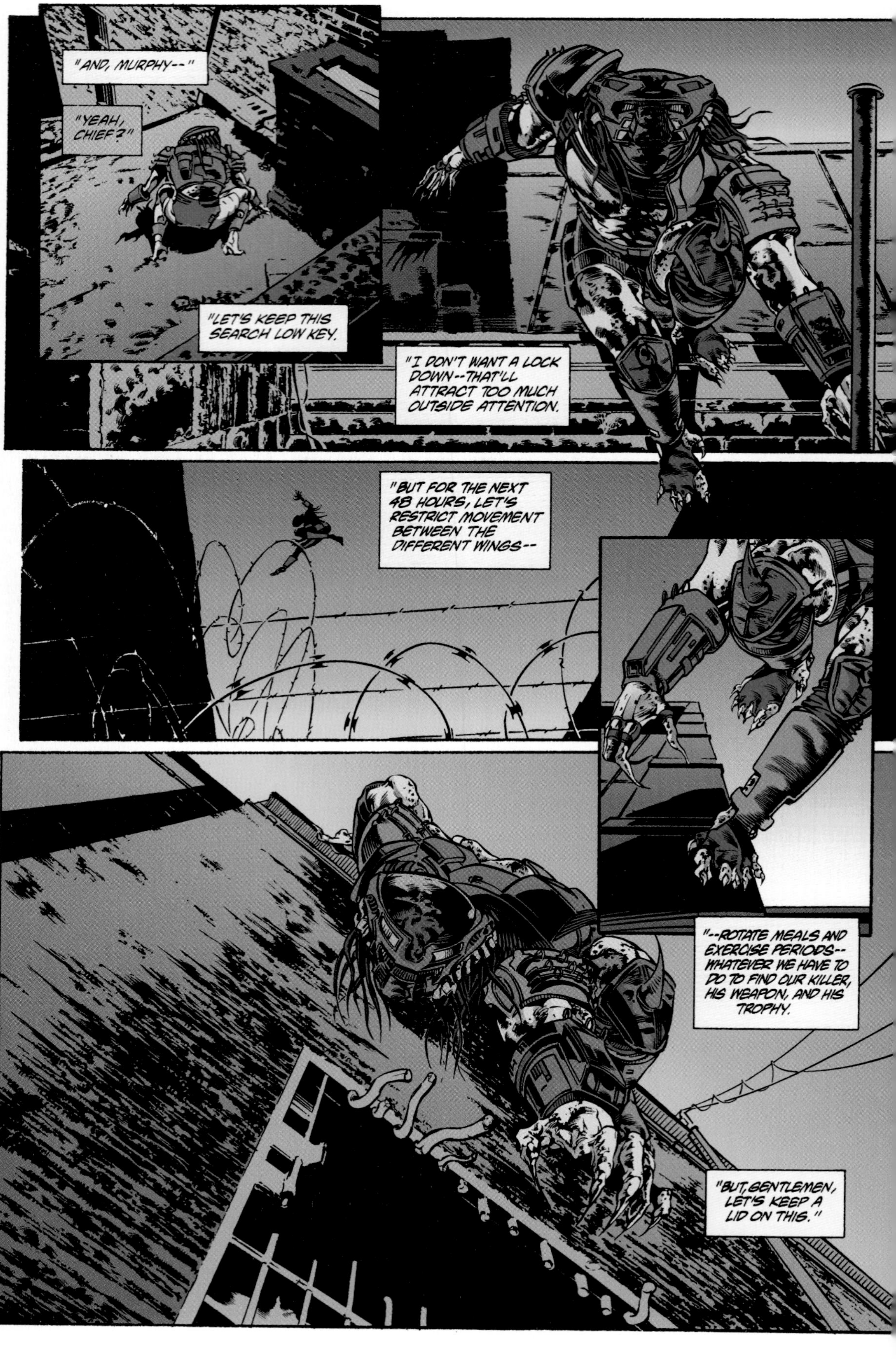
"AND, MURPHY--"
"YEAH, CHIEF?"
"LET'S KEEP THIS SEARCH LOW KEY.
"I DON'T WANT A LOCK DOWN--THAT'LL ATTRACT TOO MUCH OUTSIDE ATTENTION.
"BUT FOR THE NEXT 48 HOURS, LET'S RESTRICT MOVEMENT BETWEEN THE DIFFERENT WINGS--
"--ROTATE MEALS AND EXERCISE PERIODS--WHATEVER WE HAVE TO DO TO FIND OUR KILLER, HIS WEAPON, AND HIS TROPHY.
"BUT, GENTLEMEN, LET'S KEEP A LID ON THIS."

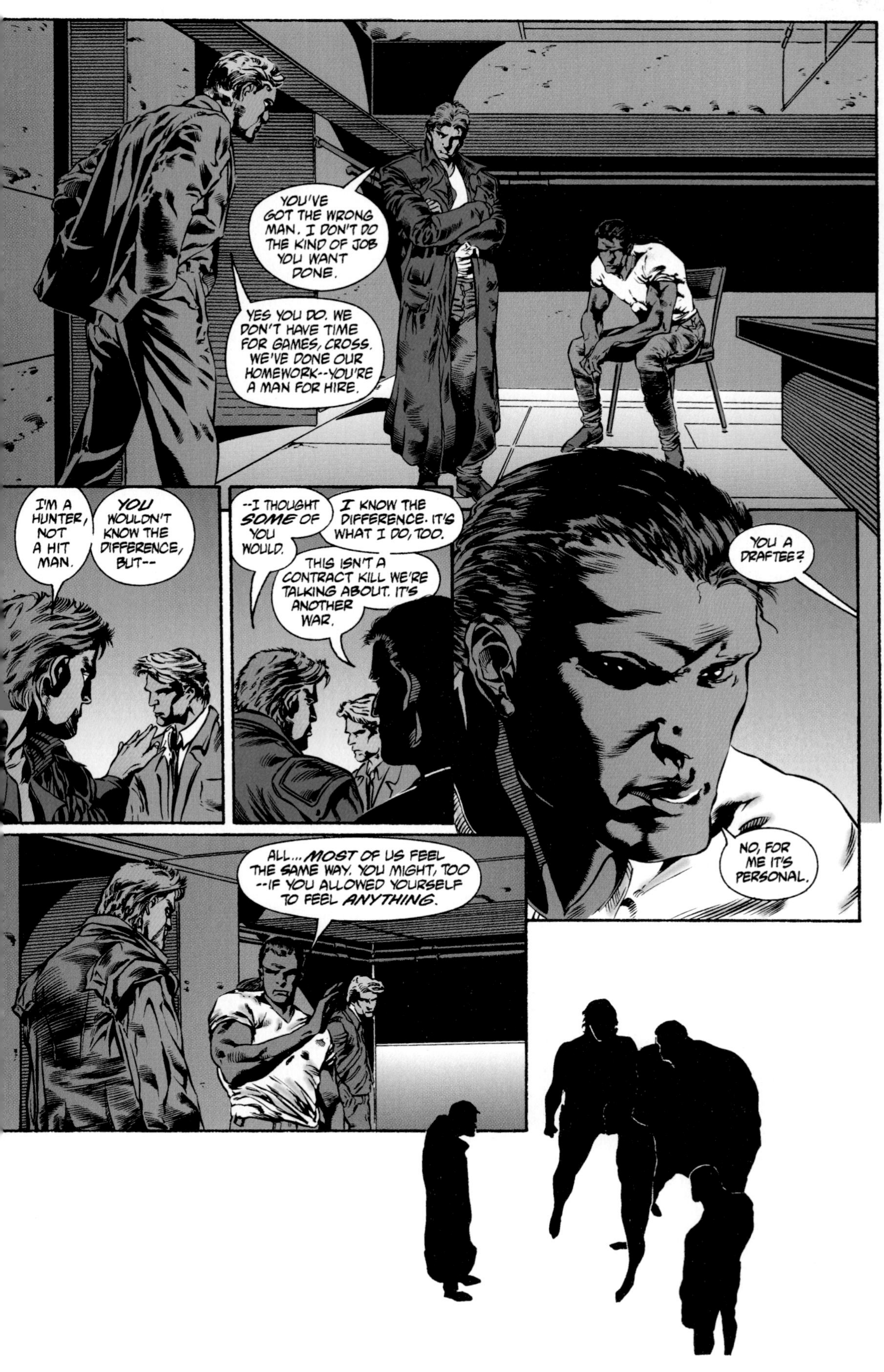
YOU'VE GOT THE WRONG MAN. I DON'T DO THE KIND OF JOB YOU WANT DONE.
YES YOU DO. WE DON'T HAVE TIME FOR GAMES, CROSS. WE'VE DONE OUR HOMEWORK--YOU'RE A MAN FOR HIRE.
I'M A HUNTER, NOT A HIT MAN.
YOU WOULDN'T KNOW THE DIFFERENCE, BUT--
--I THOUGHT SOME OF YOU WOULD.
I KNOW THE DIFFERENCE. IT'S WHAT I DO, TOO.
THIS ISN'T A CONTRACT KILL WE'RE TALKING ABOUT. IT'S ANOTHER WAR.
YOU A DRAFTEE?
NO, FOR ME IT'S PERSONAL.
ALL... MOST OF US FEEL THE SAME WAY. YOU MIGHT, TOO --IF YOU ALLOWED YOURSELF TO FEEL ANYTHING.

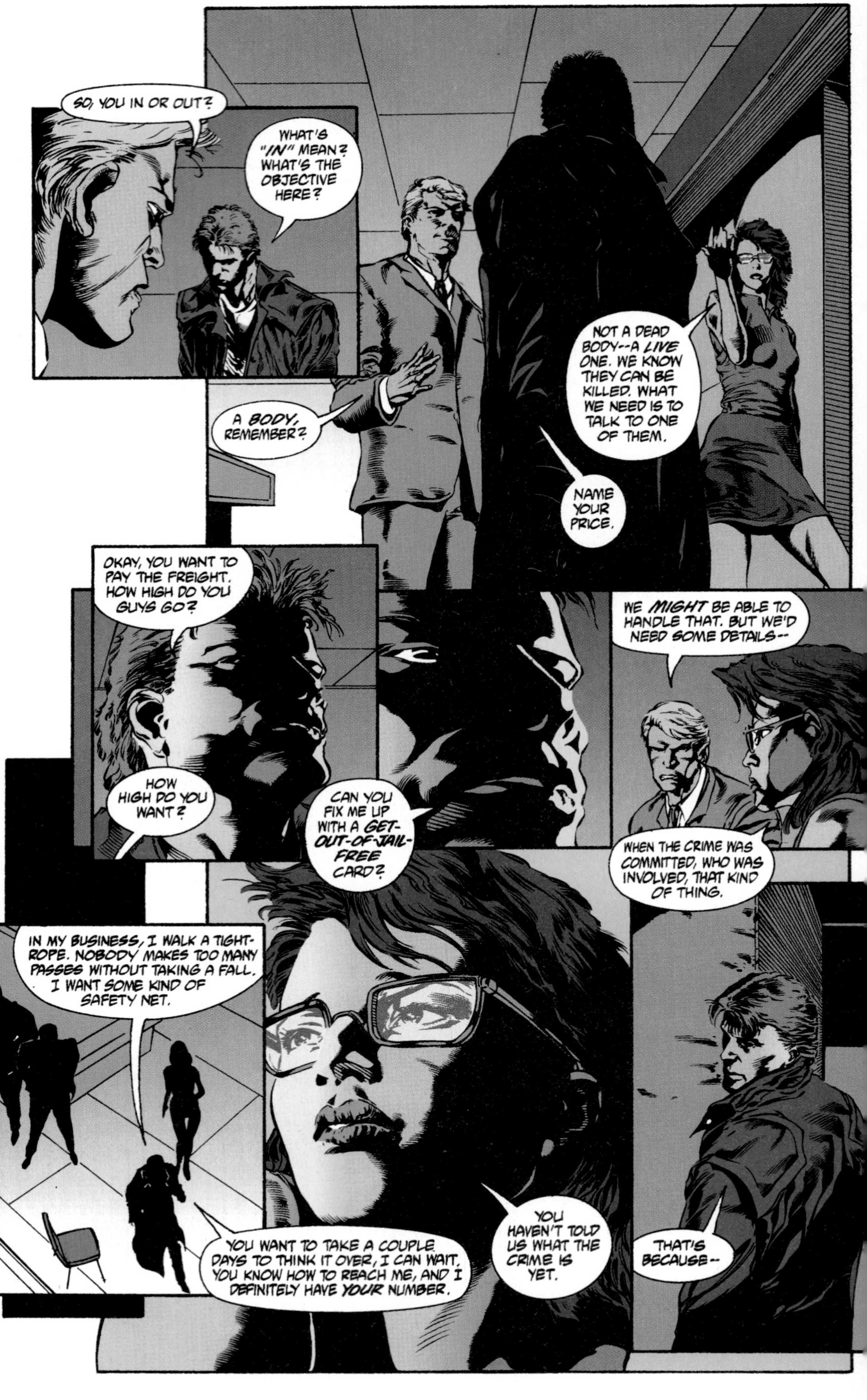
SO, YOU IN OR OUT?
WHAT'S "IN" MEAN? WHAT'S THE OBJECTIVE HERE?
A BODY, REMEMBER?
NOT A DEAD BODY--A LIVE ONE. WE KNOW THEY CAN BE KILLED. WHAT WE NEED IS TO TALK TO ONE OF THEM.
NAME YOUR PRICE.
OKAY, YOU WANT TO PAY THE FREIGHT. HOW HIGH DO YOU GUYS GO?
HOW HIGH DO YOU WANT?
CAN YOU FIX ME UP WITH A GET-OUT-OF-JAIL-FREE CARD?
WE MIGHT BE ABLE TO HANDLE THAT. BUT WE'D NEED SOME DETAILS--
WHEN THE CRIME WAS COMMITTED, WHO WAS INVOLVED, THAT KIND OF THING.
IN MY BUSINESS, I WALK A TIGHT-ROPE. NOBODY MAKES TOO MANY PASSES WITHOUT TAKING A FALL. I WANT SOME KIND OF SAFETY NET.
YOU WANT TO TAKE A COUPLE DAYS TO THINK IT OVER, I CAN WAIT. YOU KNOW HOW TO REACH ME, AND I DEFINITELY HAVE YOUR NUMBER.
YOU HAVEN'T TOLD US WHAT THE CRIME IS YET.
THAT'S BECAUSE--

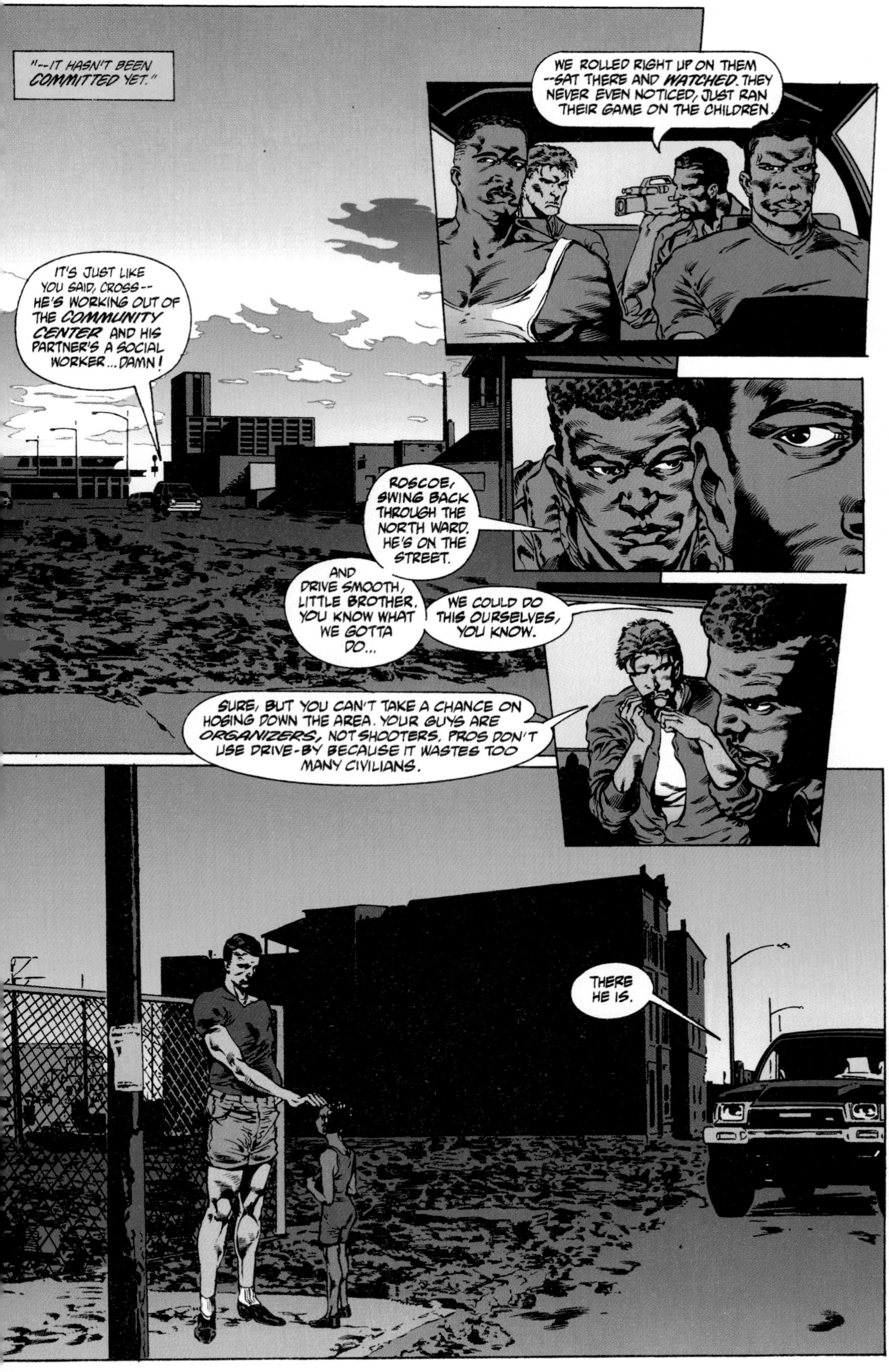
"--IT HASN'T BEEN COMMITTED YET."
WE ROLLED RIGHT UP ON THEM --SAT THERE AND WATCHED. THEY NEVER EVEN NOTICED; JUST RAN THEIR GAME ON THE CHILDREN.
IT'S JUST LIKE YOU SAID, CROSS-- HE'S WORKING OUT OF THE COMMUNITY CENTER AND HIS PARTNER'S A SOCIAL WORKER... DAMN!
ROSCOE, SWING BACK THROUGH THE NORTH WARD. HE'S ON THE STREET.
AND DRIVE SMOOTH, LITTLE BROTHER. YOU KNOW WHAT WE GOTTA DO...
WE COULD DO THIS OURSELVES, YOU KNOW.
SURE, BUT YOU CAN'T TAKE A CHANCE ON HOSING DOWN THE AREA. YOUR GUYS ARE ORGANIZERS, NOT SHOOTERS. PROS DON'T USE DRIVE-BY BECAUSE IT WASTES TOO MANY CIVILIANS.
THERE HE IS.

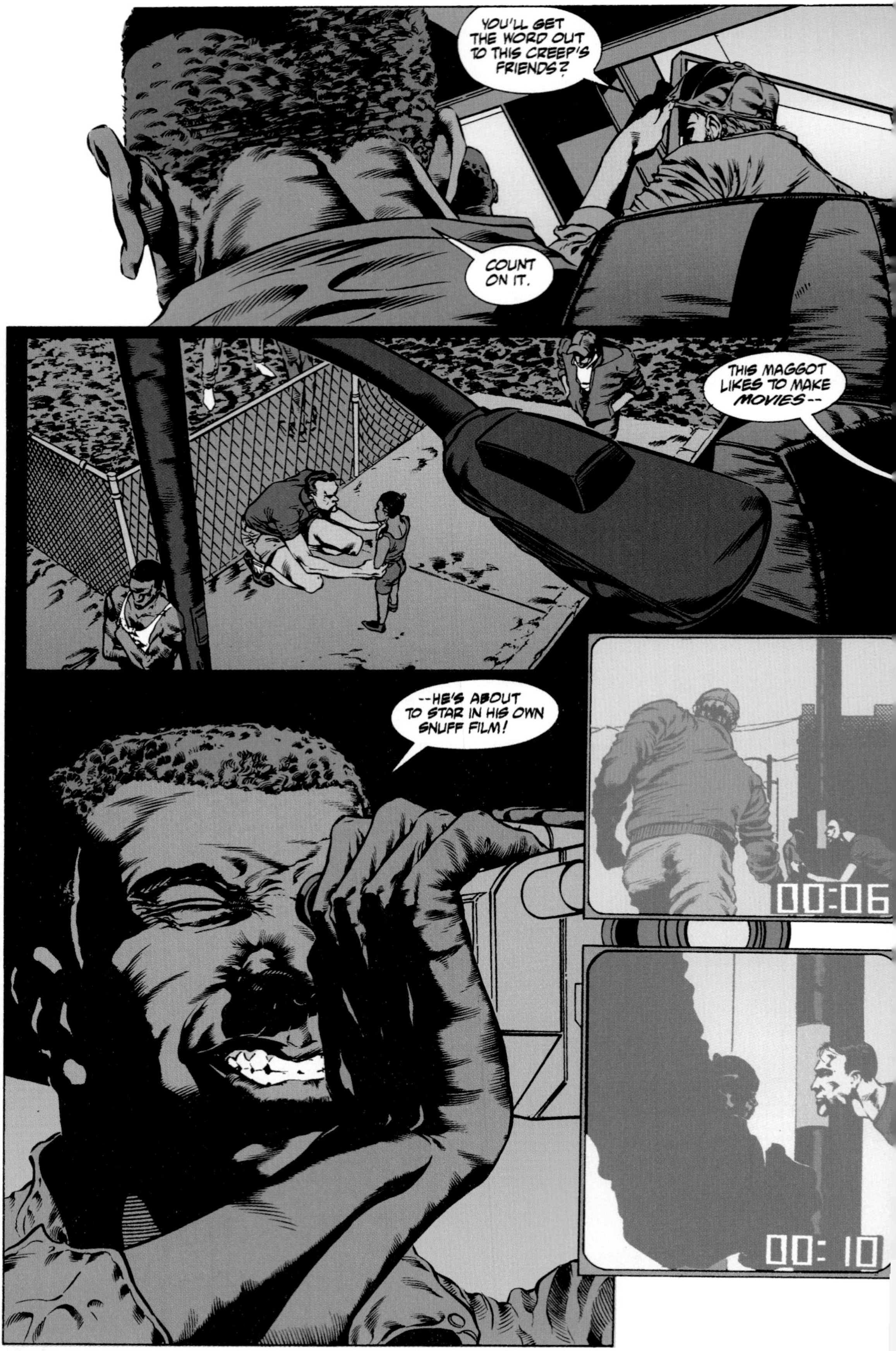

YOU'LL GET THE WORD OUT TO THIS CREEP'S FRIENDS?
COUNT ON IT.
THIS MAGGOT LIKES TO MAKE *MOVIES*--
--HE'S ABOUT TO STAR IN HIS OWN SNUFF FILM!
00:06
00:10

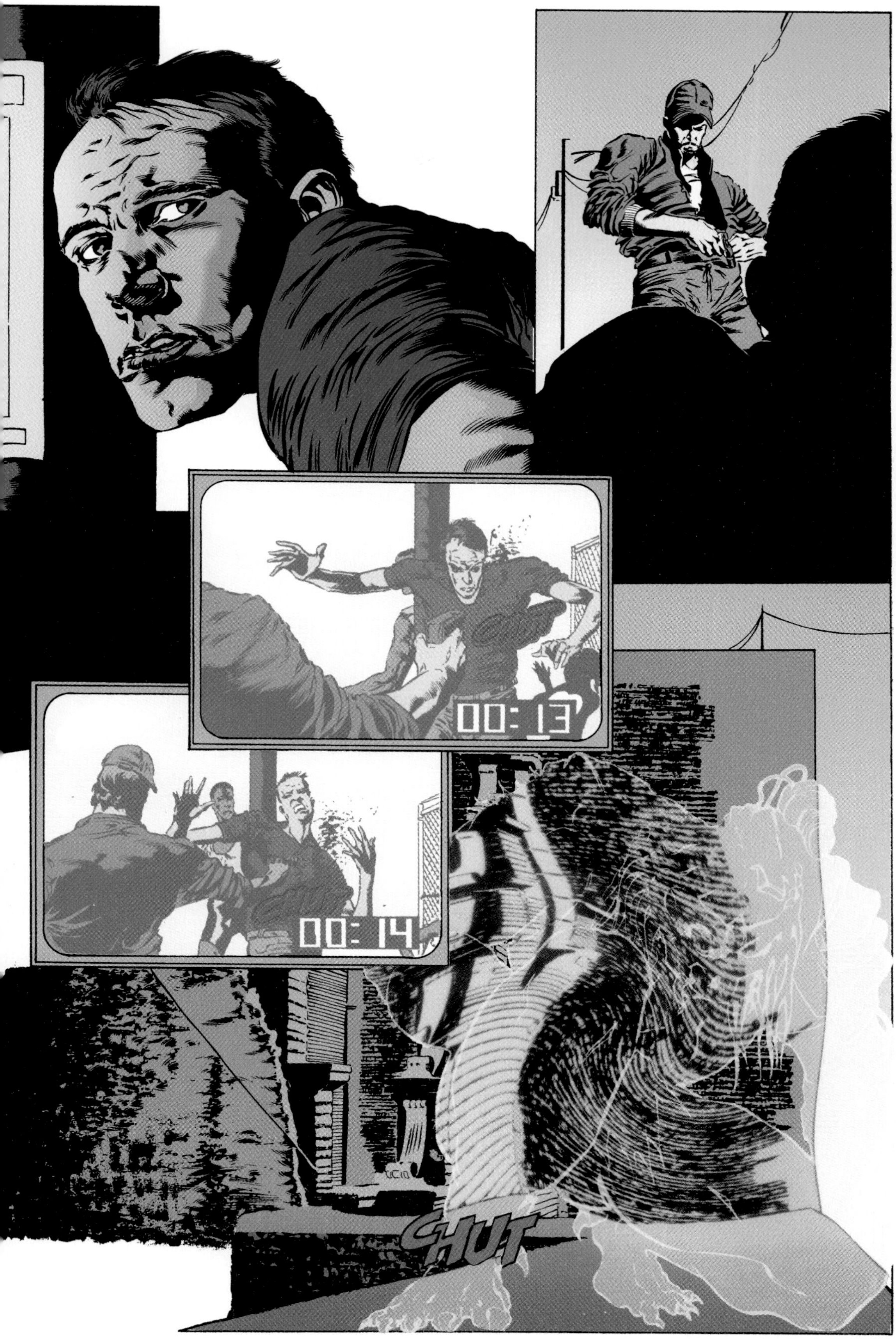
CHUT
00:13
CHUT
00:14
CHUT

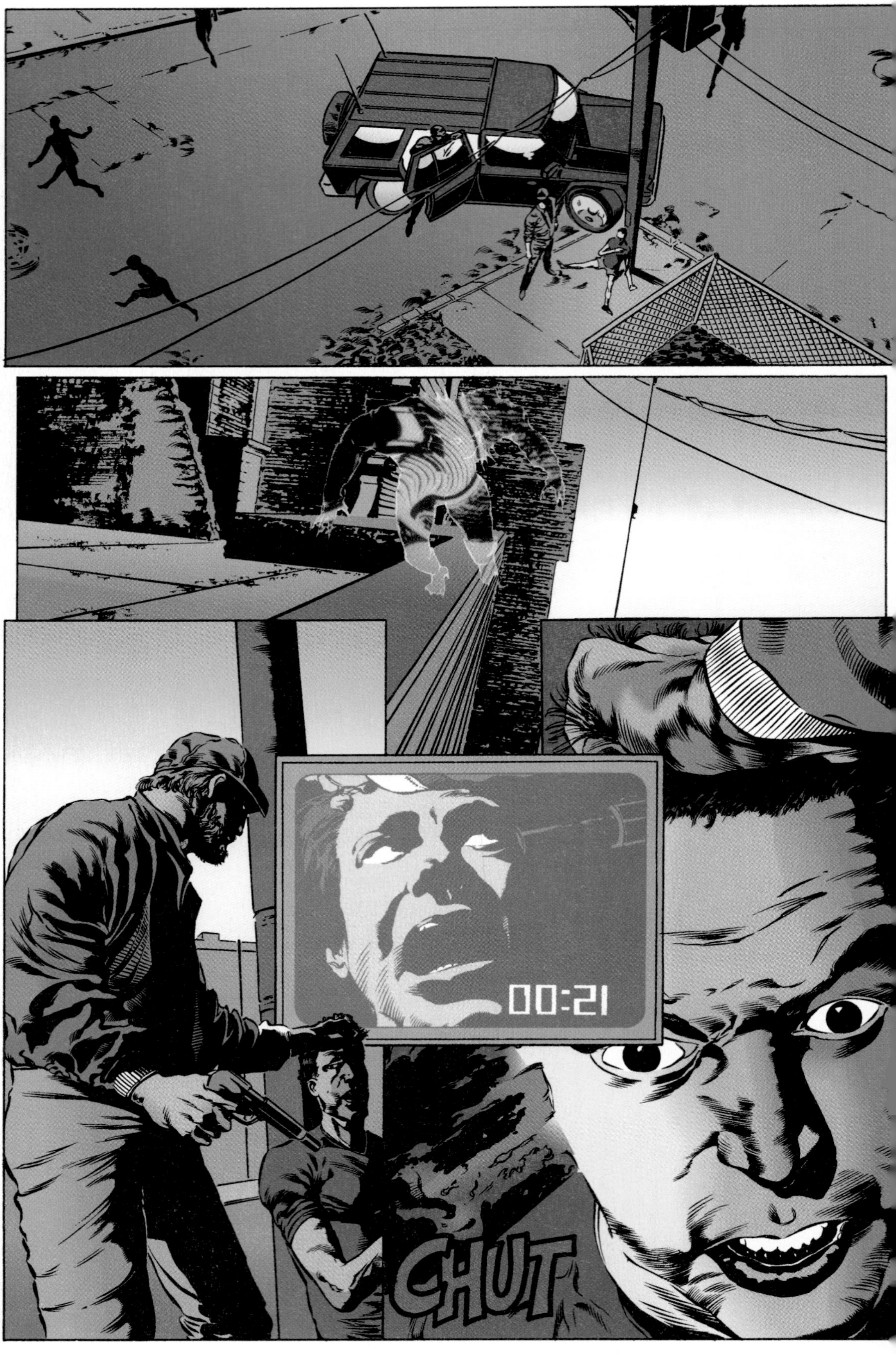
00:21
CHUT

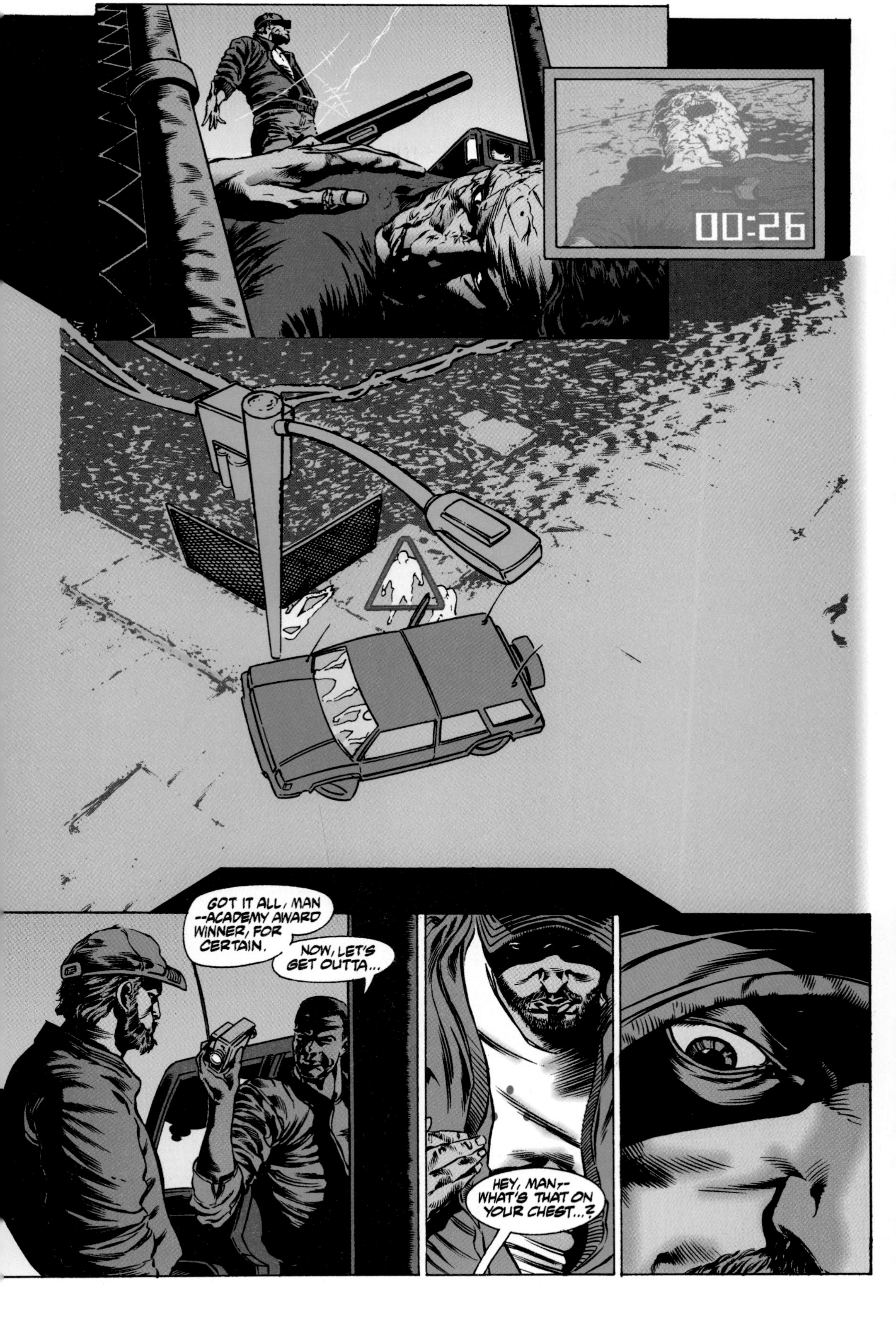
00:26
GOT IT ALL, MAN --ACADEMY AWARD WINNER, FOR CERTAIN.
NOW, LET'S GET OUTTA...
HEY, MAN,-- WHAT'S THAT ON YOUR CHEST...?

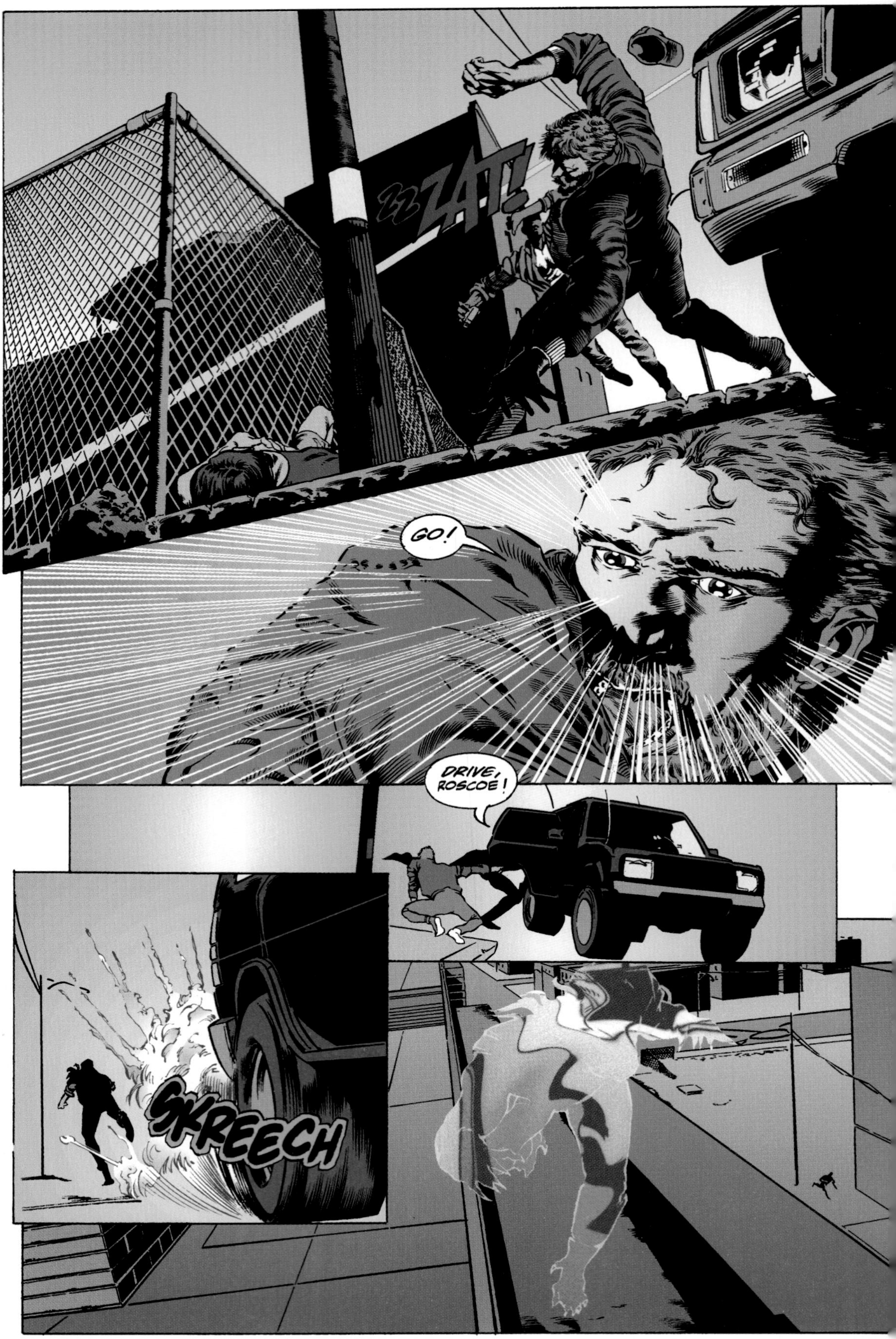
ZZ ZAT!
GO!
DRIVE, ROSCOE!
SKREECH

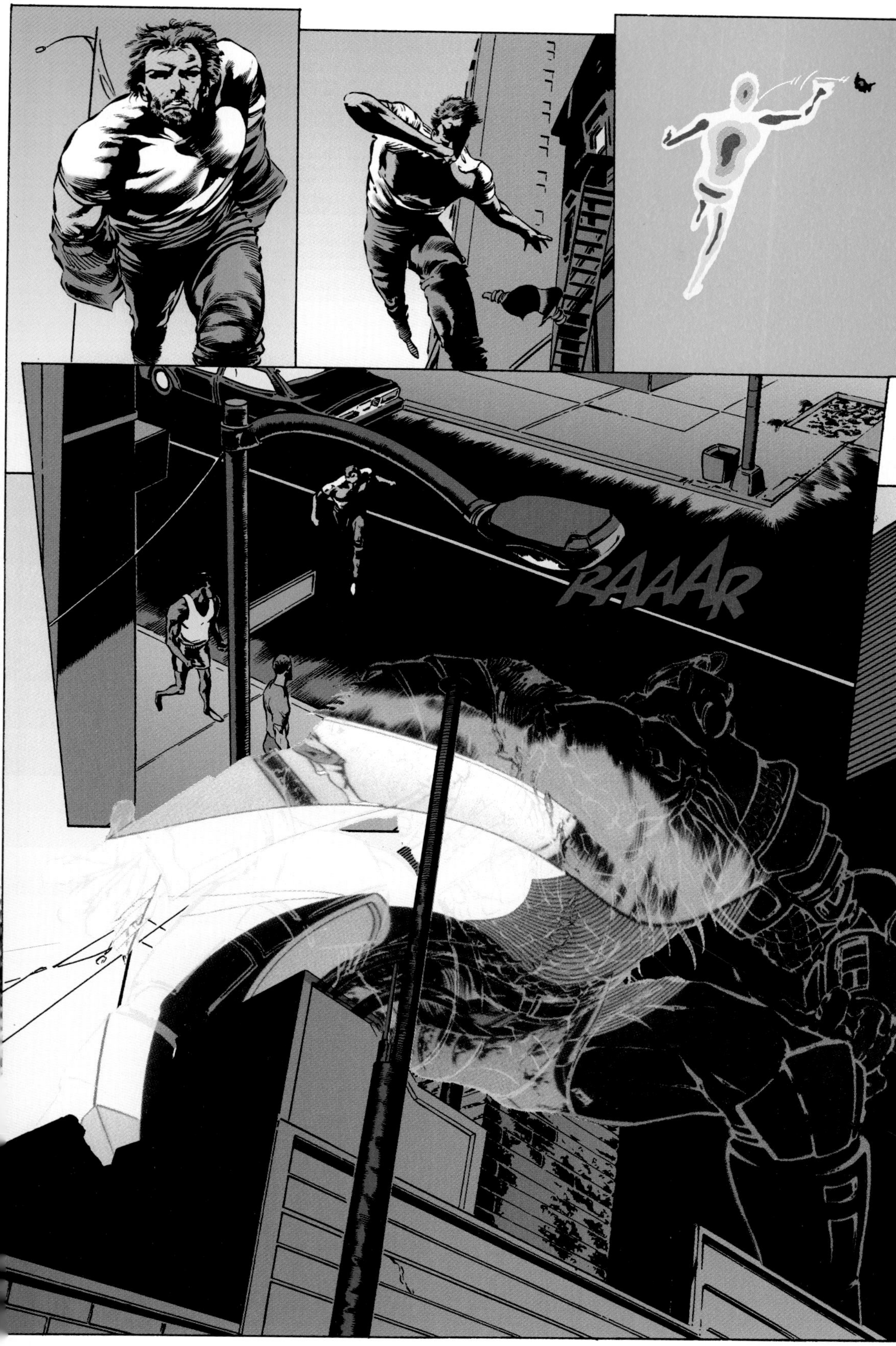
RAAAR

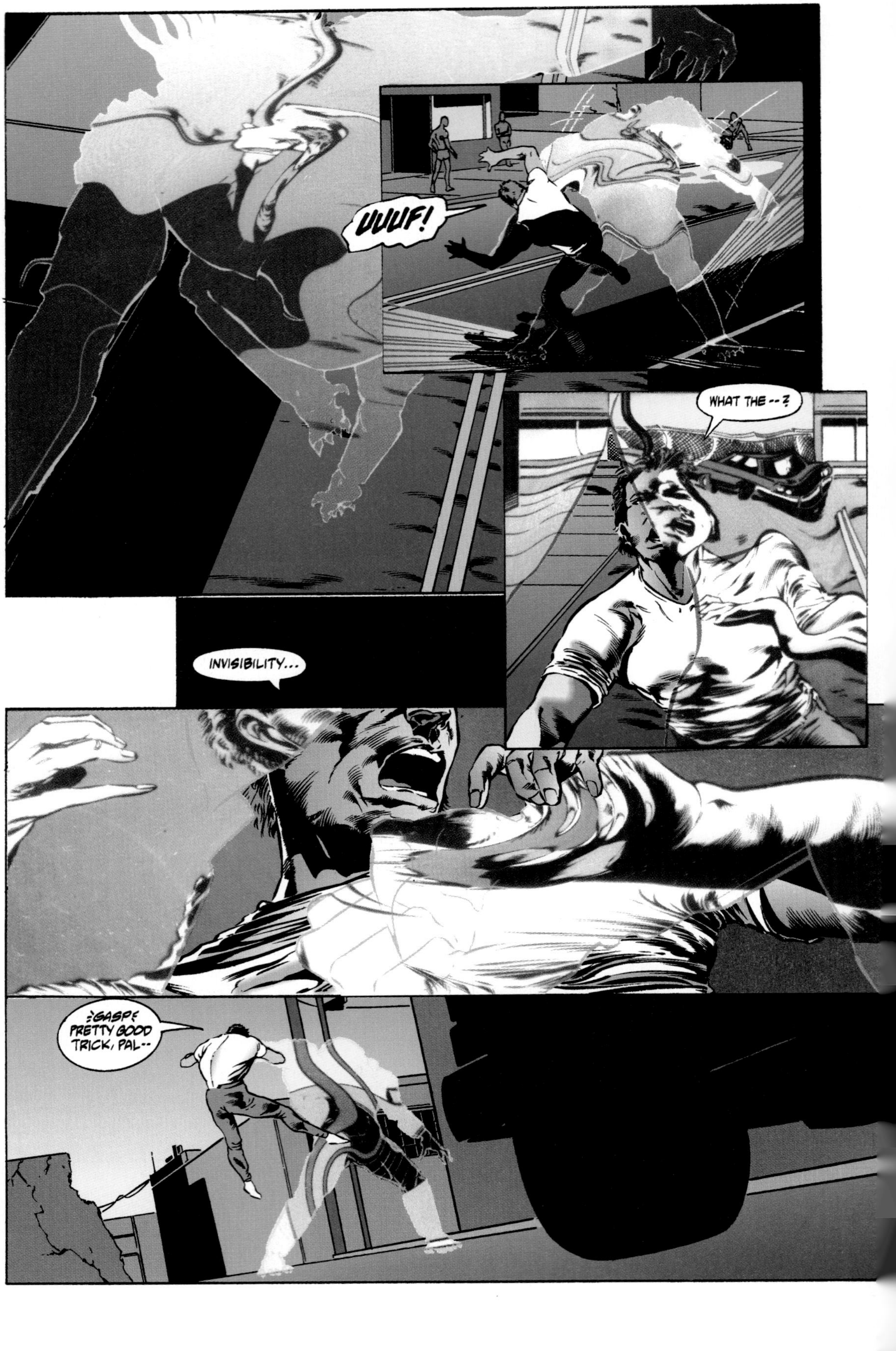
UUUF!
WHAT THE --?
INVISIBILITY...
GASP
PRETTY GOOD TRICK, PAL--

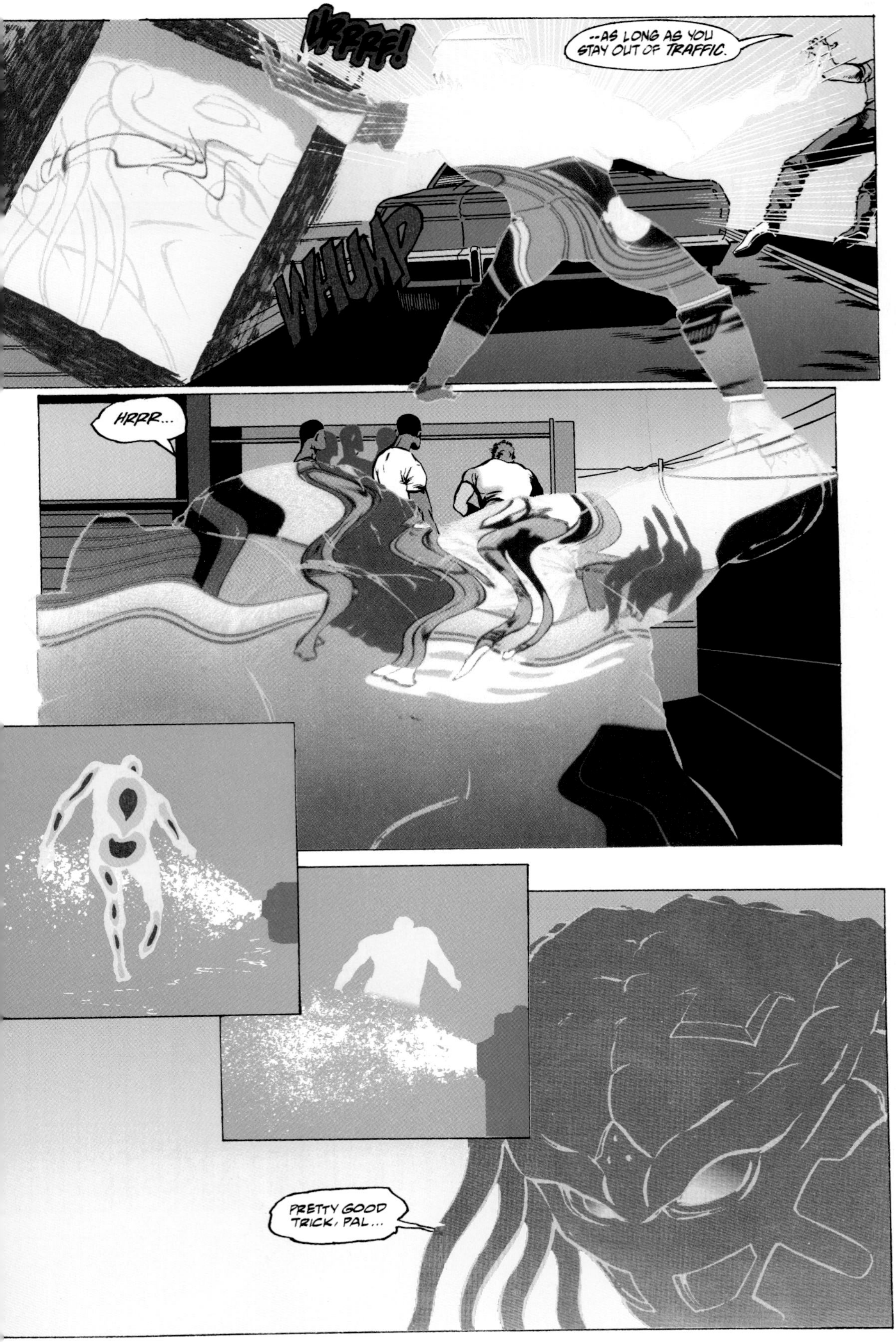
URRRF!
--AS LONG AS YOU STAY OUT OF TRAFFIC.
WHUMP
HRRR...
PRETTY GOOD TRICK, PAL...

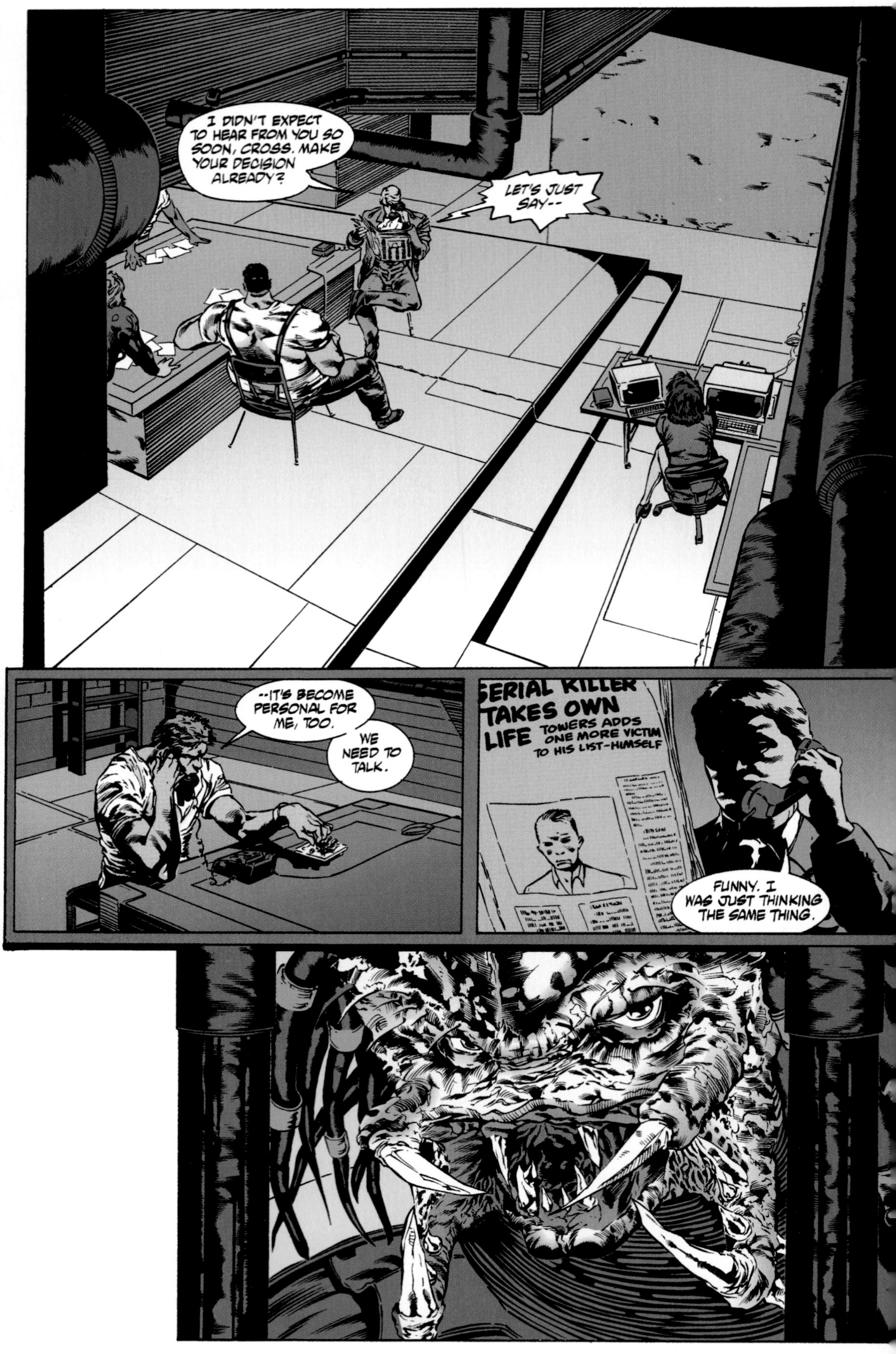
I DIDN'T EXPECT TO HEAR FROM YOU SO SOON, CROSS. MAKE YOUR DECISION ALREADY?
LET'S JUST SAY--
--IT'S BECOME PERSONAL FOR ME, TOO.
WE NEED TO TALK.
SERIAL KILLER TAKES OWN LIFE
TOWERS ADDS ONE MORE VICTIM TO HIS LIST-HIMSELF
FUNNY. I WAS JUST THINKING THE SAME THING.

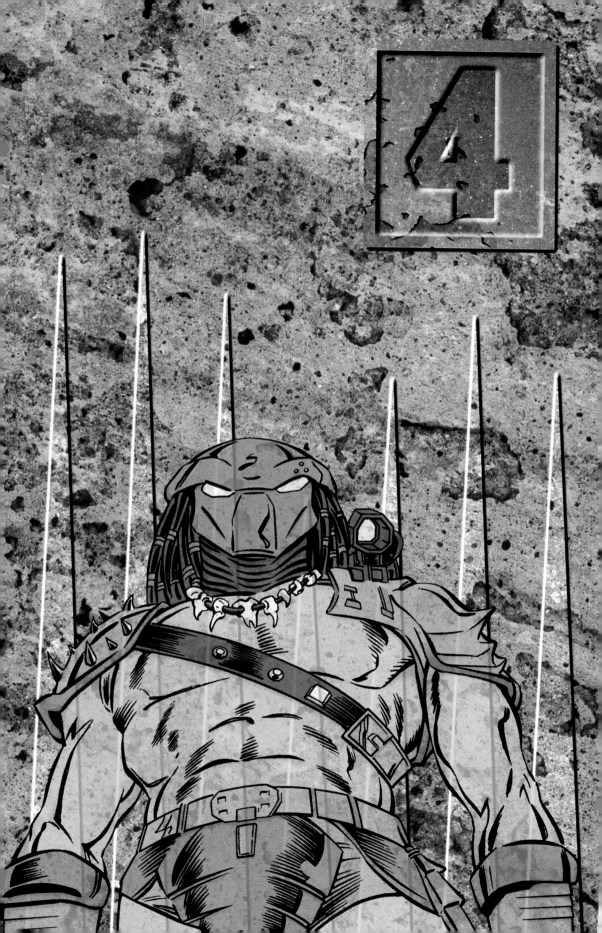

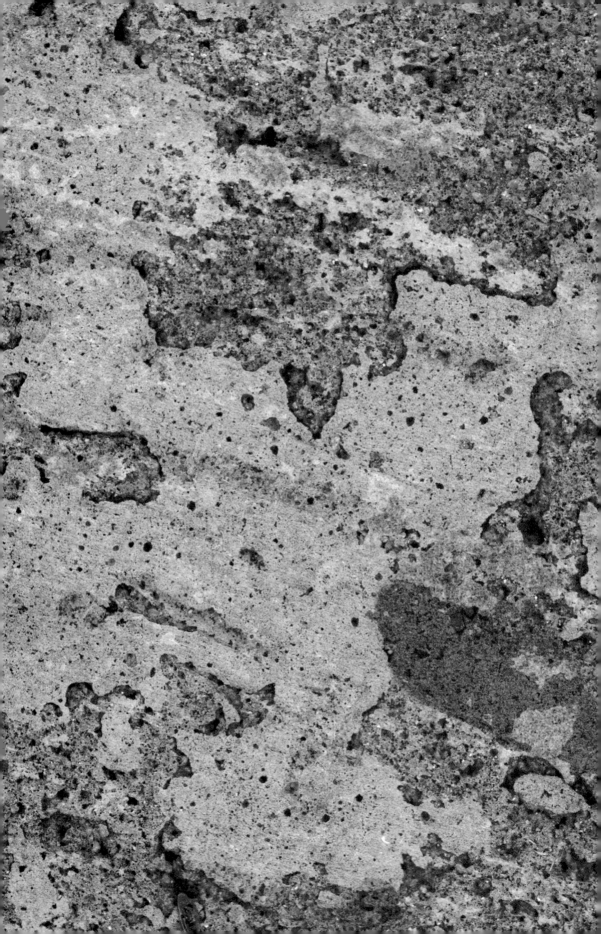

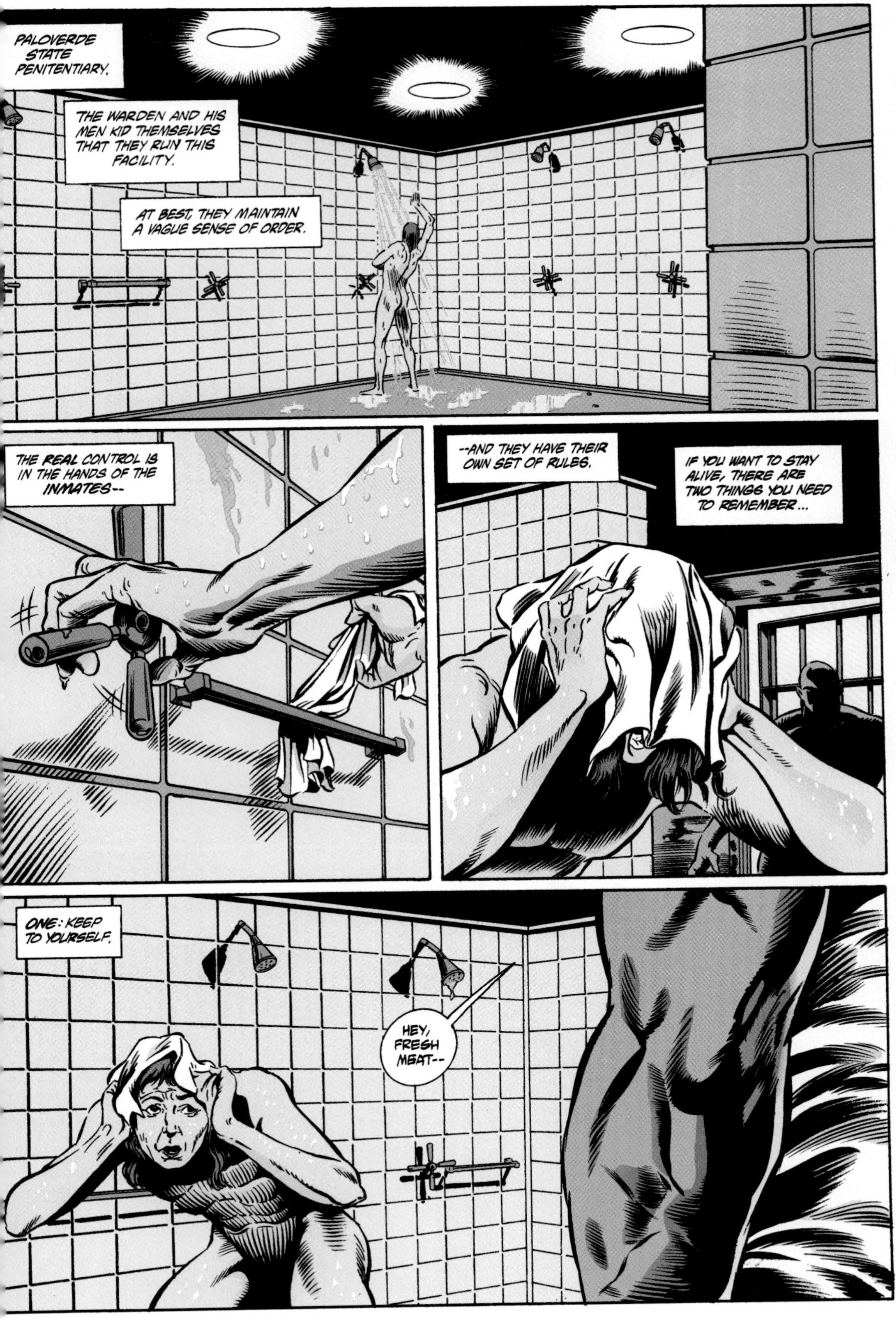
PALOVERDE STATE PENITENTIARY.
THE WARDEN AND HIS MEN KID THEMSELVES THAT THEY RUN THIS FACILITY.
AT BEST, THEY MAINTAIN A VAGUE SENSE OF ORDER.
THE REAL CONTROL IS IN THE HANDS OF THE INMATES--
--AND THEY HAVE THEIR OWN SET OF RULES.
IF YOU WANT TO STAY ALIVE, THERE ARE TWO THINGS YOU NEED TO REMEMBER...
ONE: KEEP TO YOURSELF.
HEY, FRESH MEAT--

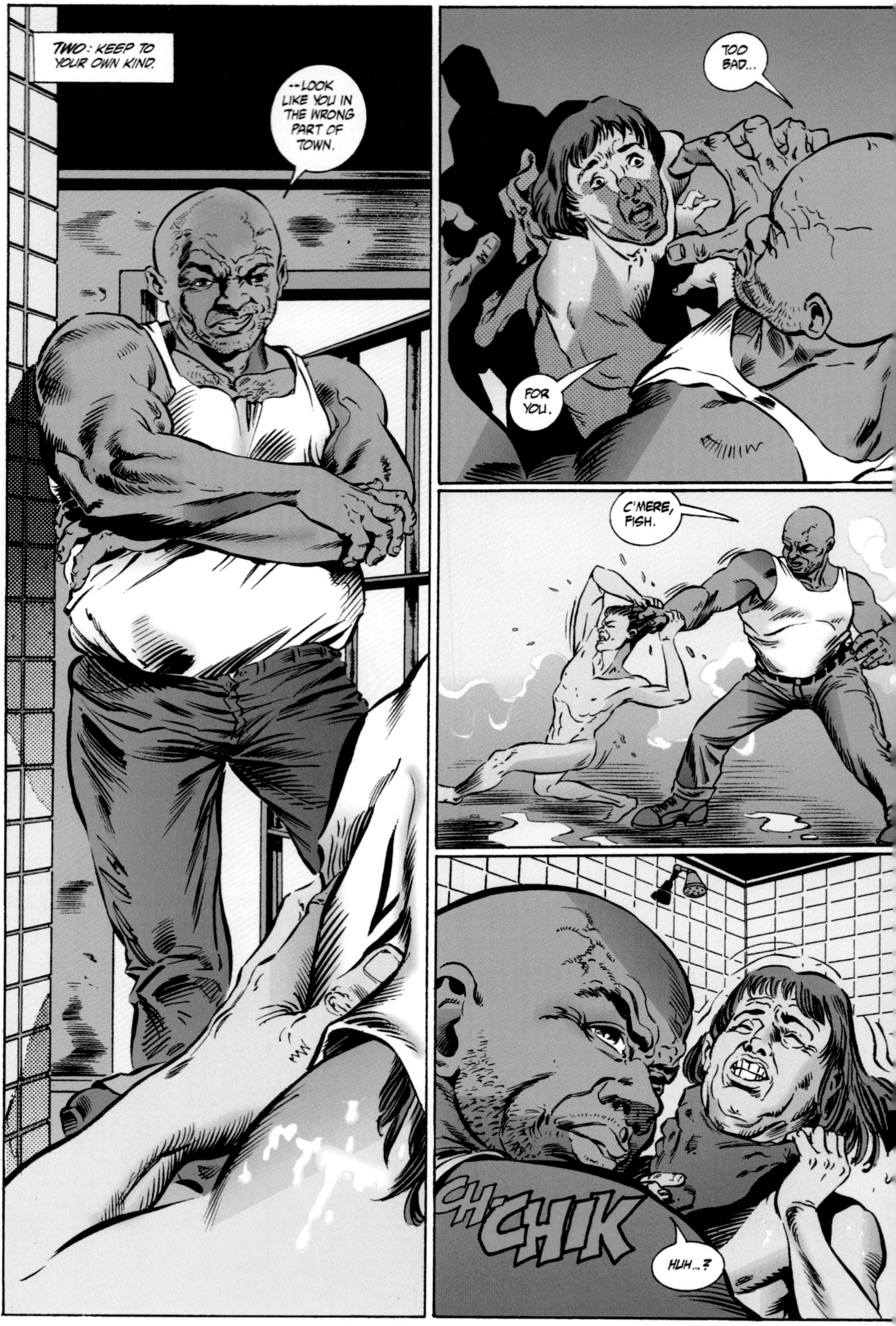
TWO: KEEP TO YOUR OWN KIND.
--LOOK LIKE YOU IN THE WRONG PART OF TOWN.
TOO BAD...
FOR YOU.
C'MERE, FISH.
CH-CHIK
HUH...?

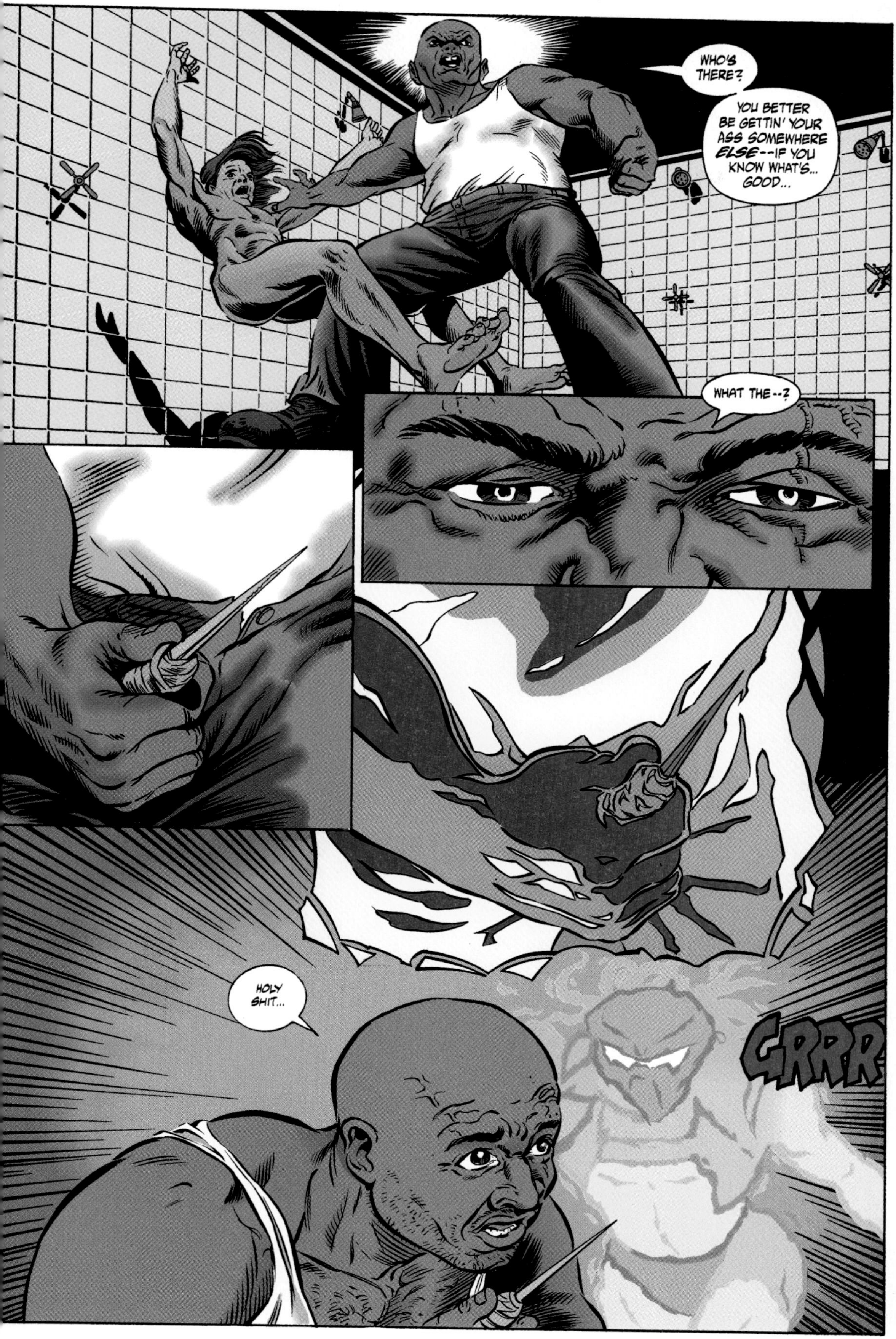
WHO'S THERE?
YOU BETTER BE GETTIN' YOUR ASS SOMEWHERE *ELSE*--IF YOU KNOW WHAT'S... GOOD...
WHAT THE--?
HOLY SHIT...
GRRR

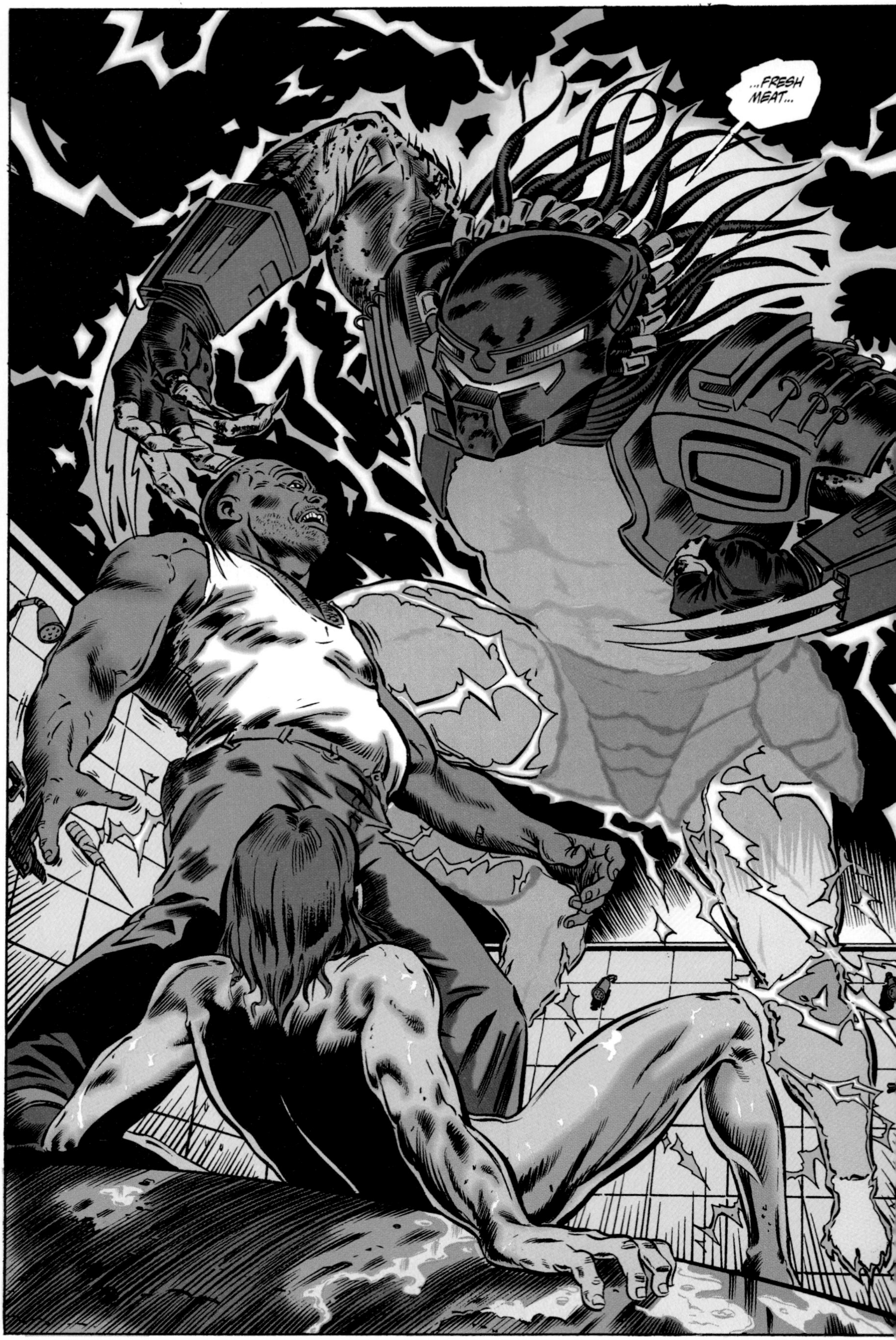
...FRESH MEAT...

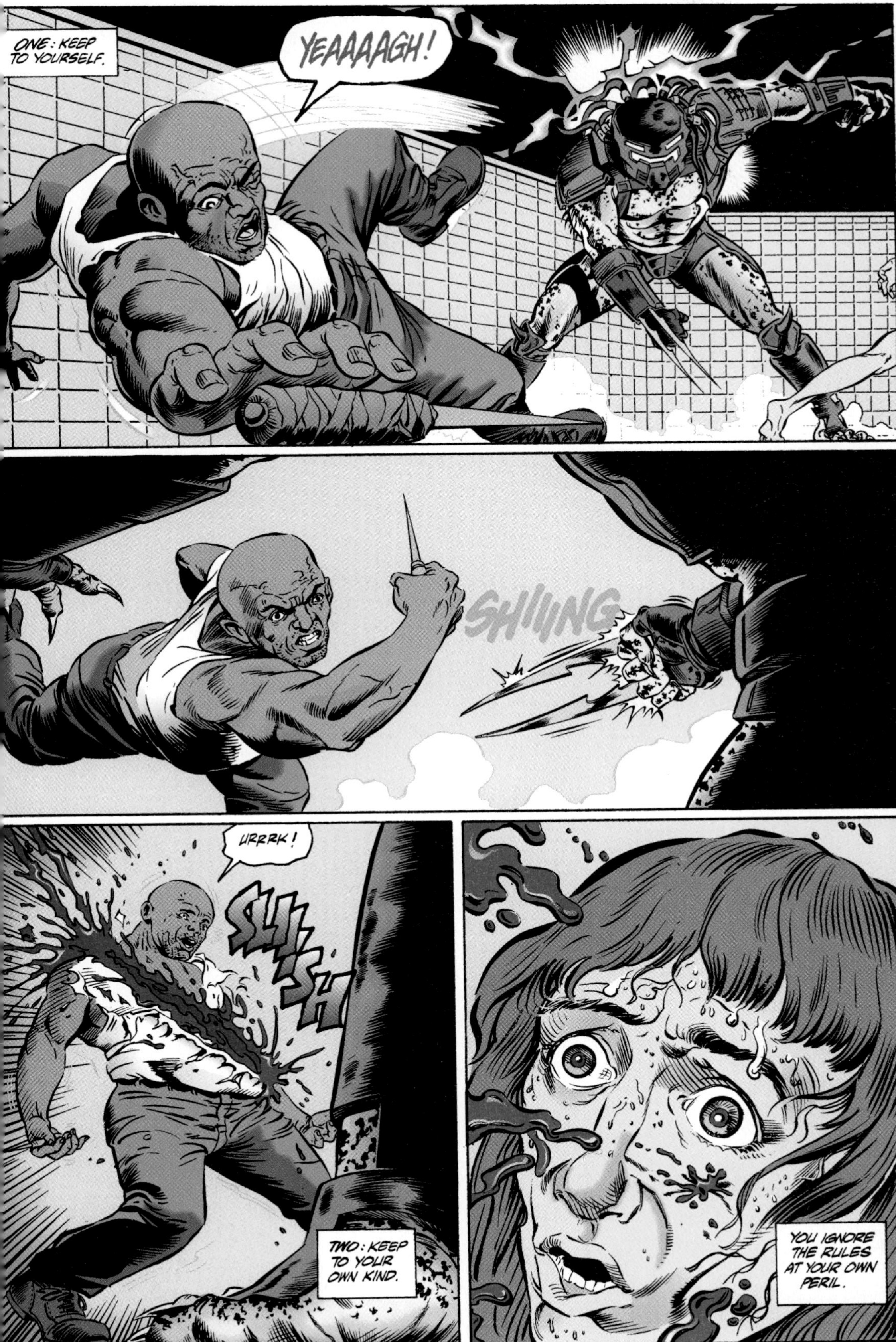
ONE: KEEP TO YOURSELF.
YEAAAAGH!
SHIIING
URRRK!
SLISH
TWO: KEEP TO YOUR OWN KIND.
YOU IGNORE THE RULES AT YOUR OWN PERIL.

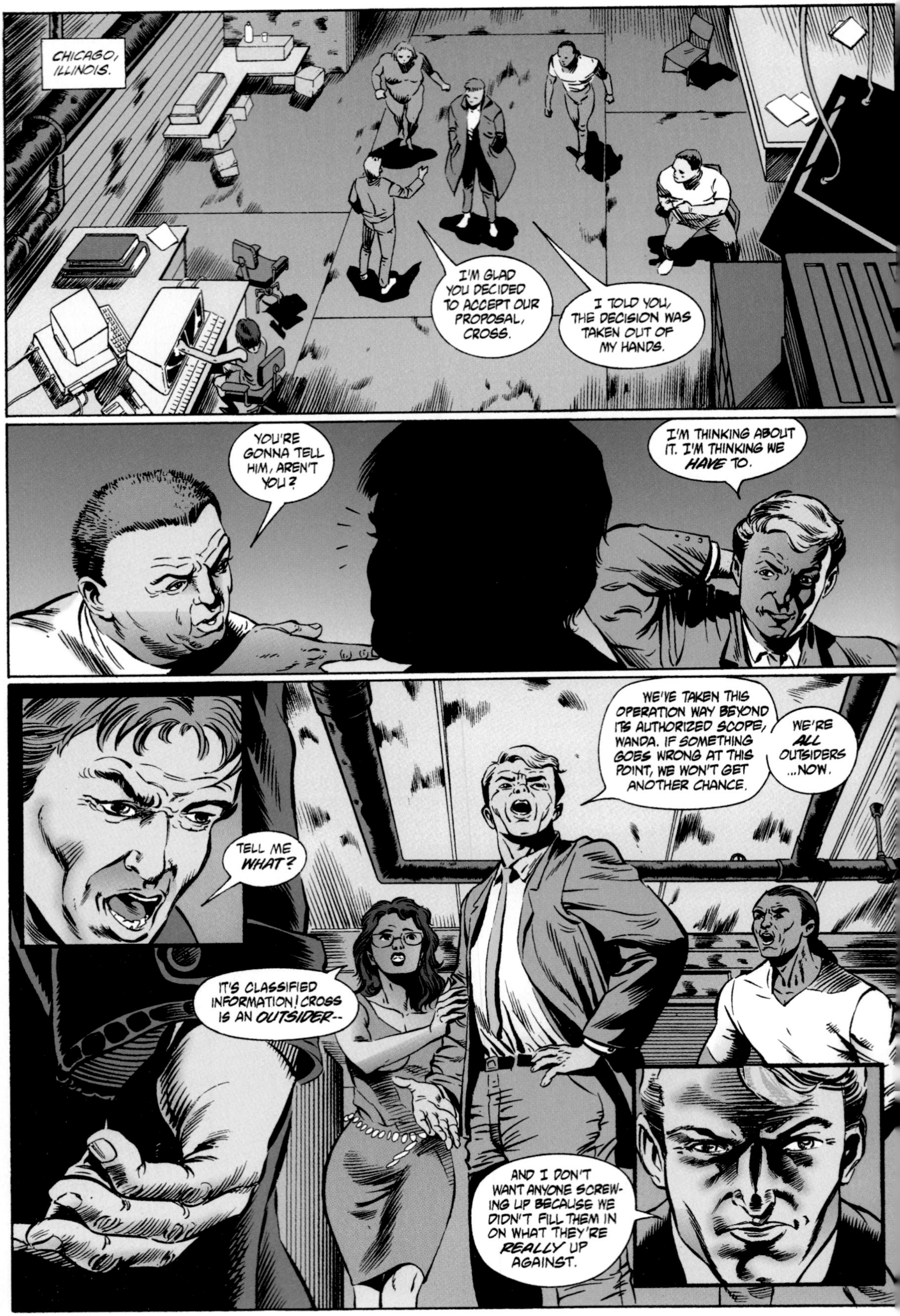
CHICAGO, ILLINOIS.
I'M GLAD YOU DECIDED TO ACCEPT OUR PROPOSAL, CROSS.
I TOLD YOU, THE DECISION WAS TAKEN OUT OF MY HANDS.
YOU'RE GONNA TELL HIM, AREN'T YOU?
I'M THINKING ABOUT IT. I'M THINKING WE HAVE TO.
TELL ME WHAT?
WE'VE TAKEN THIS OPERATION WAY BEYOND ITS AUTHORIZED SCOPE, WANDA. IF SOMETHING GOES WRONG AT THIS POINT, WE WON'T GET ANOTHER CHANCE.
WE'RE ALL OUTSIDERS ...NOW.
IT'S CLASSIFIED INFORMATION! CROSS IS AN OUTSIDER--
AND I DON'T WANT ANYONE SCREWING UP BECAUSE WE DIDN'T FILL THEM IN ON WHAT THEY'RE REALLY UP AGAINST.

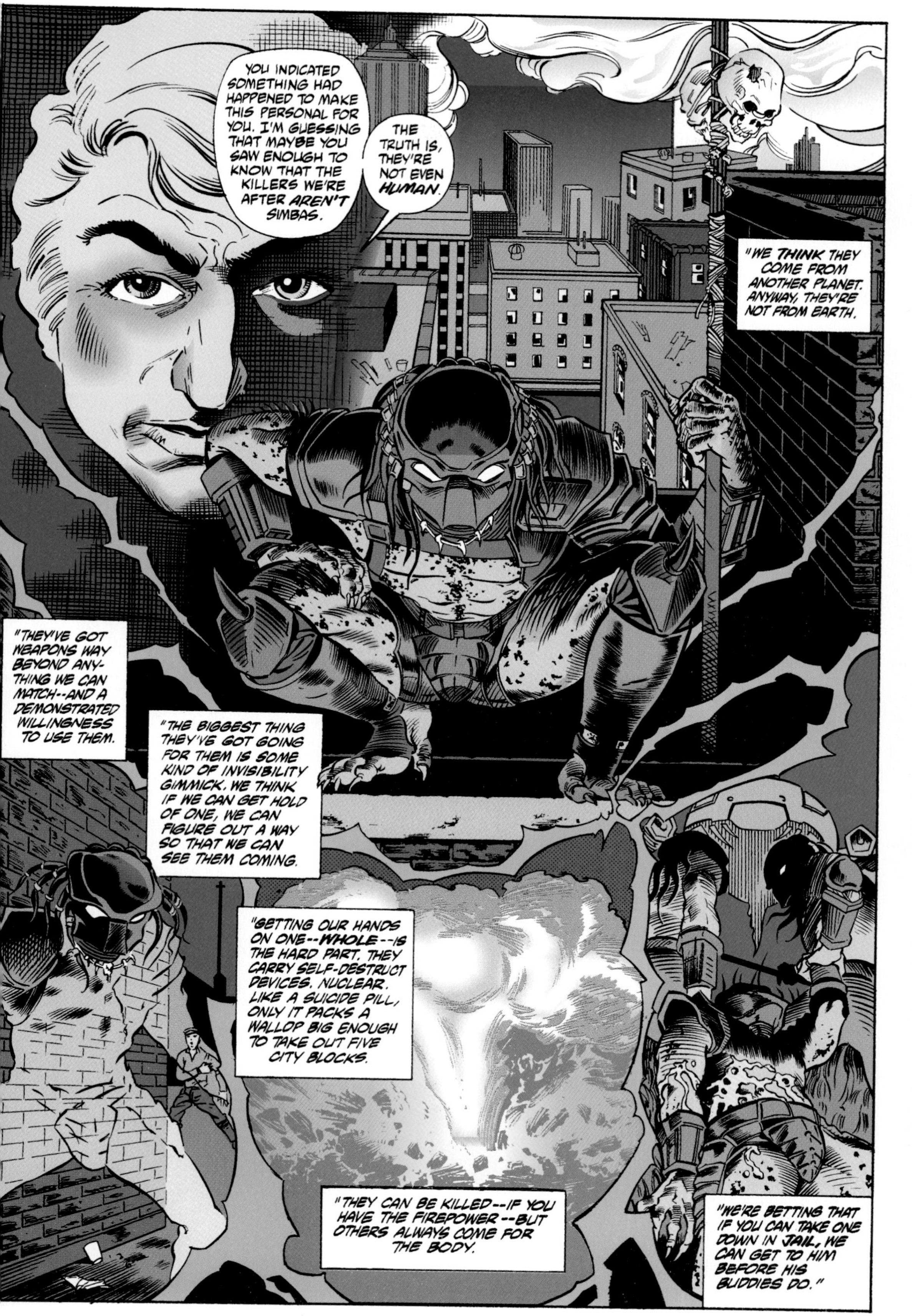
YOU INDICATED SOMETHING HAD HAPPENED TO MAKE THIS PERSONAL FOR YOU. I'M GUESSING THAT MAYBE YOU SAW ENOUGH TO KNOW THAT THE KILLERS WE'RE AFTER AREN'T SIMBAS.
THE TRUTH IS, THEY'RE NOT EVEN HUMAN.
"WE THINK THEY COME FROM ANOTHER PLANET. ANYWAY, THEY'RE NOT FROM EARTH.
"THEY'VE GOT WEAPONS WAY BEYOND ANYTHING WE CAN MATCH--AND A DEMONSTRATED WILLINGNESS TO USE THEM.
"THE BIGGEST THING THEY'VE GOT GOING FOR THEM IS SOME KIND OF INVISIBILITY GIMMICK. WE THINK IF WE CAN GET HOLD OF ONE, WE CAN FIGURE OUT A WAY SO THAT WE CAN SEE THEM COMING.
"GETTING OUR HANDS ON ONE--WHOLE--IS THE HARD PART. THEY CARRY SELF-DESTRUCT DEVICES. NUCLEAR. LIKE A SUICIDE PILL, ONLY IT PACKS A WALLOP BIG ENOUGH TO TAKE OUT FIVE CITY BLOCKS.
"THEY CAN BE KILLED--IF YOU HAVE THE FIREPOWER--BUT OTHERS ALWAYS COME FOR THE BODY.
"WE'RE BETTING THAT IF YOU CAN TAKE ONE DOWN IN JAIL, WE CAN GET TO HIM BEFORE HIS BUDDIES DO."

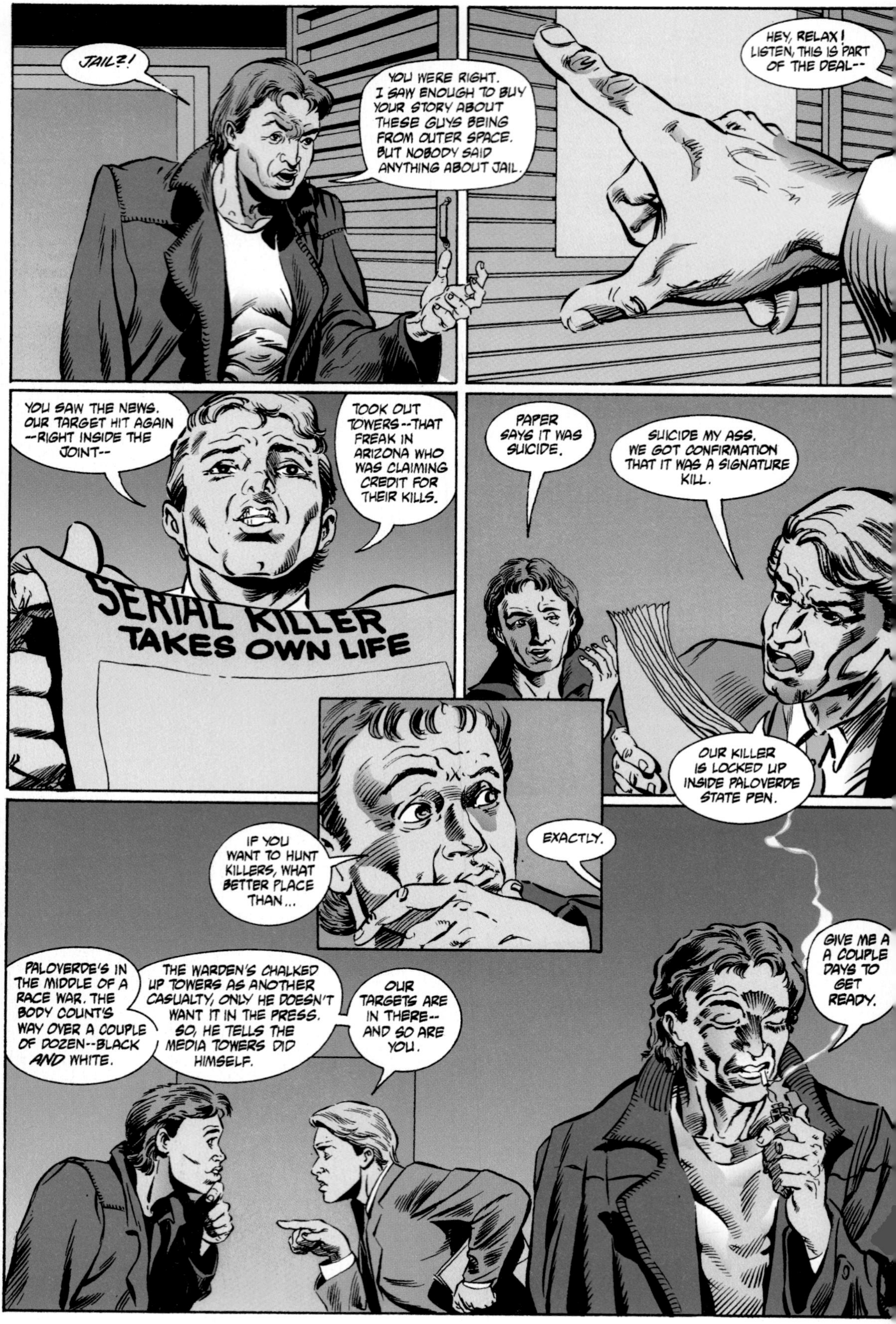

JAIL?!
YOU WERE RIGHT. I SAW ENOUGH TO BUY YOUR STORY ABOUT THESE GUYS BEING FROM OUTER SPACE. BUT NOBODY SAID ANYTHING ABOUT JAIL.
HEY, RELAX! LISTEN, THIS IS PART OF THE DEAL--
YOU SAW THE NEWS. OUR TARGET HIT AGAIN --RIGHT INSIDE THE JOINT--
TOOK OUT TOWERS--THAT FREAK IN ARIZONA WHO WAS CLAIMING CREDIT FOR THEIR KILLS.
SERIAL KILLER
TAKES OWN LIFE
PAPER SAYS IT WAS SUICIDE.
SUICIDE MY ASS. WE GOT CONFIRMATION THAT IT WAS A SIGNATURE KILL.
OUR KILLER IS LOCKED UP INSIDE PALOVERDE STATE PEN.
IF YOU WANT TO HUNT KILLERS, WHAT BETTER PLACE THAN...
EXACTLY.
PALOVERDE'S IN THE MIDDLE OF A RACE WAR. THE BODY COUNT'S WAY OVER A COUPLE OF DOZEN--BLACK AND WHITE.
THE WARDEN'S CHALKED UP TOWERS AS ANOTHER CASUALTY, ONLY HE DOESN'T WANT IT IN THE PRESS. SO, HE TELLS THE MEDIA TOWERS DID HIMSELF.
OUR TARGETS ARE IN THERE-- AND SO ARE YOU.
GIVE ME A A COUPLE DAYS TO GET READY.

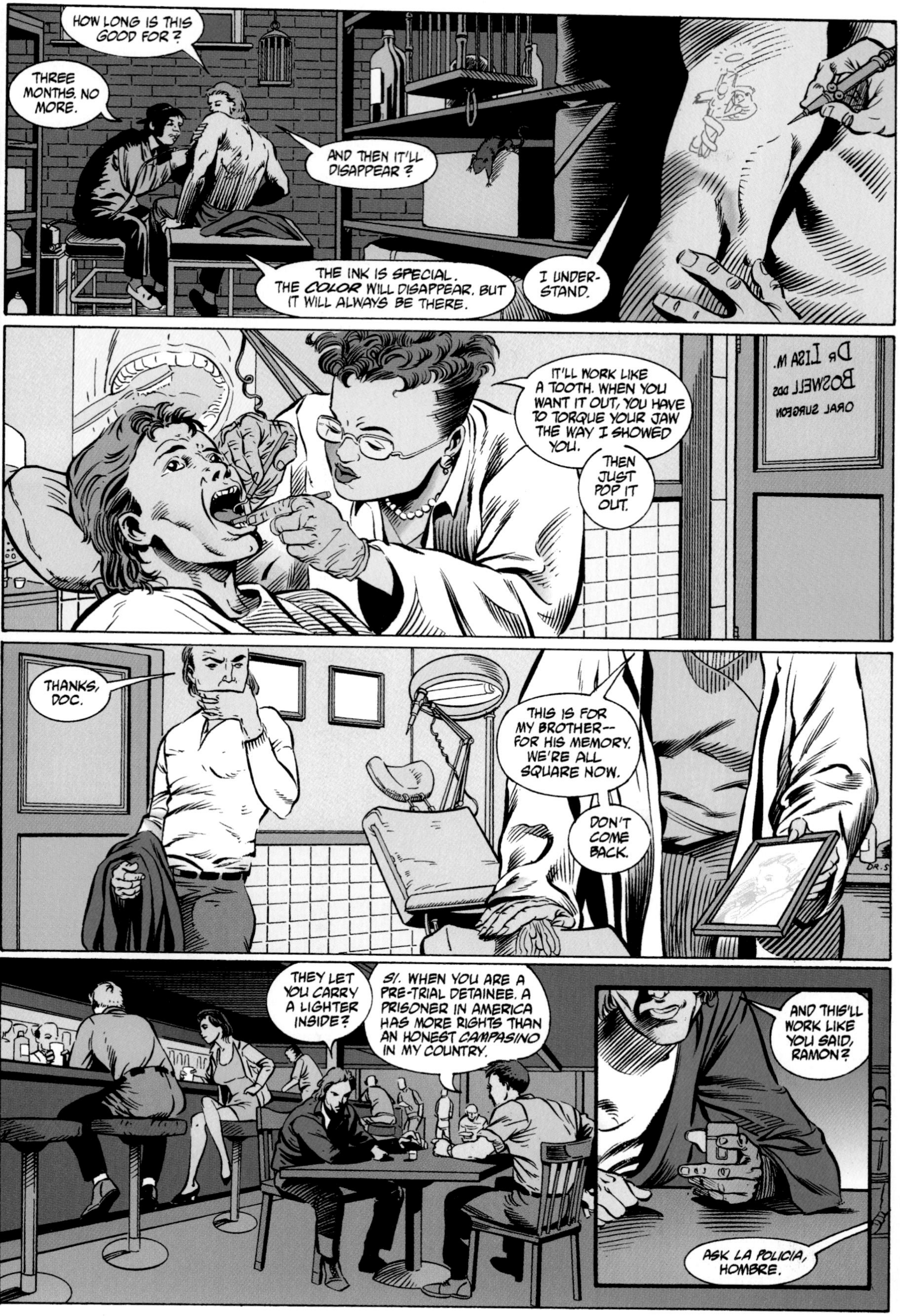
HOW LONG IS THIS GOOD FOR?
THREE MONTHS. NO MORE.
AND THEN IT'LL DISAPPEAR?
THE INK IS SPECIAL. THE COLOR WILL DISAPPEAR, BUT IT WILL ALWAYS BE THERE.
I UNDERSTAND.
DR LISA M. BOSWELL DDS ORAL SURGEON
IT'LL WORK LIKE A TOOTH. WHEN YOU WANT IT OUT, YOU HAVE TO TORQUE YOUR JAW THE WAY I SHOWED YOU.
THEN JUST POP IT OUT.
THANKS, DOC.
THIS IS FOR MY BROTHER-- FOR HIS MEMORY. WE'RE ALL SQUARE NOW.
DON'T COME BACK.
THEY LET YOU CARRY A LIGHTER INSIDE?
SI. WHEN YOU ARE A PRE-TRIAL DETAINEE, A PRISONER IN AMERICA HAS MORE RIGHTS THAN AN HONEST CAMPASINO IN MY COUNTRY.
AND THIS'LL WORK LIKE YOU SAID, RAMON?
ASK LA POLICIA, HOMBRE.

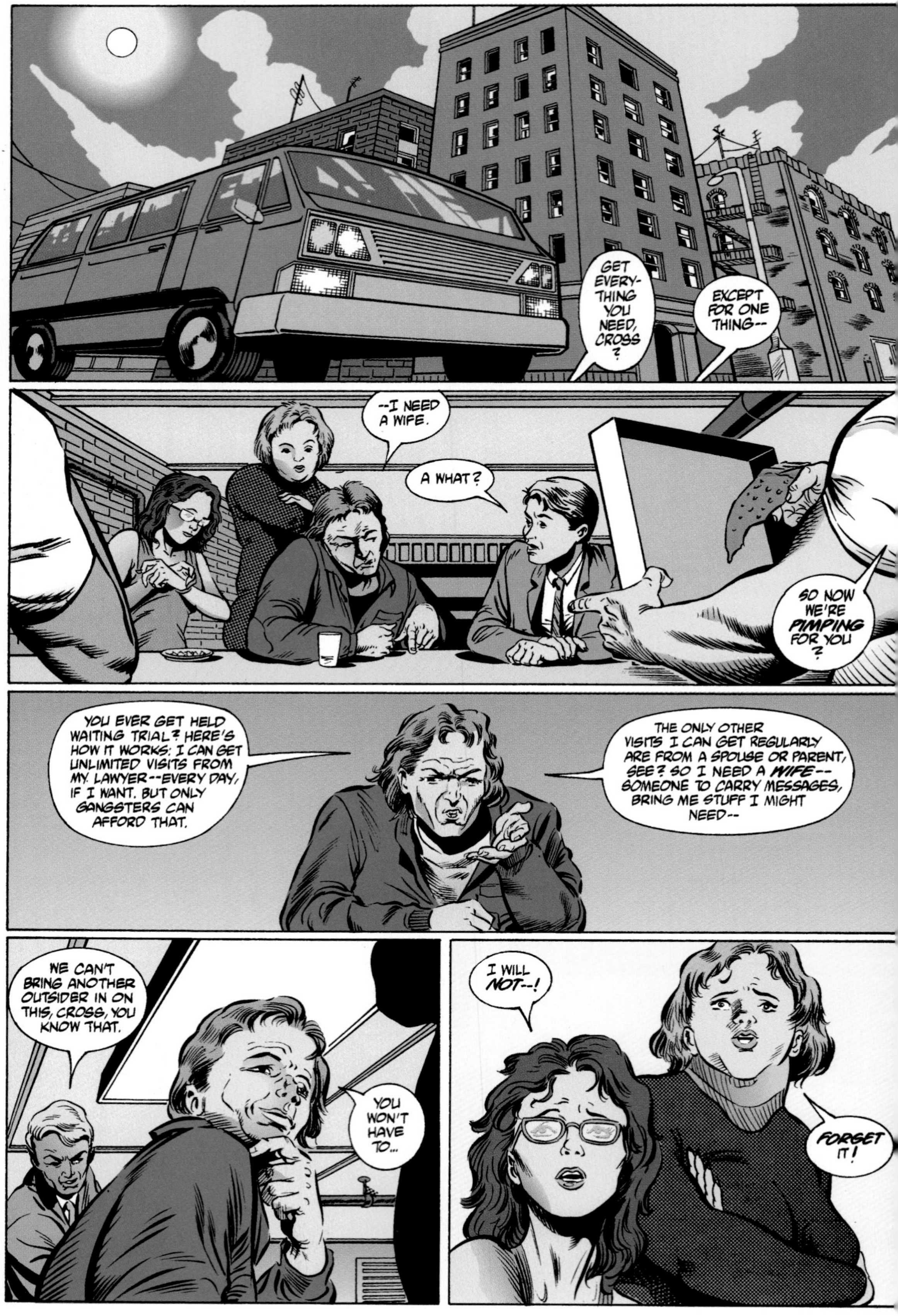
GET EVERY-THING YOU NEED, CROSS?
EXCEPT FOR ONE THING--
--I NEED A WIFE.
A WHAT?
SO NOW WE'RE PIMPING FOR YOU?
YOU EVER GET HELD WAITING TRIAL? HERE'S HOW IT WORKS: I CAN GET UNLIMITED VISITS FROM MY LAWYER--EVERY DAY, IF I WANT. BUT ONLY GANGSTERS CAN AFFORD THAT.
THE ONLY OTHER VISITS I CAN GET REGULARLY ARE FROM A SPOUSE OR PARENT, SEE? SO I NEED A WIFE-- SOMEONE TO CARRY MESSAGES, BRING ME STUFF I MIGHT NEED--
WE CAN'T BRING ANOTHER OUTSIDER IN ON THIS, CROSS, YOU KNOW THAT.
YOU WON'T HAVE TO...
I WILL NOT--!
FORGET IT!

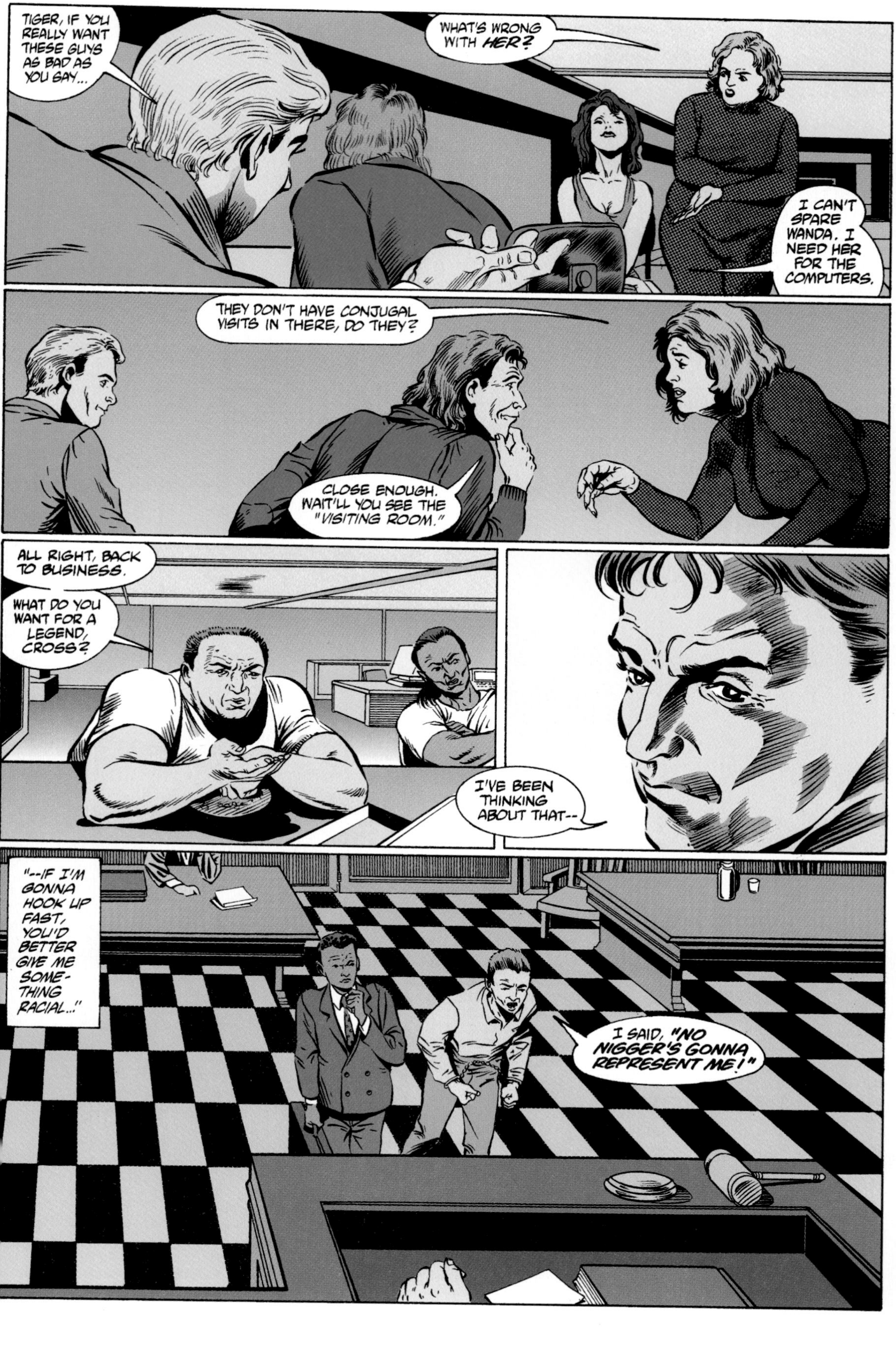
TIGER, IF YOU REALLY WANT THESE GUYS AS BAD AS YOU SAY...
WHAT'S WRONG WITH HER?
I CAN'T SPARE WANDA. I NEED HER FOR THE COMPUTERS.
THEY DON'T HAVE CONJUGAL VISITS IN THERE, DO THEY?
CLOSE ENOUGH. WAIT'LL YOU SEE THE "VISITING ROOM."
ALL RIGHT, BACK TO BUSINESS.
WHAT DO YOU WANT FOR A LEGEND, CROSS?
I'VE BEEN THINKING ABOUT THAT--
"--IF I'M GONNA HOOK UP FAST, YOU'D BETTER GIVE ME SOME-THING RACIAL..."
I SAID, "NO NIGGER'S GONNA REPRESENT ME!"

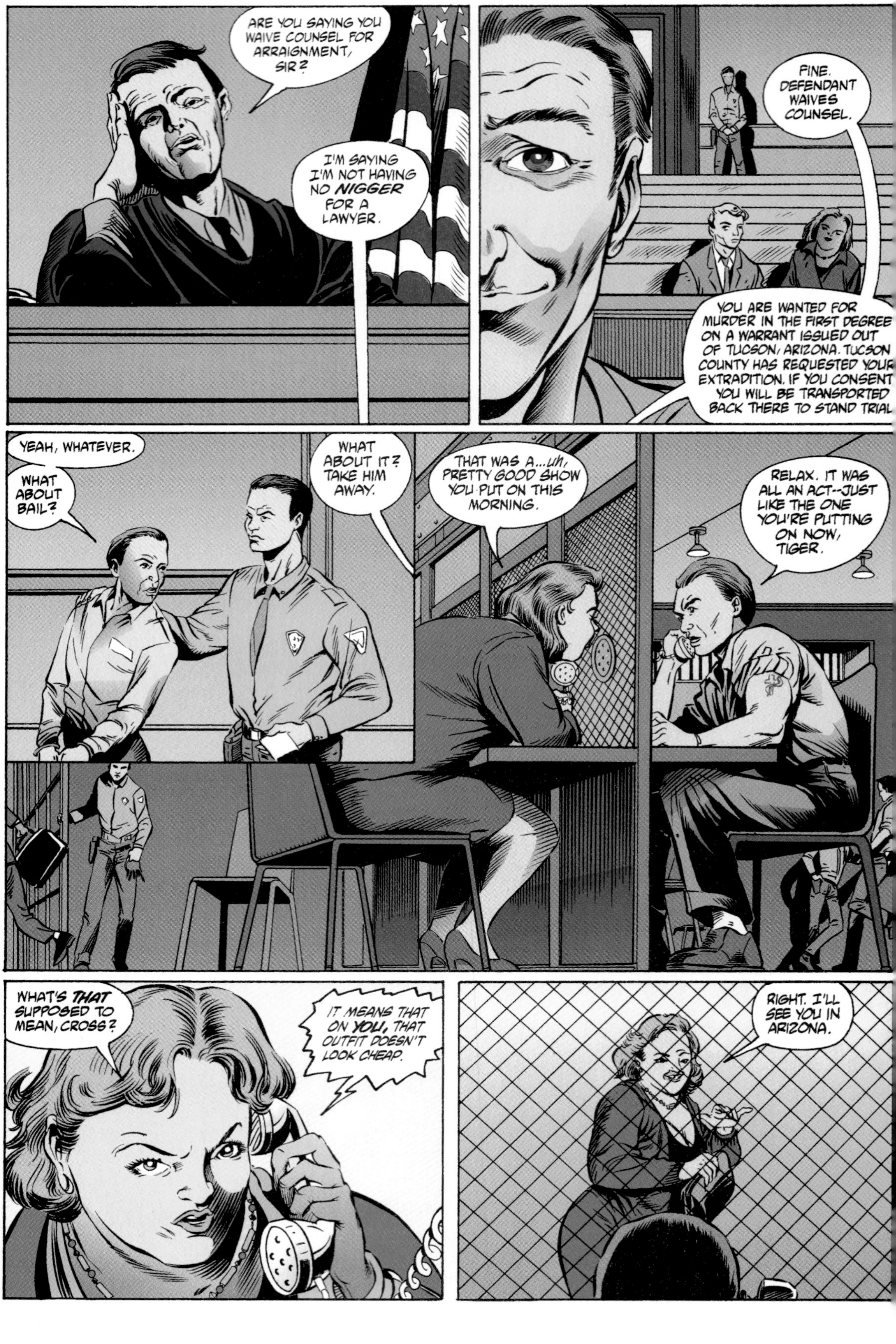
ARE YOU SAYING YOU WAIVE COUNSEL FOR ARRAIGNMENT, SIR?
I'M SAYING I'M NOT HAVING NO **NIGGER** FOR A LAWYER.
FINE. DEFENDANT WAIVES COUNSEL.
YOU ARE WANTED FOR MURDER IN THE FIRST DEGREE ON A WARRANT ISSUED OUT OF TUCSON, ARIZONA. TUCSON COUNTY HAS REQUESTED YOUR EXTRADITION. IF YOU CONSENT YOU WILL BE TRANSPORTED BACK THERE TO STAND TRIAL
YEAH, WHATEVER.
WHAT ABOUT BAIL?
WHAT ABOUT IT? TAKE HIM AWAY.
THAT WAS A...*uh*, PRETTY GOOD SHOW YOU PUT ON THIS MORNING.
RELAX. IT WAS ALL AN ACT--JUST LIKE THE ONE YOU'RE PUTTING ON NOW, TIGER.
WHAT'S ***THAT*** SUPPOSED TO MEAN, CROSS?
IT MEANS THAT ON ***YOU***, THAT OUTFIT DOESN'T LOOK CHEAP.
RIGHT. I'LL SEE YOU IN ARIZONA.

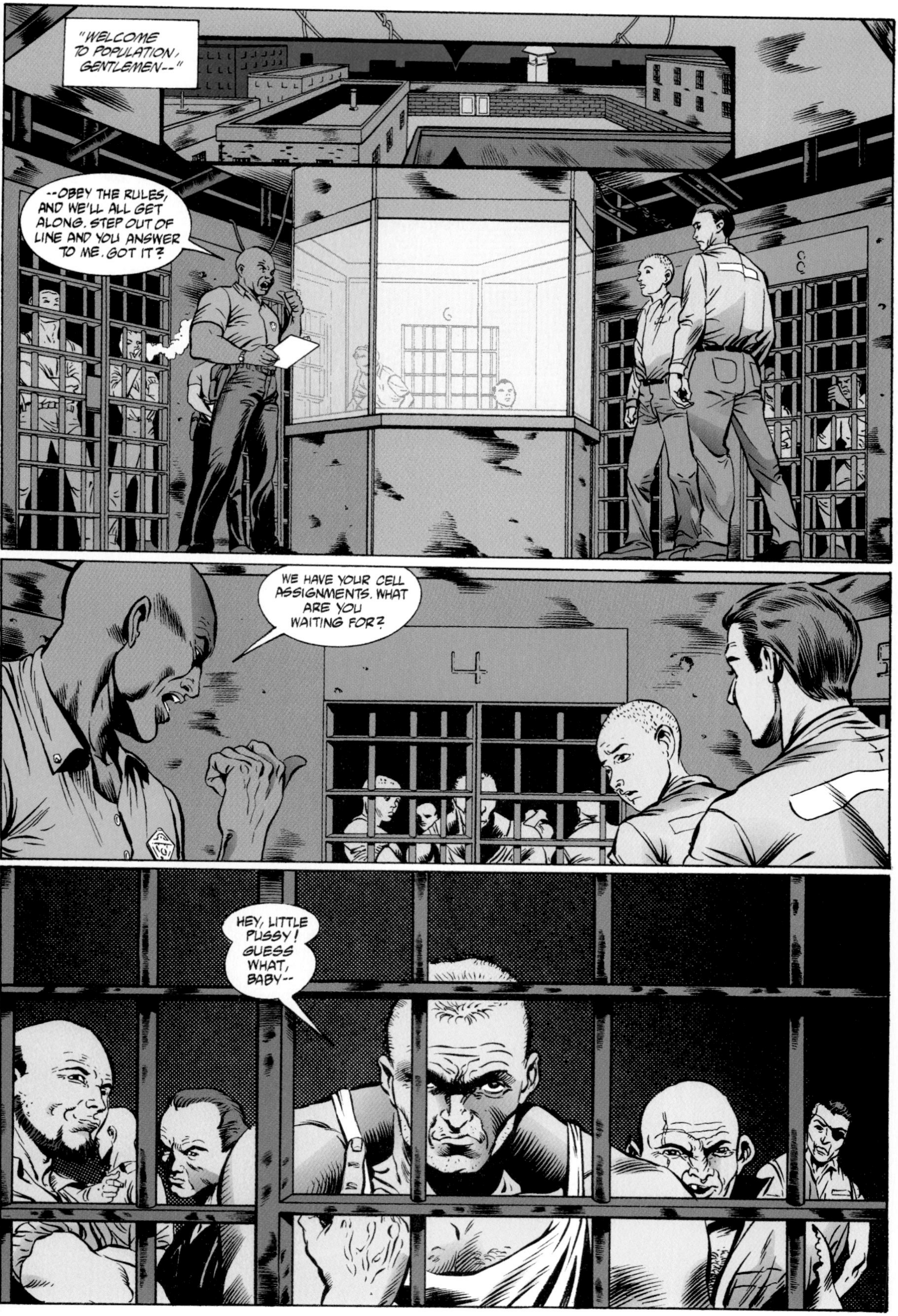
"WELCOME TO POPULATION, GENTLEMEN--"
--OBEY THE RULES, AND WE'LL ALL GET ALONG. STEP OUT OF LINE AND YOU ANSWER TO ME. GOT IT?
WE HAVE YOUR CELL ASSIGNMENTS. WHAT ARE YOU WAITING FOR?
HEY, LITTLE PUSSY! GUESS WHAT, BABY--

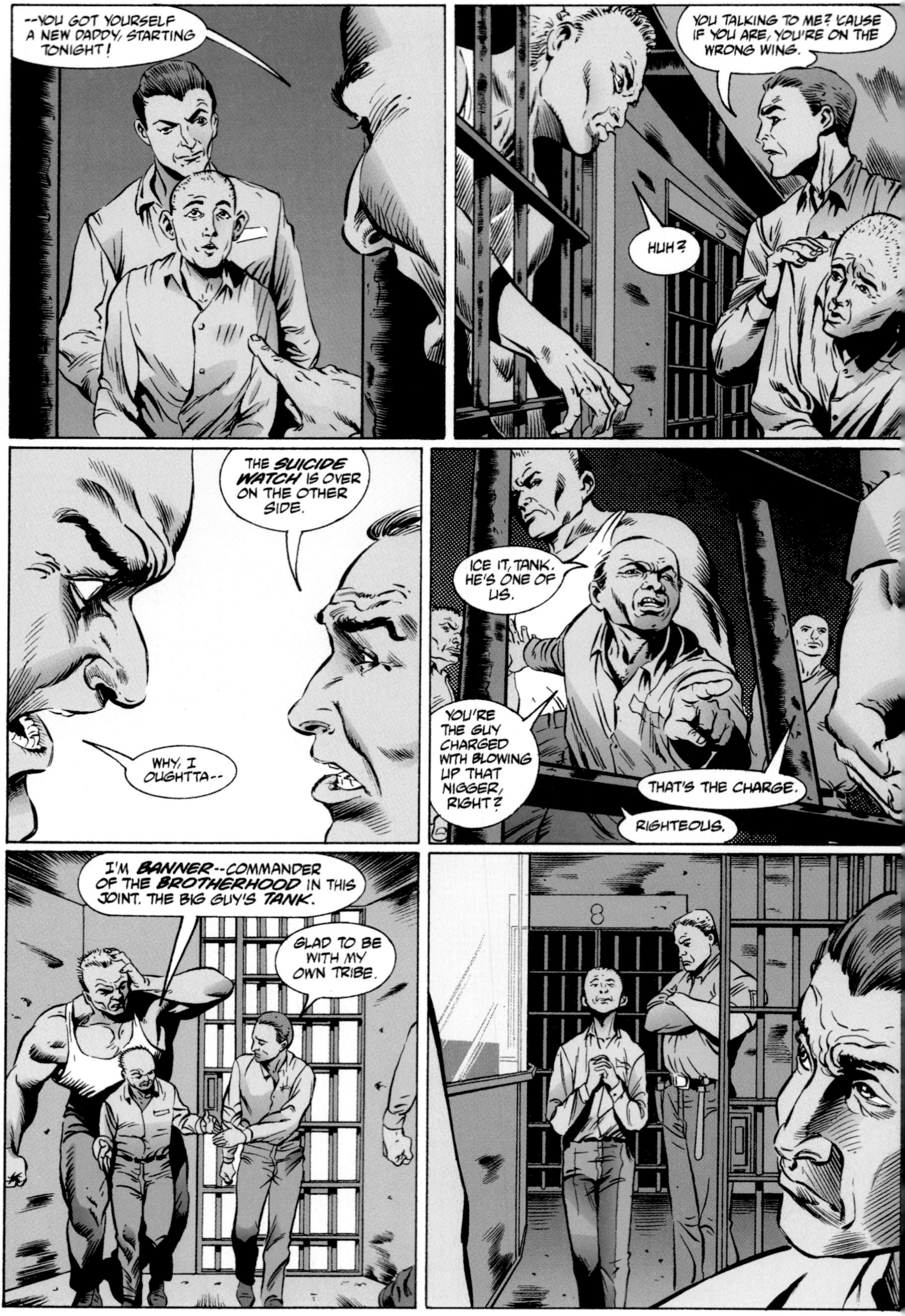
--YOU GOT YOURSELF A NEW DADDY, STARTING TONIGHT!
YOU TALKING TO ME? 'CAUSE IF YOU ARE, YOU'RE ON THE WRONG WING.
HUH?
THE SUICIDE WATCH IS OVER ON THE OTHER SIDE.
WHY, I OUGHTTA--
ICE IT, TANK. HE'S ONE OF US.
YOU'RE THE GUY CHARGED WITH BLOWING UP THAT NIGGER, RIGHT?
THAT'S THE CHARGE.
RIGHTEOUS.
I'M BANNER--COMMANDER OF THE BROTHERHOOD IN THIS JOINT. THE BIG GUY'S TANK.
GLAD TO BE WITH MY OWN TRIBE.

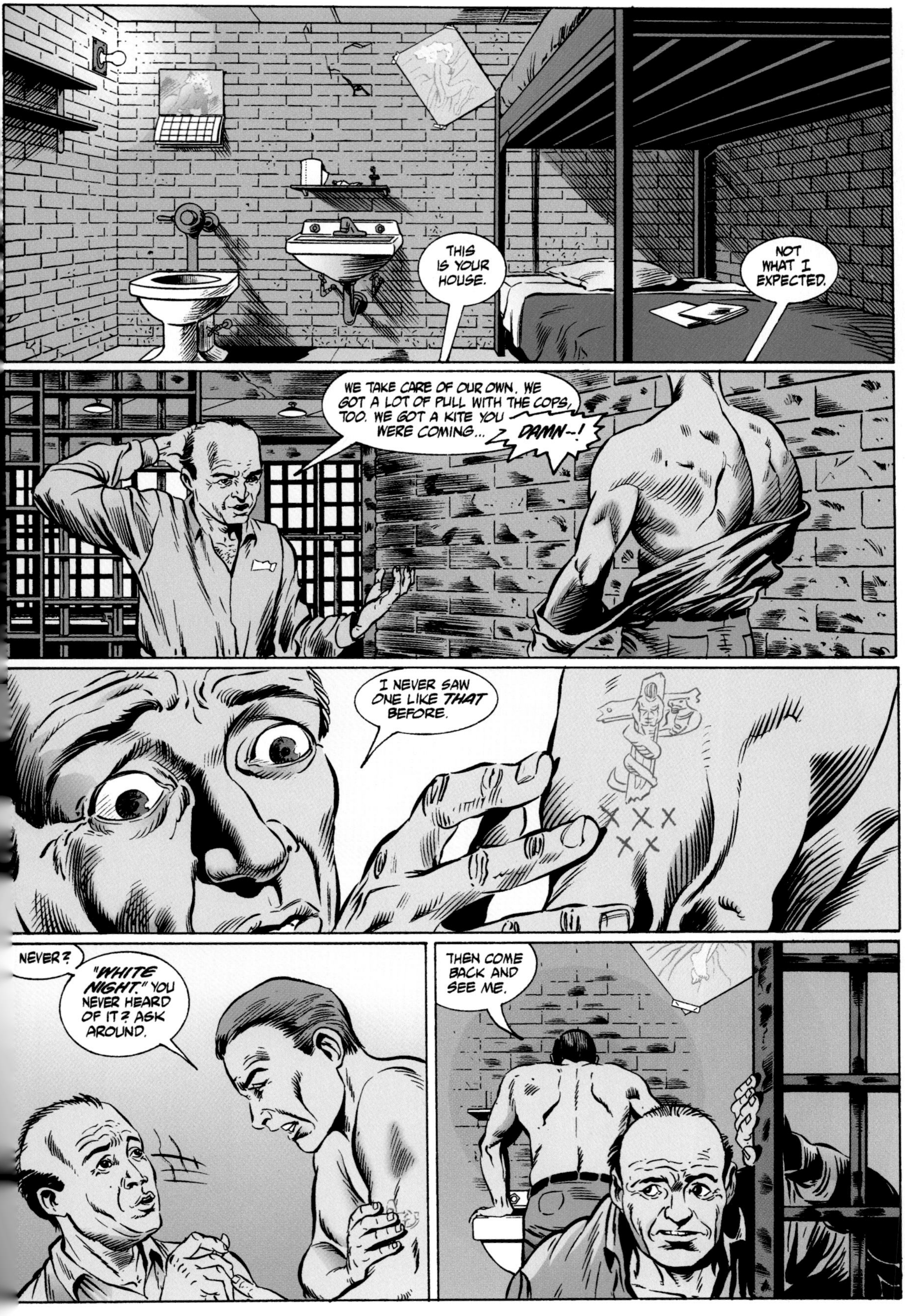
THIS IS YOUR HOUSE.
NOT WHAT I EXPECTED.
WE TAKE CARE OF OUR OWN. WE GOT A LOT OF PULL WITH THE COPS, TOO. WE GOT A KITE YOU WERE COMING...
DAMN--!
I NEVER SAW ONE LIKE THAT BEFORE.
NEVER?
"WHITE NIGHT." YOU NEVER HEARD OF IT? ASK AROUND.
THEN COME BACK AND SEE ME.

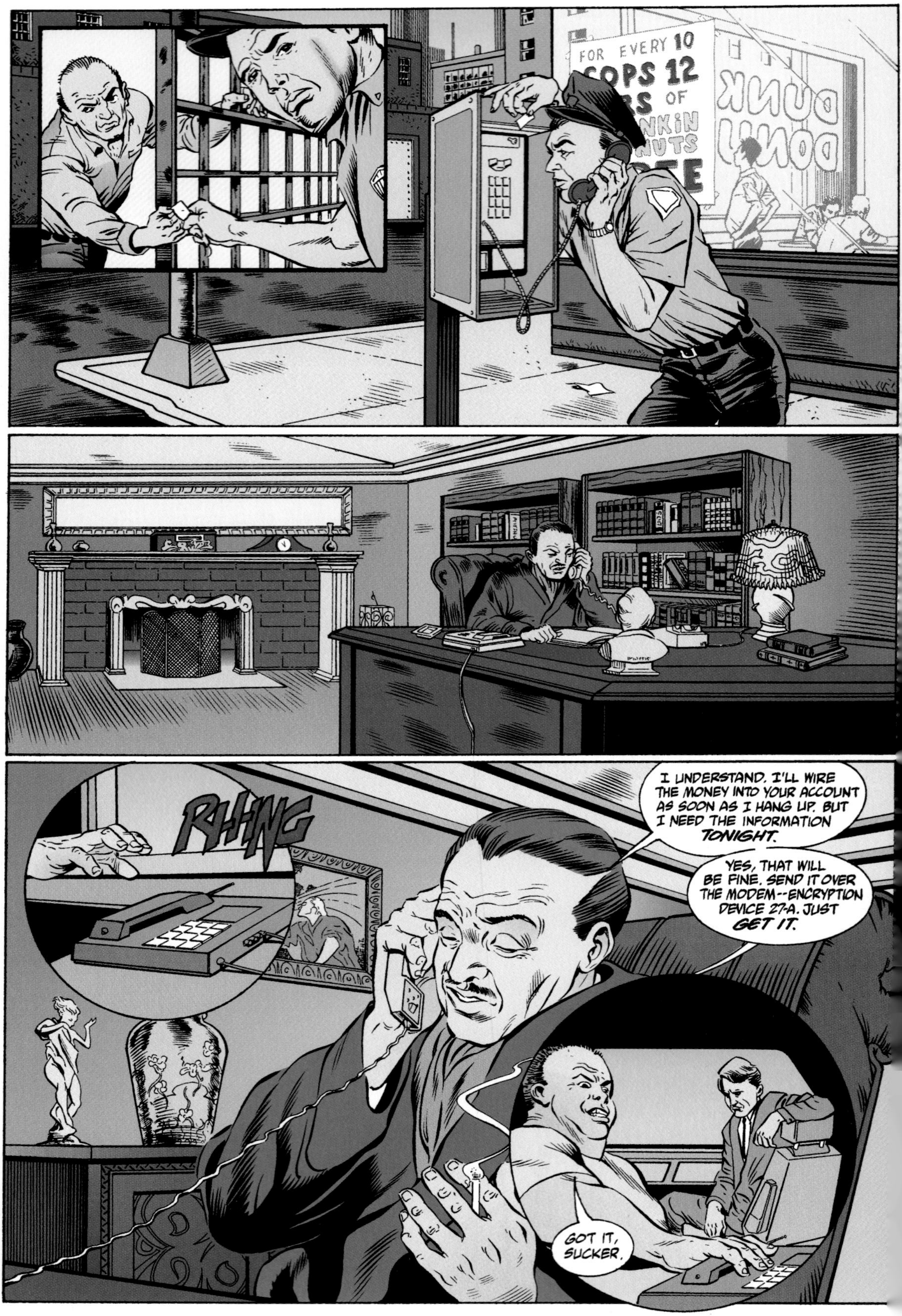

FOR EVERY 10
COPS 12
RHHNG
I UNDERSTAND. I'LL WIRE THE MONEY INTO YOUR ACCOUNT AS SOON AS I HANG UP. BUT I NEED THE INFORMATION *TONIGHT*.
YES, THAT WILL BE FINE. SEND IT OVER THE MODEM--ENCRYPTION DEVICE 27-A. JUST *GET IT*.
GOT IT, SUCKER.

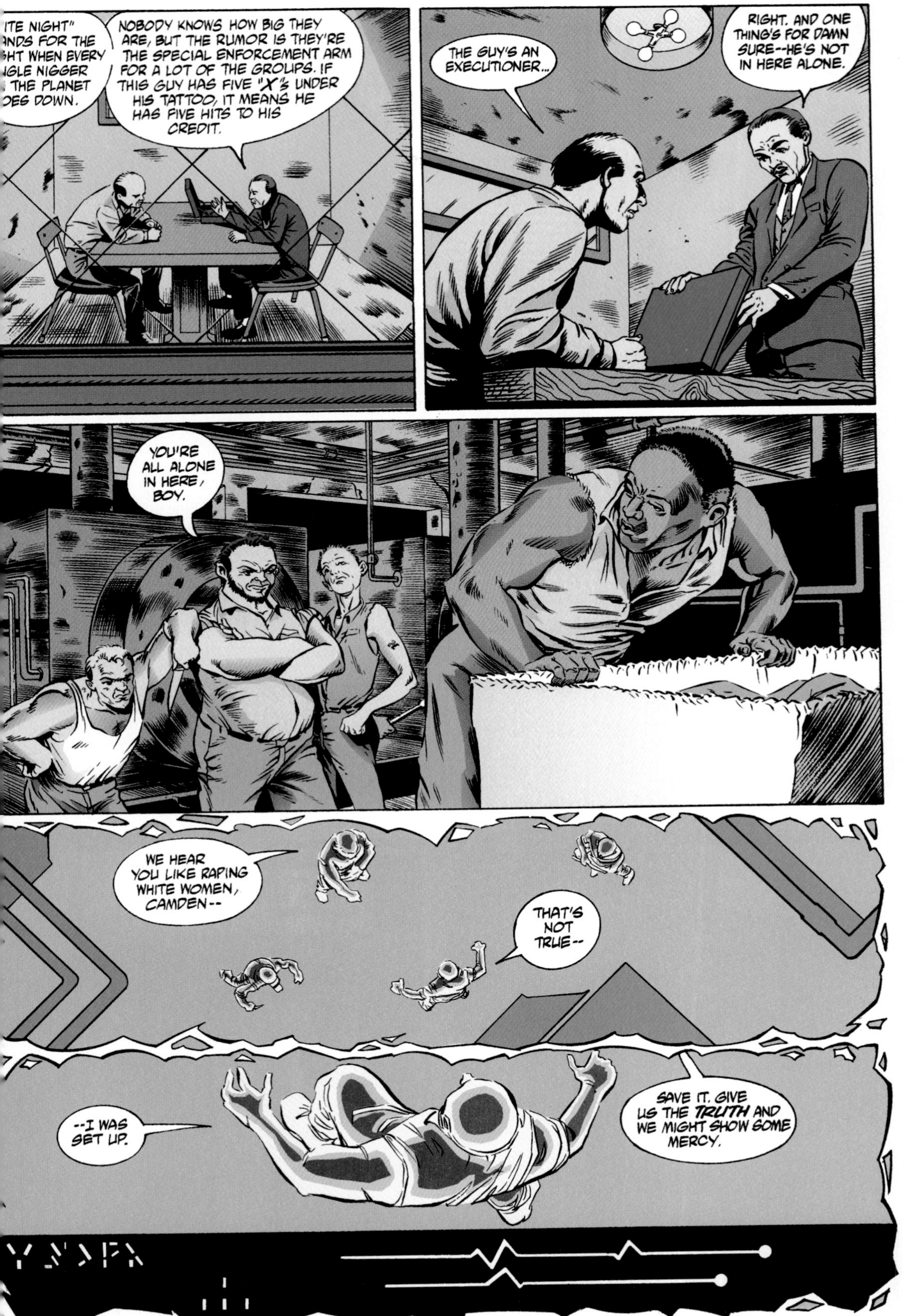

ITE NIGHT" ANDS FOR THE IGHT WHEN EVERY NGLE NIGGER THE PLANET OES DOWN.
NOBODY KNOWS HOW BIG THEY ARE, BUT THE RUMOR IS THEY'RE THE SPECIAL ENFORCEMENT ARM FOR A LOT OF THE GROUPS. IF THIS GUY HAS FIVE "X"'s UNDER HIS TATTOO, IT MEANS HE HAS FIVE HITS TO HIS CREDIT.
THE GUY'S AN EXECUTIONER...
RIGHT. AND ONE THING'S FOR DAMN SURE--HE'S NOT IN HERE ALONE.
YOU'RE ALL ALONE IN HERE, BOY.
WE HEAR YOU LIKE RAPING WHITE WOMEN, CAMDEN--
THAT'S NOT TRUE--
--I WAS SET UP.
SAVE IT. GIVE US THE TRUTH AND WE MIGHT SHOW SOME MERCY.

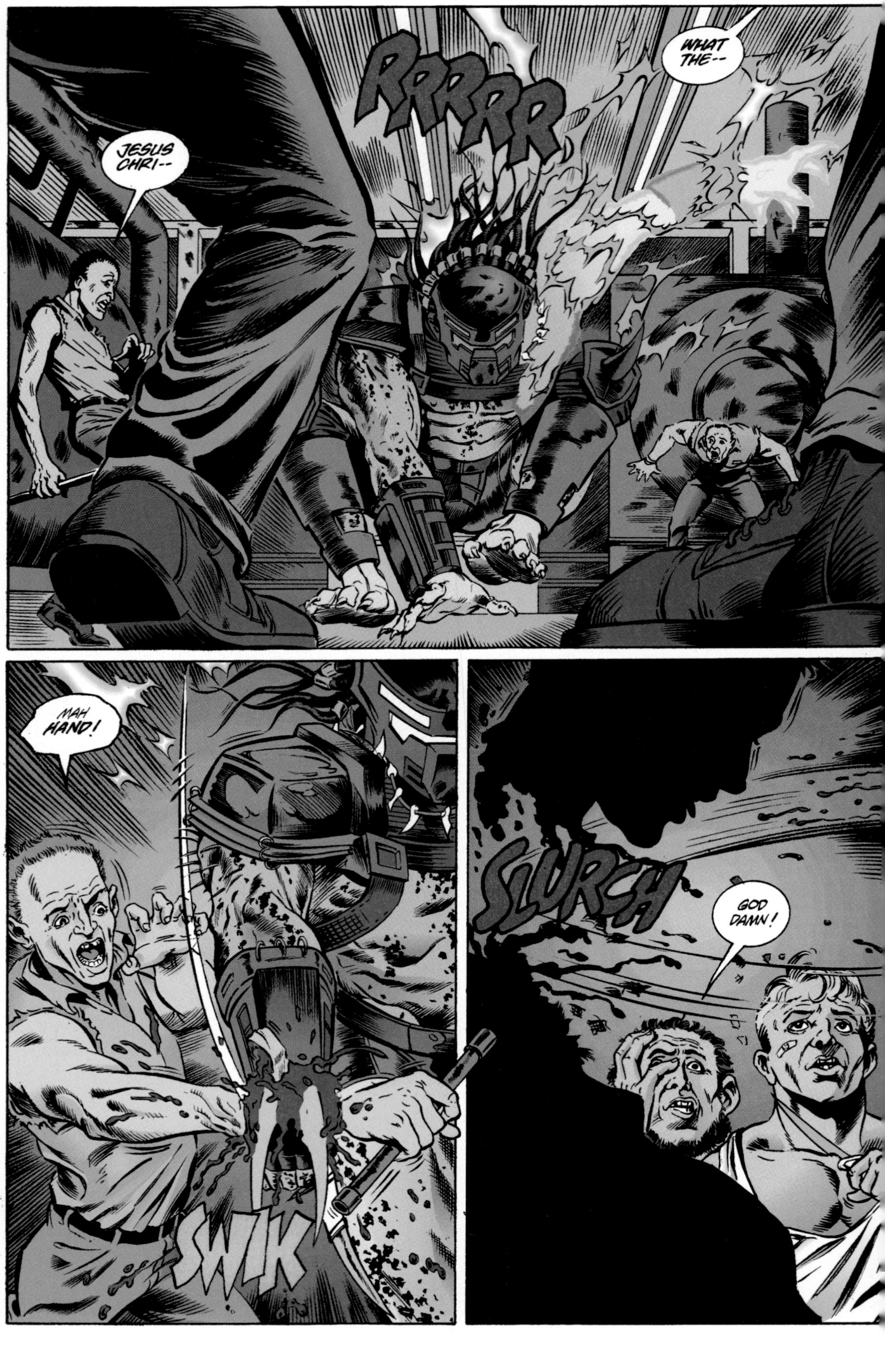
RRRRR
JESUS CHRI--
WHAT THE--
MAH HAND!
SWIK
SLURCH
GOD DAMN!

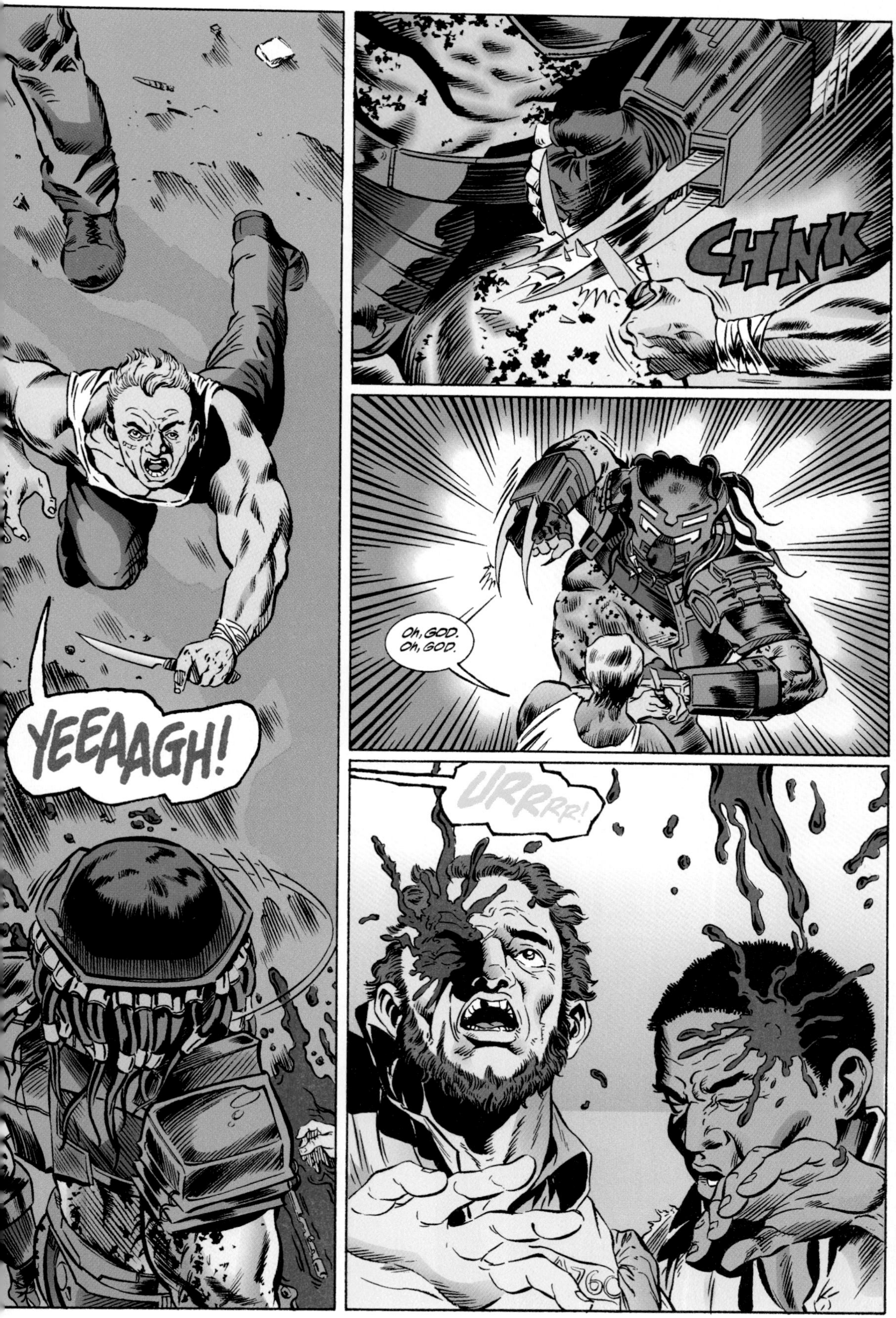
YEEAAGH!
CHINK
Oh, GOD. Oh, GOD.
URRrrr!

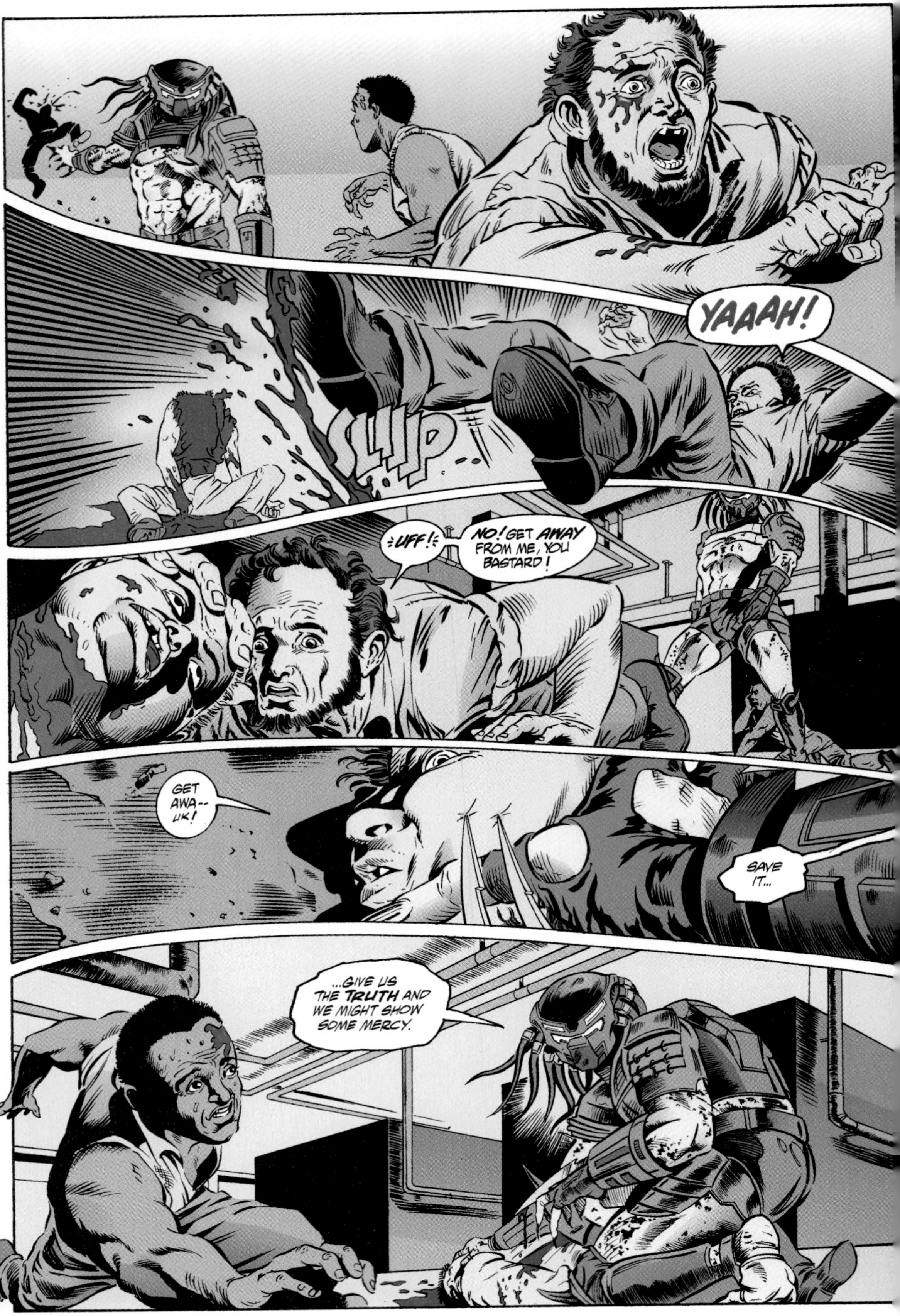
YAAAH!
SLIIP
UFF!
NO! GET AWAY FROM ME, YOU BASTARD!
GET AWA-- UK!
SAVE IT...
...GIVE US THE TRUTH AND WE MIGHT SHOW SOME MERCY.

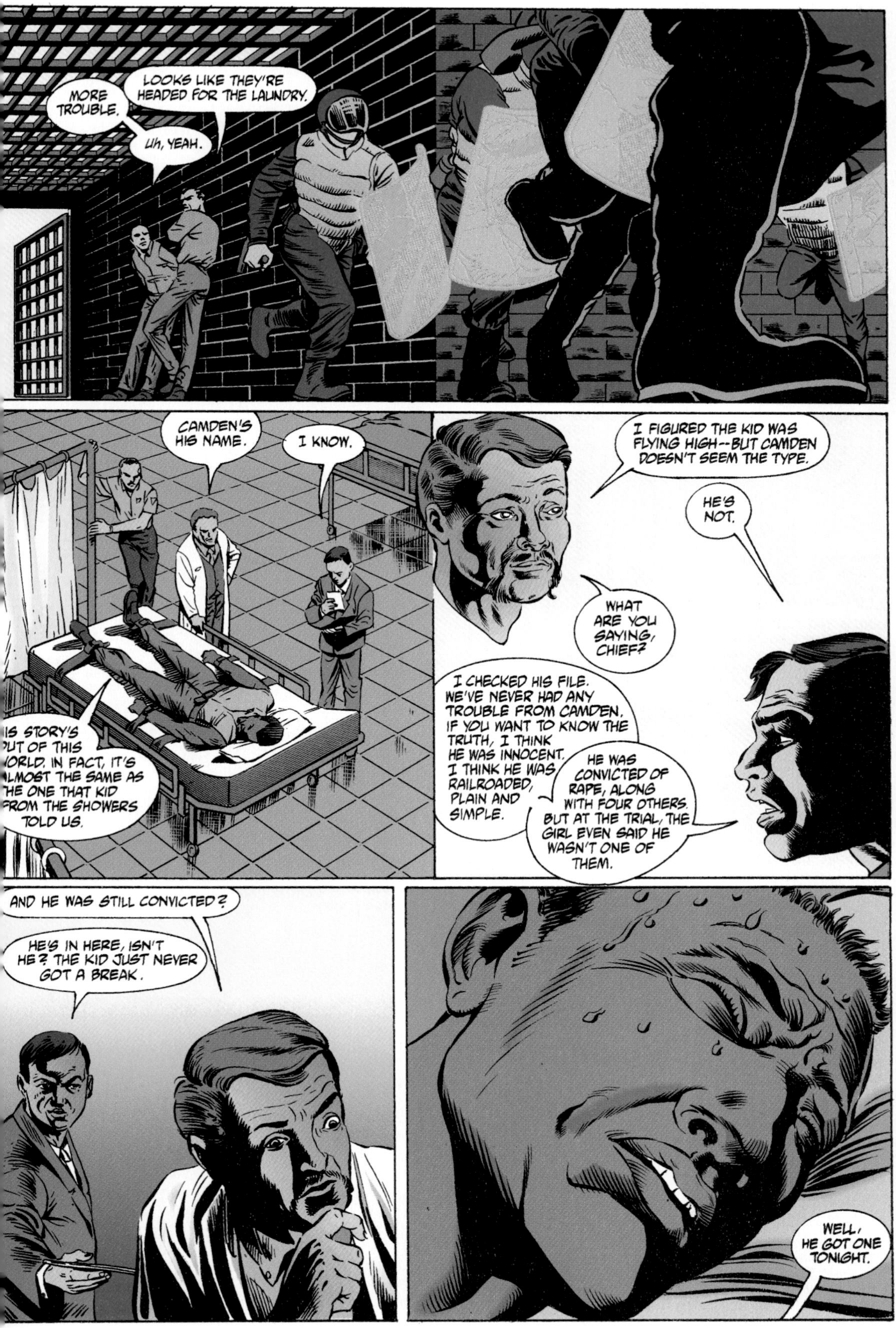
MORE TROUBLE.
LOOKS LIKE THEY'RE HEADED FOR THE LAUNDRY.
UH, YEAH.
CAMDEN'S HIS NAME.
I KNOW.
IS STORY'S
UT OF THIS
ORLD. IN FACT, IT'S
LMOST THE SAME AS
HE ONE THAT KID
ROM THE SHOWERS
TOLD US.
I FIGURED THE KID WAS FLYING HIGH--BUT CAMDEN DOESN'T SEEM THE TYPE.
HE'S NOT.
WHAT ARE YOU SAYING, CHIEF?
I CHECKED HIS FILE. WE'VE NEVER HAD ANY TROUBLE FROM CAMDEN. IF YOU WANT TO KNOW THE TRUTH, I THINK HE WAS INNOCENT. I THINK HE WAS RAILROADED, PLAIN AND SIMPLE.
HE WAS CONVICTED OF RAPE, ALONG WITH FOUR OTHERS. BUT AT THE TRIAL, THE GIRL EVEN SAID HE WASN'T ONE OF THEM.
AND HE WAS STILL CONVICTED?
HE'S IN HERE, ISN'T HE? THE KID JUST NEVER GOT A BREAK.
WELL, HE GOT ONE TONIGHT.

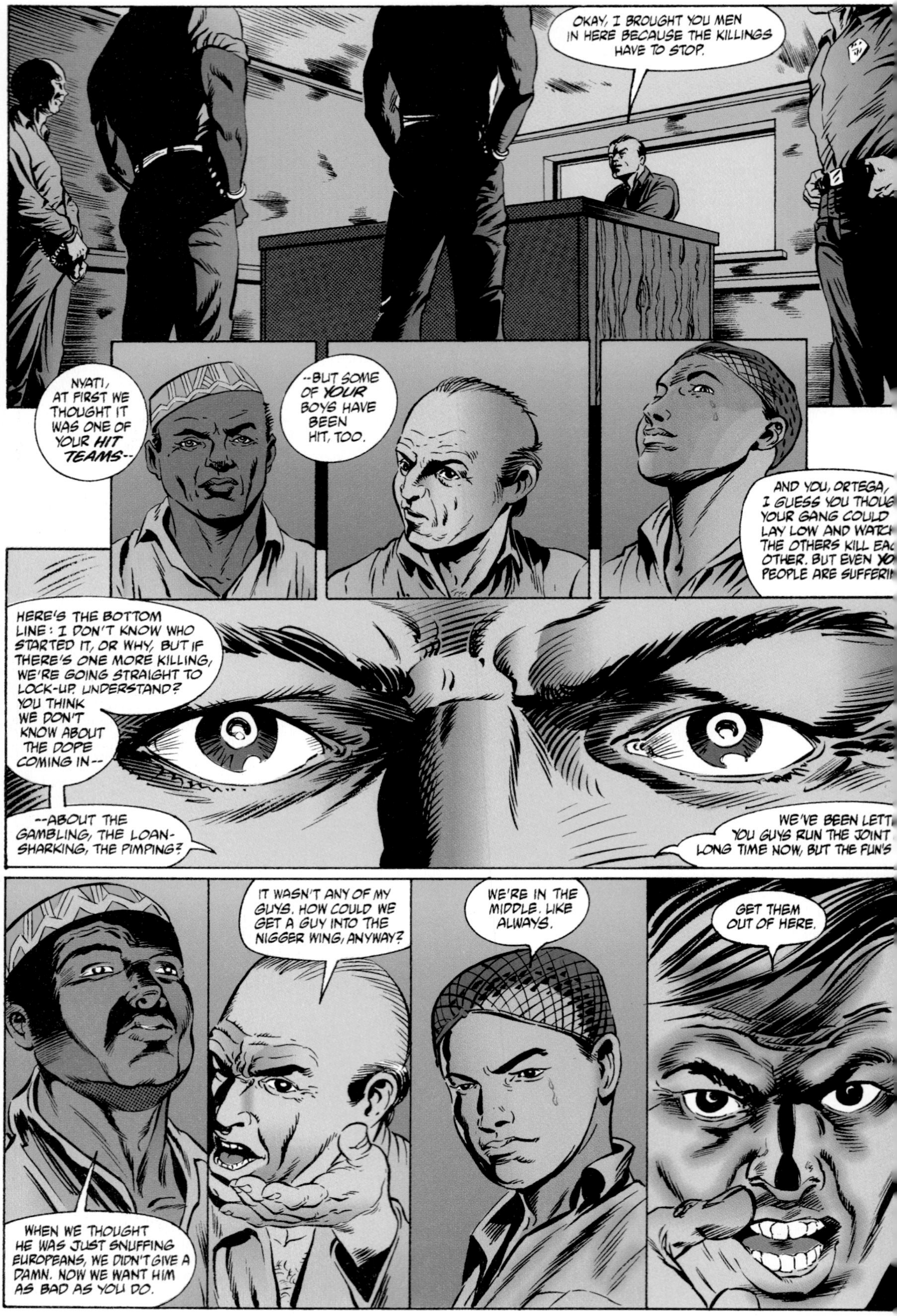

OKAY, I BROUGHT YOU MEN IN HERE BECAUSE THE KILLINGS HAVE TO STOP.
NYATI, AT FIRST WE THOUGHT IT WAS ONE OF YOUR HIT TEAMS--
--BUT SOME OF YOUR BOYS HAVE BEEN HIT, TOO.
AND YOU, ORTEGA, I GUESS YOU THOUG YOUR GANG COULD LAY LOW AND WATCH THE OTHERS KILL EAC OTHER. BUT EVEN YO PEOPLE ARE SUFFERI
HERE'S THE BOTTOM LINE: I DON'T KNOW WHO STARTED IT, OR WHY, BUT IF THERE'S ONE MORE KILLING, WE'RE GOING STRAIGHT TO LOCK-UP. UNDERSTAND? YOU THINK WE DON'T KNOW ABOUT THE DOPE COMING IN--
--ABOUT THE GAMBLING, THE LOAN-SHARKING, THE PIMPING?
WE'VE BEEN LETT YOU GUYS RUN THE JOINT LONG TIME NOW, BUT THE FUN'S
WHEN WE THOUGHT HE WAS JUST SNUFFING EUROPEANS, WE DIDN'T GIVE A DAMN. NOW WE WANT HIM AS BAD AS YOU DO.
IT WASN'T ANY OF MY GUYS. HOW COULD WE GET A GUY INTO THE NIGGER WING, ANYWAY?
WE'RE IN THE MIDDLE. LIKE ALWAYS.
GET THEM OUT OF HERE.

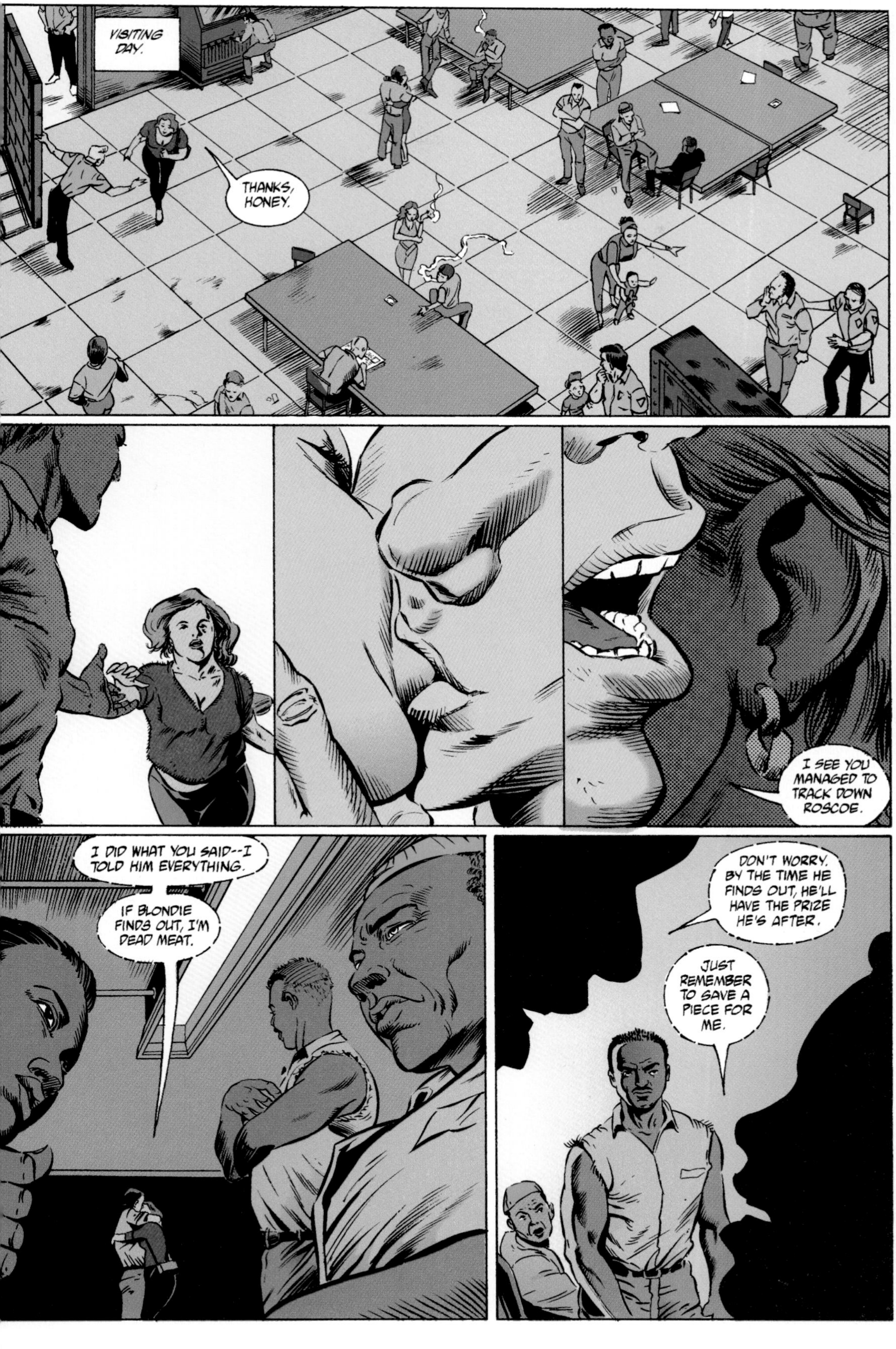
VISITING DAY.
THANKS, HONEY.
I SEE YOU MANAGED TO TRACK DOWN ROSCOE.
I DID WHAT YOU SAID--I TOLD HIM EVERYTHING.
IF BLONDIE FINDS OUT, I'M DEAD MEAT.
DON'T WORRY. BY THE TIME HE FINDS OUT, HE'LL HAVE THE PRIZE HE'S AFTER.
JUST REMEMBER TO SAVE A PIECE FOR ME.

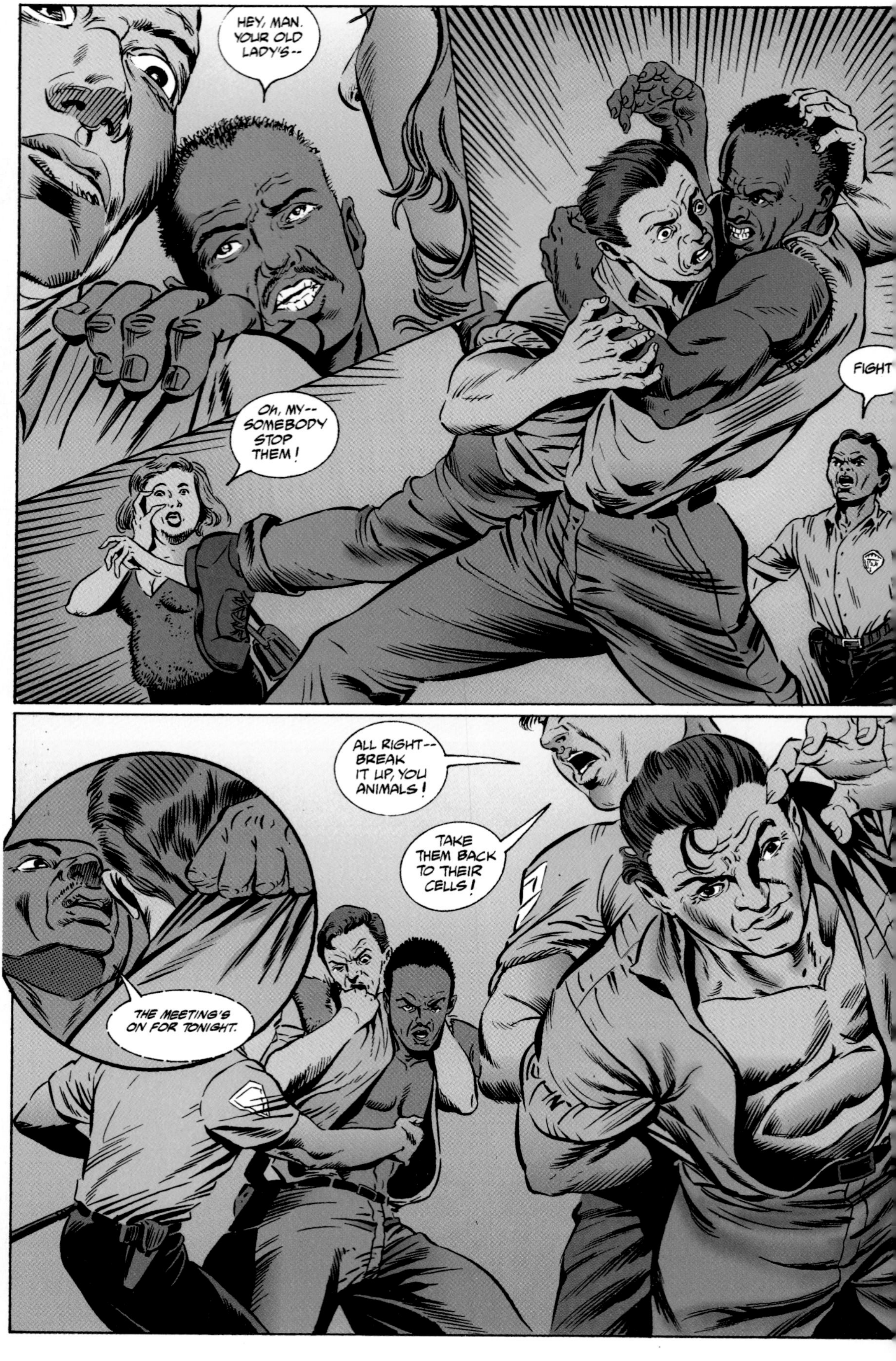
HEY, MAN. YOUR OLD LADY'S--
Oh, MY-- SOMEBODY STOP THEM!
FIGHT
ALL RIGHT-- BREAK IT UP, YOU ANIMALS!
TAKE THEM BACK TO THEIR CELLS!
THE MEETING'S ON FOR TONIGHT.

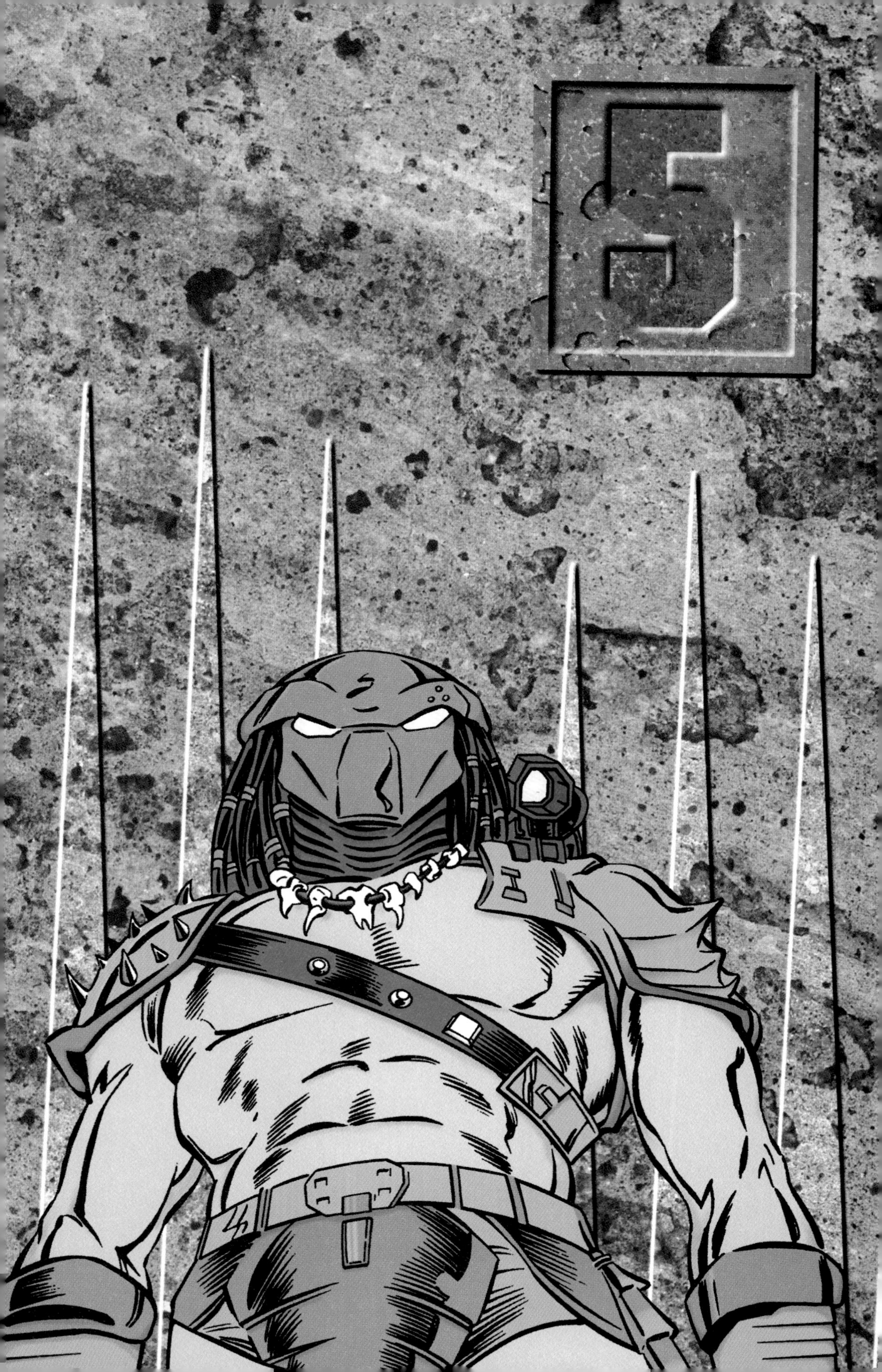
5

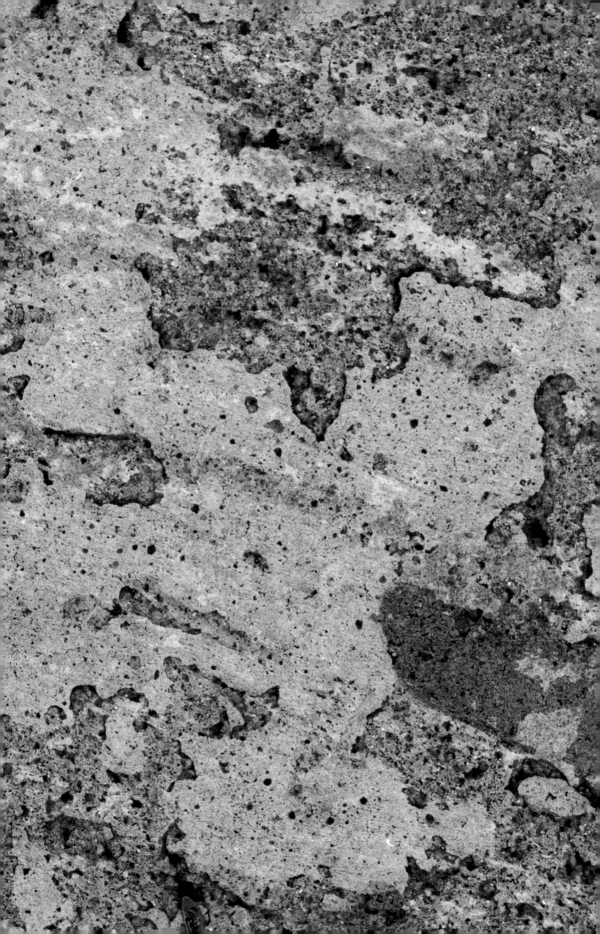

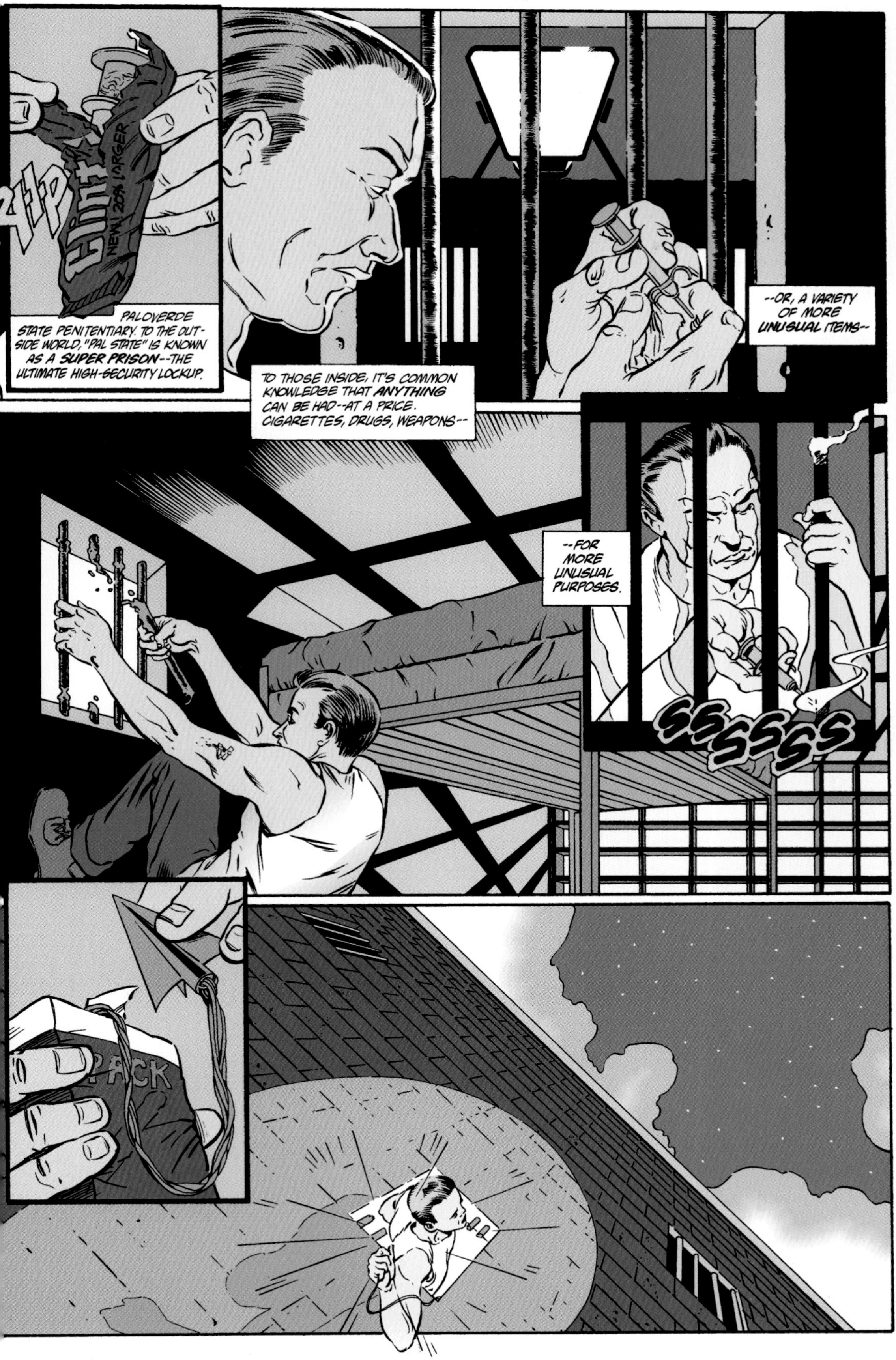
GIANT NEW! 20% LARGER
ZIIP
PALOVERDE STATE PENITENTIARY. TO THE OUTSIDE WORLD, "PAL STATE" IS KNOWN AS A SUPER PRISON--THE ULTIMATE HIGH-SECURITY LOCKUP.
TO THOSE INSIDE, IT'S COMMON KNOWLEDGE THAT ANYTHING CAN BE HAD--AT A PRICE. CIGARETTES, DRUGS, WEAPONS--
--OR, A VARIETY OF MORE UNUSUAL ITEMS--
--FOR MORE UNUSUAL PURPOSES.
SSSSSSS
PACK

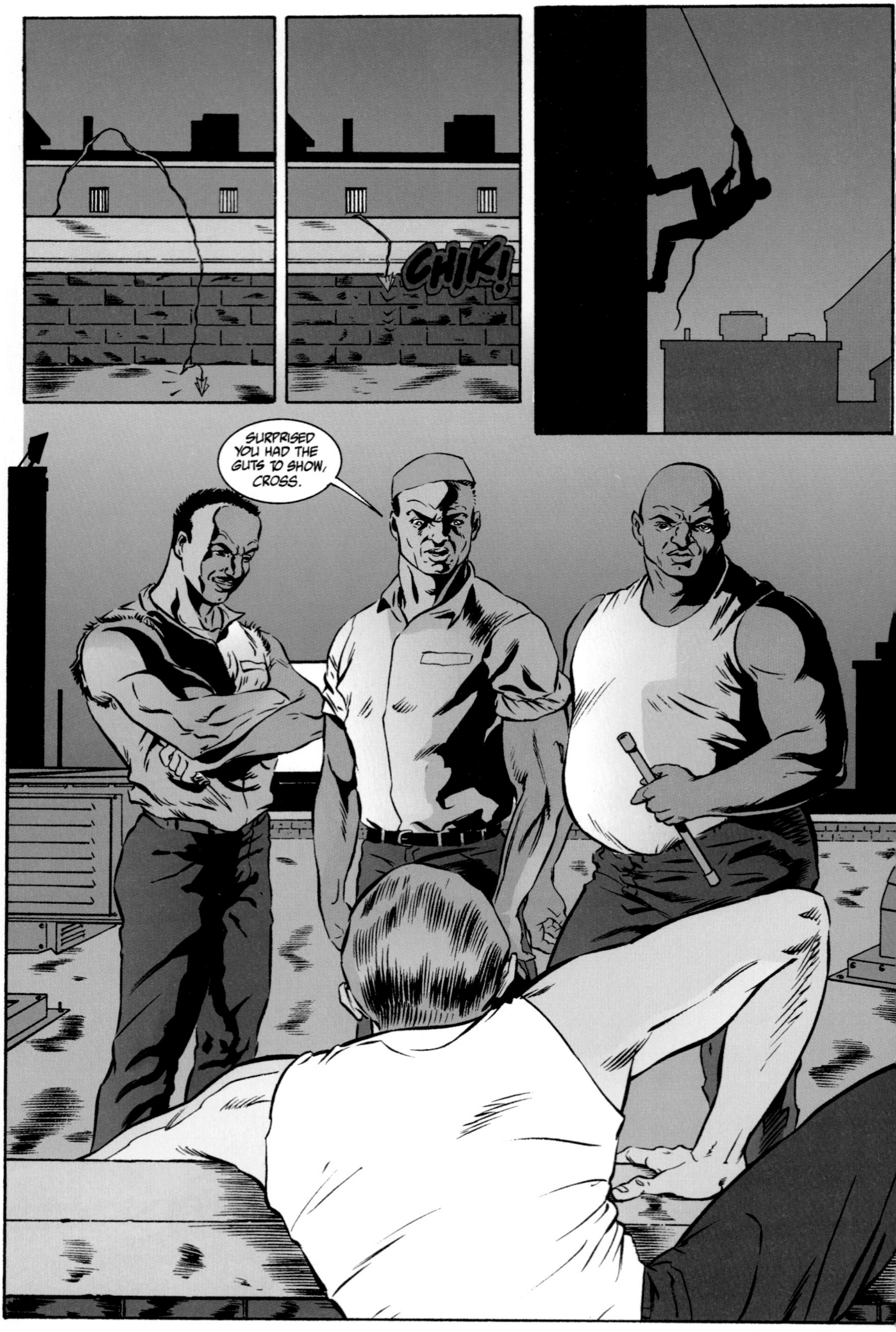
CHIK!
SURPRISED YOU HAD THE GUTS TO SHOW, CROSS.

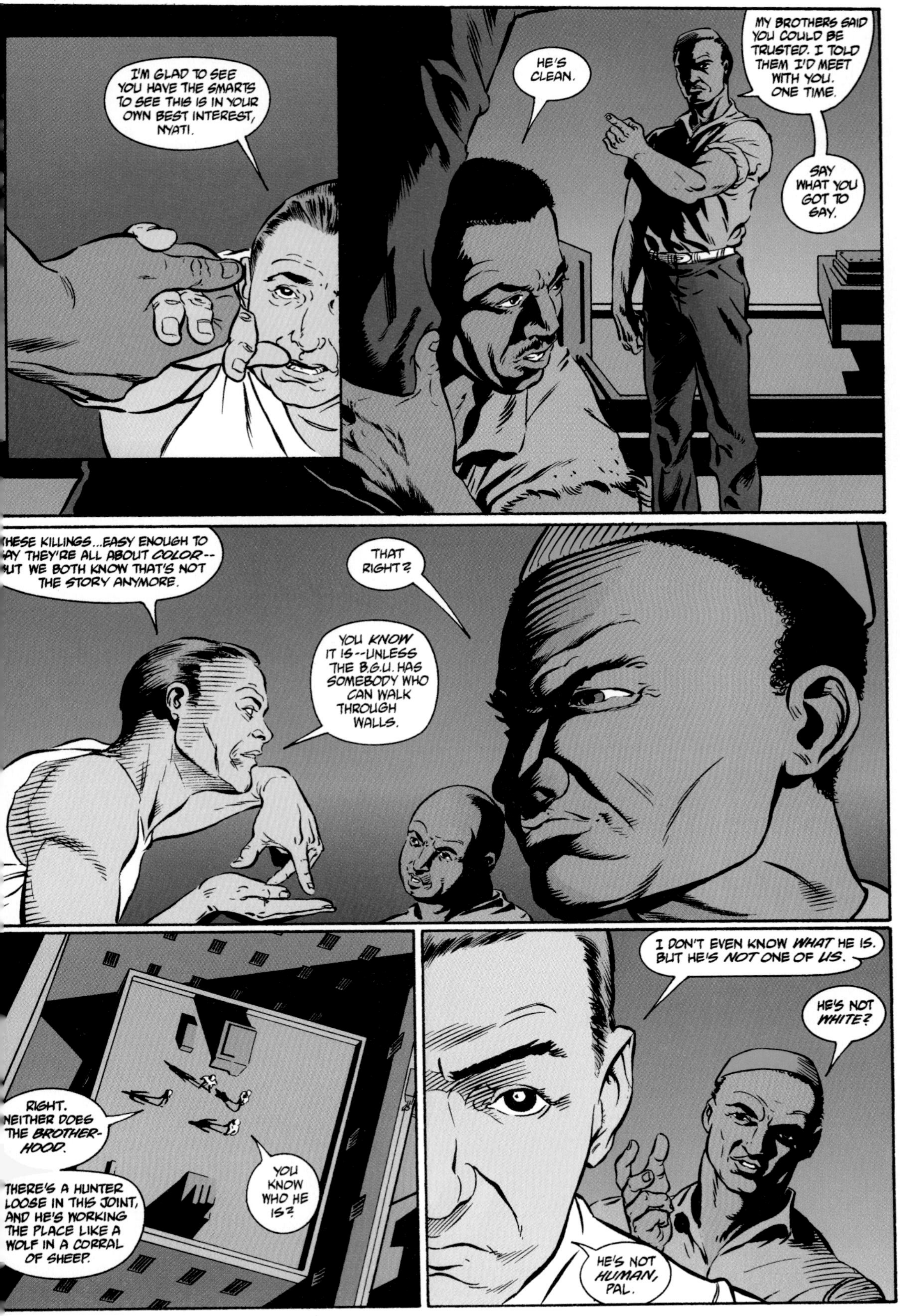
I'M GLAD TO SEE YOU HAVE THE SMARTS TO SEE THIS IS IN YOUR OWN BEST INTEREST, NYATI.
HE'S CLEAN.
MY BROTHERS SAID YOU COULD BE TRUSTED. I TOLD THEM I'D MEET WITH YOU. ONE TIME.
SAY WHAT YOU GOT TO SAY.
THESE KILLINGS...EASY ENOUGH TO SAY THEY'RE ALL ABOUT COLOR-- BUT WE BOTH KNOW THAT'S NOT THE STORY ANYMORE.
THAT RIGHT?
YOU KNOW IT IS--UNLESS THE B.G.U. HAS SOMEBODY WHO CAN WALK THROUGH WALLS.
RIGHT. NEITHER DOES THE BROTHER-HOOD.
THERE'S A HUNTER LOOSE IN THIS JOINT, AND HE'S WORKING THE PLACE LIKE A WOLF IN A CORRAL OF SHEEP.
YOU KNOW WHO HE IS?
I DON'T EVEN KNOW WHAT HE IS. BUT HE'S NOT ONE OF US.
HE'S NOT WHITE?
HE'S NOT HUMAN, PAL.

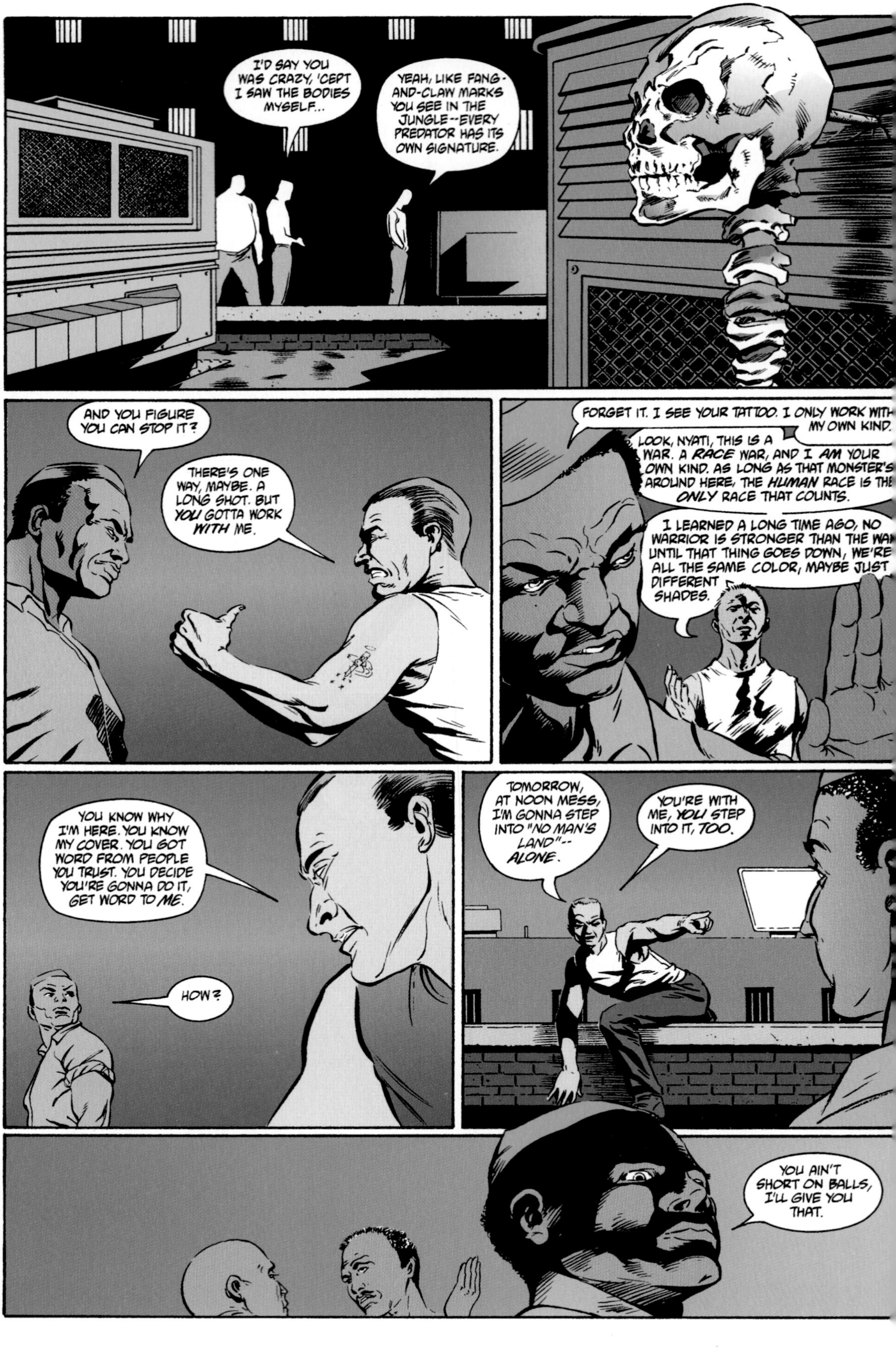
I'D SAY YOU WAS CRAZY, 'CEPT I SAW THE BODIES MYSELF...
YEAH, LIKE FANG-AND-CLAW MARKS YOU SEE IN THE JUNGLE--EVERY PREDATOR HAS ITS OWN SIGNATURE.
AND YOU FIGURE YOU CAN STOP IT?
THERE'S ONE WAY, MAYBE. A LONG SHOT. BUT YOU GOTTA WORK WITH ME.
FORGET IT. I SEE YOUR TATTOO. I ONLY WORK WITH MY OWN KIND.
LOOK, NYATI, THIS IS A WAR. A RACE WAR, AND I AM YOUR OWN KIND. AS LONG AS THAT MONSTER'S AROUND HERE, THE HUMAN RACE IS THE ONLY RACE THAT COUNTS.
I LEARNED A LONG TIME AGO, NO WARRIOR IS STRONGER THAN THE WAR. UNTIL THAT THING GOES DOWN, WE'RE ALL THE SAME COLOR, MAYBE JUST DIFFERENT SHADES.
YOU KNOW WHY I'M HERE. YOU KNOW MY COVER. YOU GOT WORD FROM PEOPLE YOU TRUST. YOU DECIDE YOU'RE GONNA DO IT, GET WORD TO ME.
HOW?
TOMORROW, AT NOON MESS, I'M GONNA STEP INTO "NO MAN'S LAND"--ALONE.
YOU'RE WITH ME, YOU STEP INTO IT, TOO.
YOU AIN'T SHORT ON BALLS, I'LL GIVE YOU THAT.

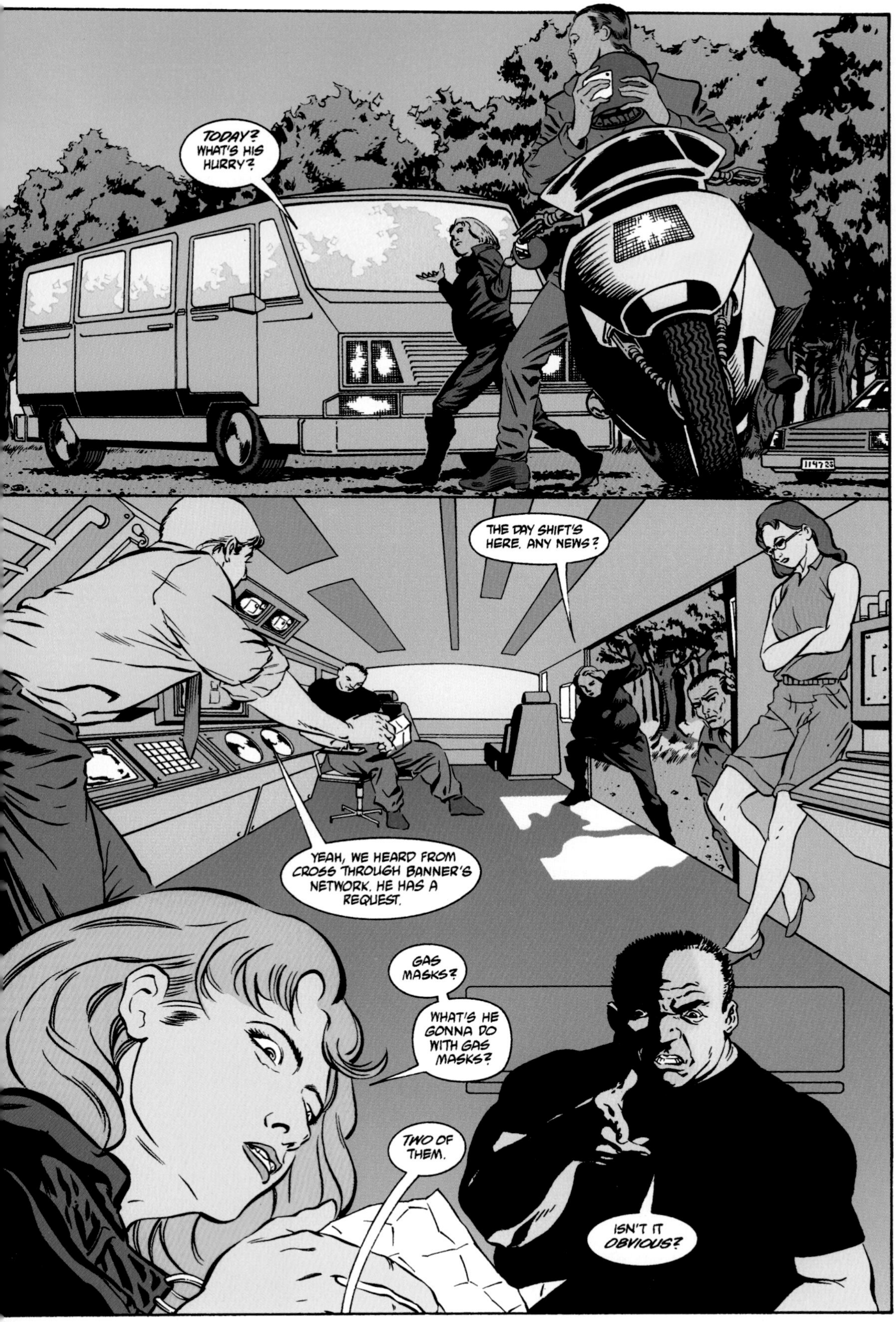
TODAY? WHAT'S HIS HURRY?
THE DAY SHIFT'S HERE. ANY NEWS?
YEAH, WE HEARD FROM CROSS THROUGH BANNER'S NETWORK. HE HAS A REQUEST.
GAS MASKS?
WHAT'S HE GONNA DO WITH GAS MASKS?
TWO OF THEM.
ISN'T IT OBVIOUS?

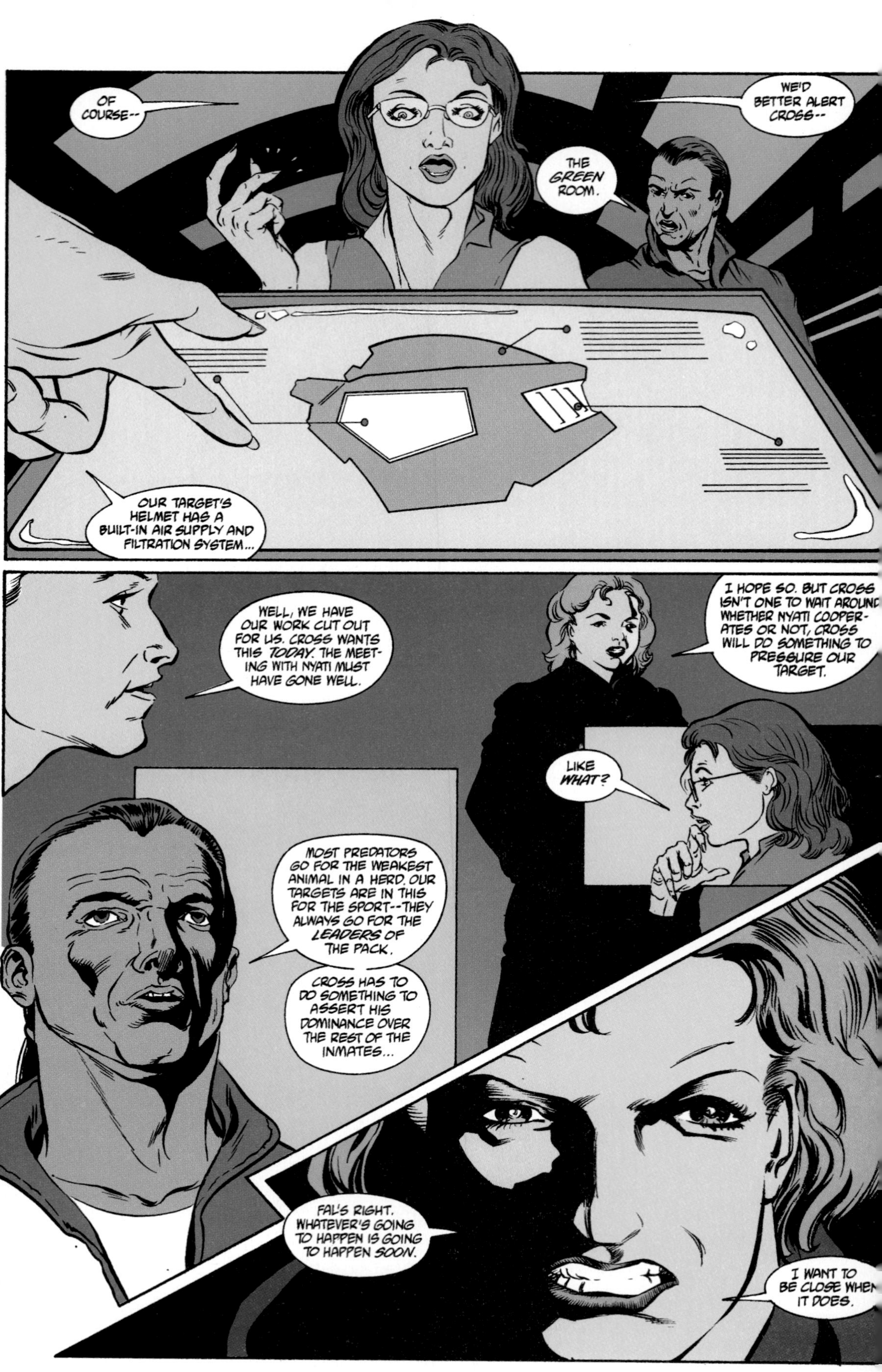
OF COURSE--
WE'D BETTER ALERT CROSS--
THE GREEN ROOM.
OUR TARGET'S HELMET HAS A BUILT-IN AIR SUPPLY AND FILTRATION SYSTEM...
WELL, WE HAVE OUR WORK CUT OUT FOR US. CROSS WANTS THIS TODAY. THE MEETING WITH NYATI MUST HAVE GONE WELL.
I HOPE SO. BUT CROSS ISN'T ONE TO WAIT AROUND WHETHER NYATI COOPERATES OR NOT, CROSS WILL DO SOMETHING TO PRESSURE OUR TARGET.
LIKE WHAT?
MOST PREDATORS GO FOR THE WEAKEST ANIMAL IN A HERD. OUR TARGETS ARE IN THIS FOR THE SPORT--THEY ALWAYS GO FOR THE LEADERS OF THE PACK.
CROSS HAS TO DO SOMETHING TO ASSERT HIS DOMINANCE OVER THE REST OF THE INMATES...
FAL'S RIGHT. WHATEVER'S GOING TO HAPPEN IS GOING TO HAPPEN SOON.
I WANT TO BE CLOSE WHEN IT DOES.

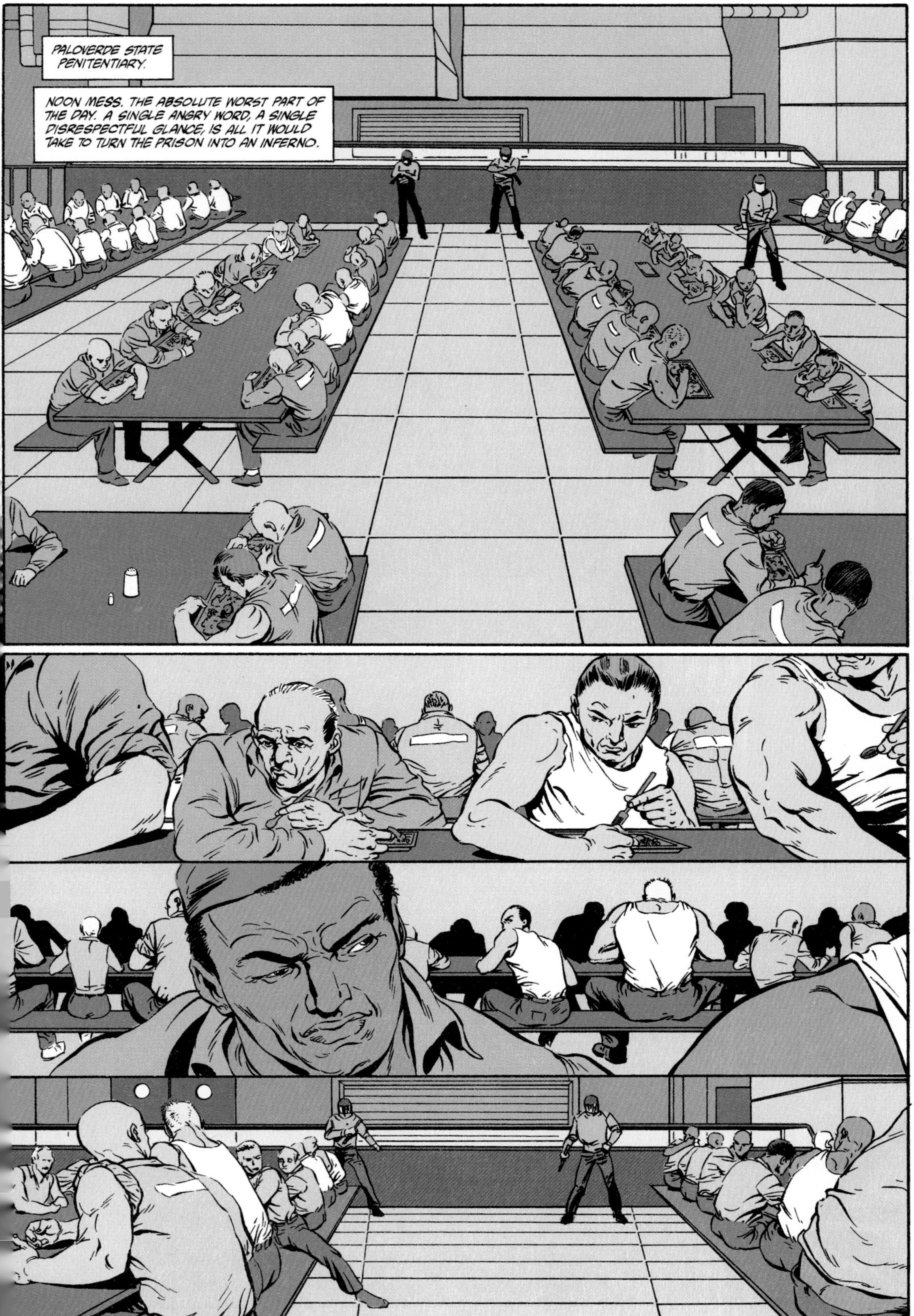
PALOVERDE STATE PENITENTIARY.
NOON MESS. THE ABSOLUTE WORST PART OF THE DAY. A SINGLE ANGRY WORD, A SINGLE DISRESPECTFUL GLANCE, IS ALL IT WOULD TAKE TO TURN THE PRISON INTO AN INFERNO.

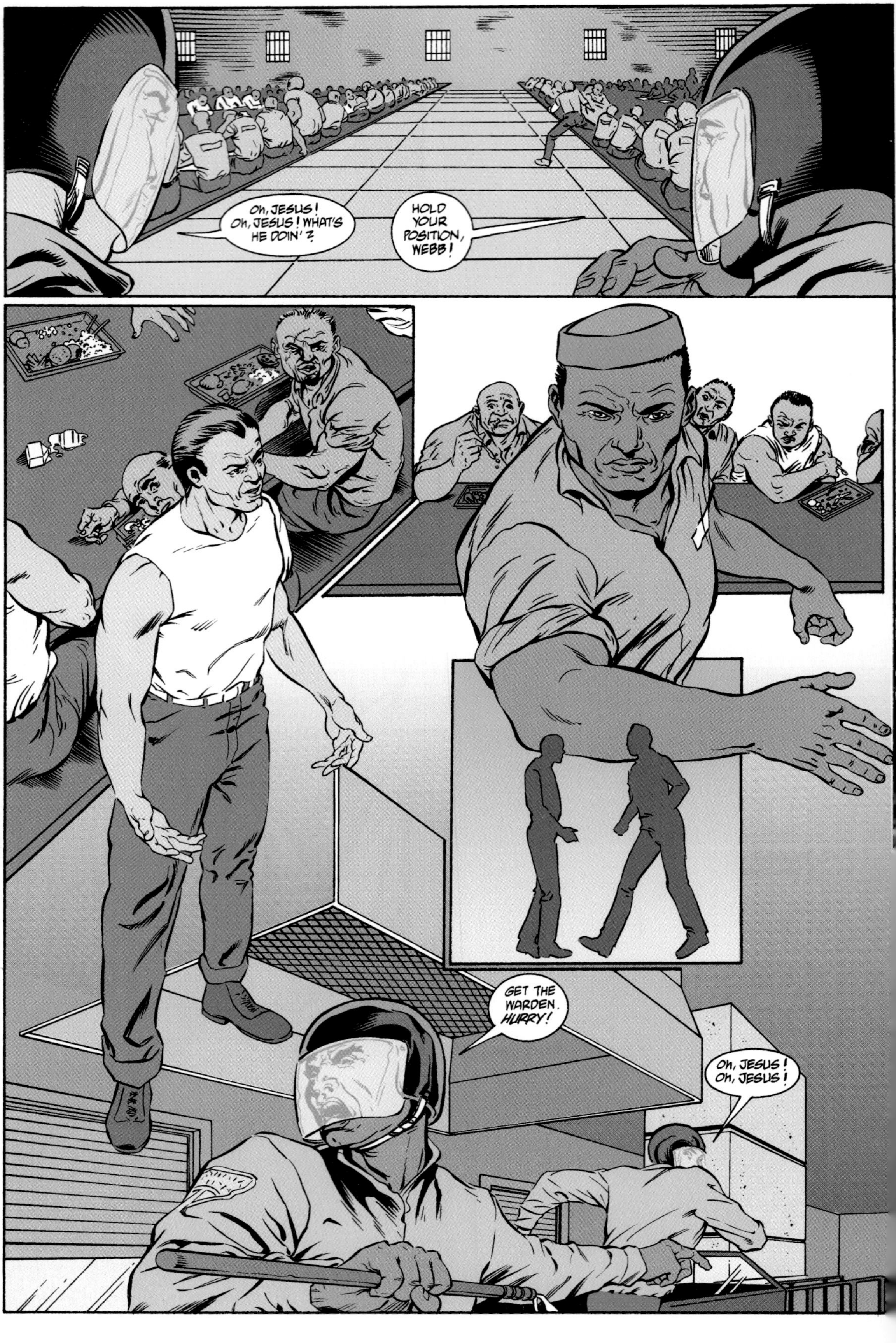
Oh, JESUS! Oh, JESUS! WHAT'S HE DOIN' ?
HOLD YOUR POSITION, WEBB!
GET THE WARDEN. HURRY!
Oh, JESUS! Oh, JESUS!

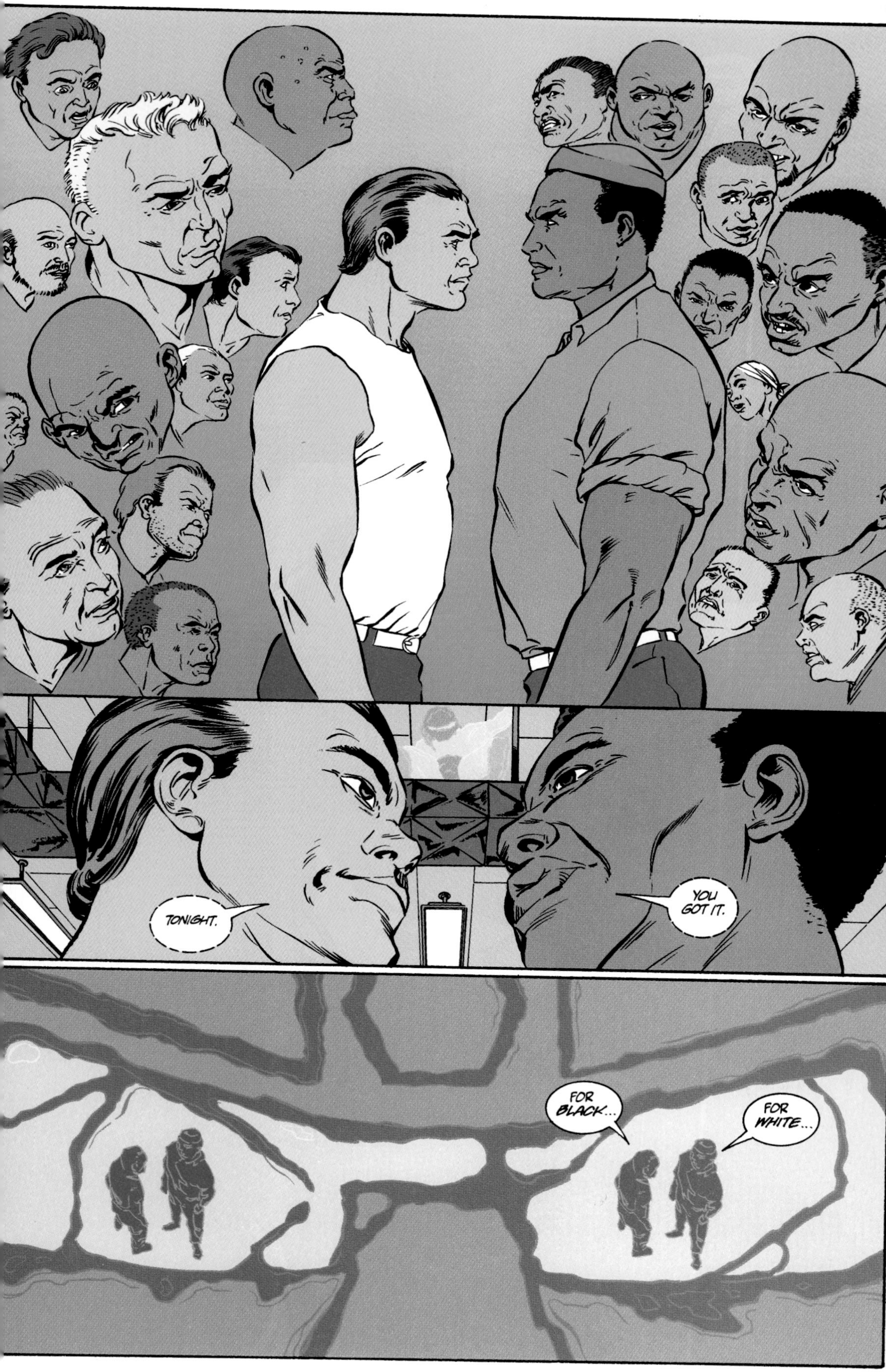
TONIGHT.
YOU GOT IT.
FOR BLACK...
FOR WHITE...

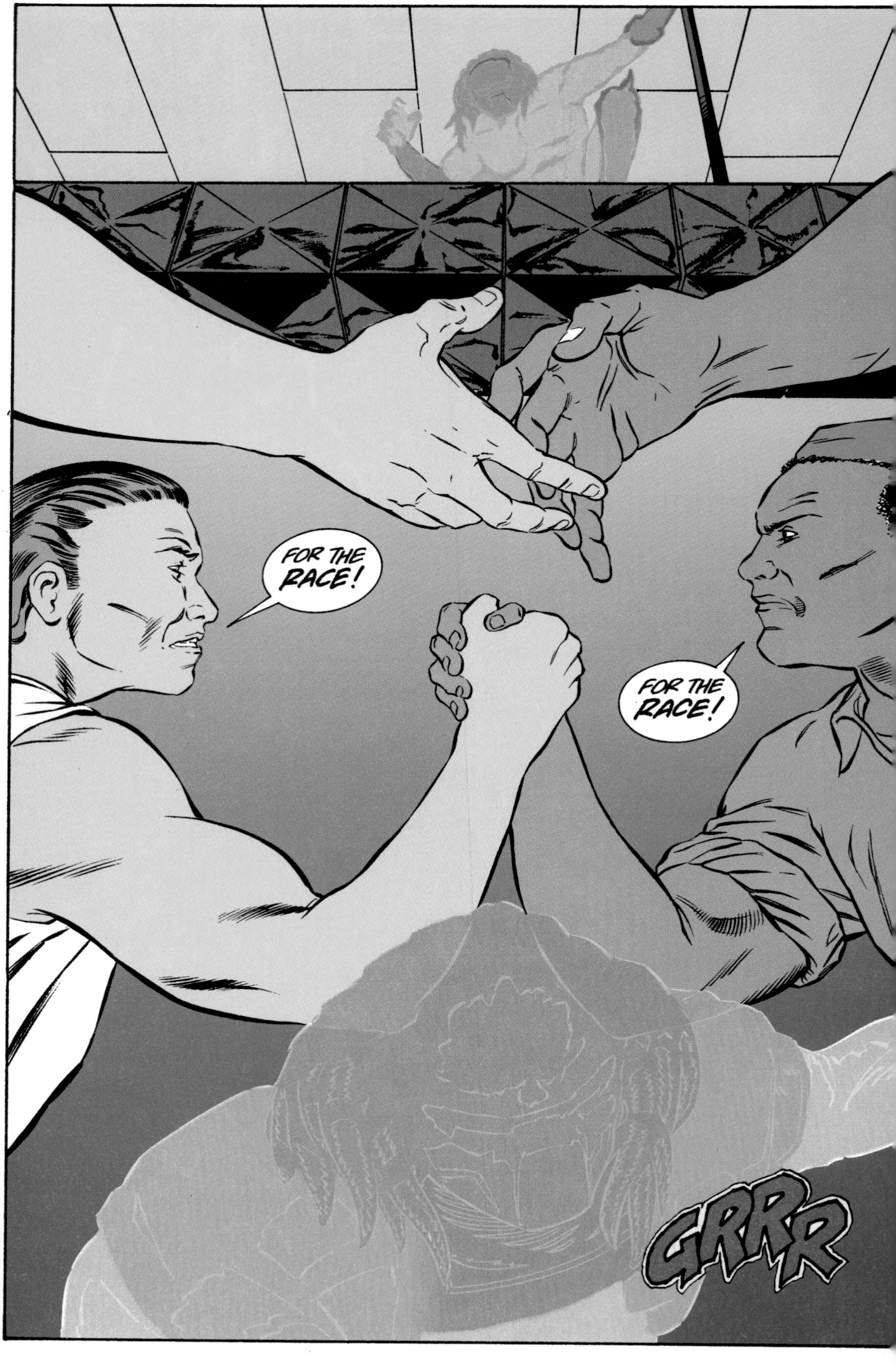
FOR THE RACE!
FOR THE RACE!
GRRR

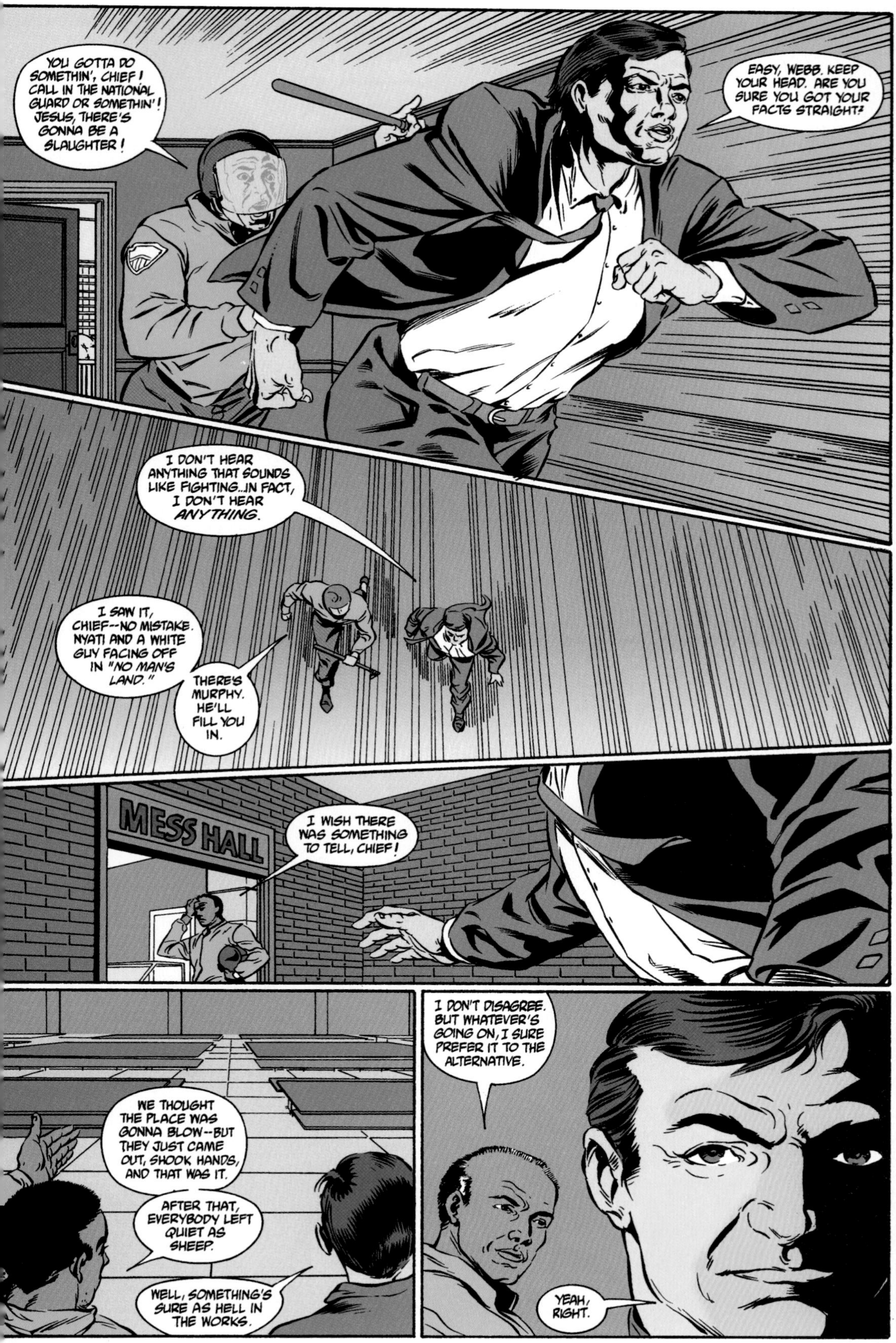

YOU GOTTA DO SOMETHIN', CHIEF! CALL IN THE NATIONAL GUARD OR SOMETHIN'! JESUS, THERE'S GONNA BE A SLAUGHTER!
EASY, WEBB. KEEP YOUR HEAD. ARE YOU SURE YOU GOT YOUR FACTS STRAIGHT?
I DON'T HEAR ANYTHING THAT SOUNDS LIKE FIGHTING...IN FACT, I DON'T HEAR *ANYTHING*.
I SAW IT, CHIEF--NO MISTAKE. NYATI AND A WHITE GUY FACING OFF IN "NO MAN'S LAND."
THERE'S MURPHY. HE'LL FILL YOU IN.
MESS HALL
I WISH THERE WAS SOMETHING TO TELL, CHIEF!
WE THOUGHT THE PLACE WAS GONNA BLOW--BUT THEY JUST CAME OUT, SHOOK HANDS, AND THAT WAS IT.
AFTER THAT, EVERYBODY LEFT QUIET AS SHEEP.
WELL, SOMETHING'S SURE AS HELL IN THE WORKS.
I DON'T DISAGREE. BUT WHATEVER'S GOING ON, I SURE PREFER IT TO THE ALTERNATIVE.
YEAH, RIGHT.

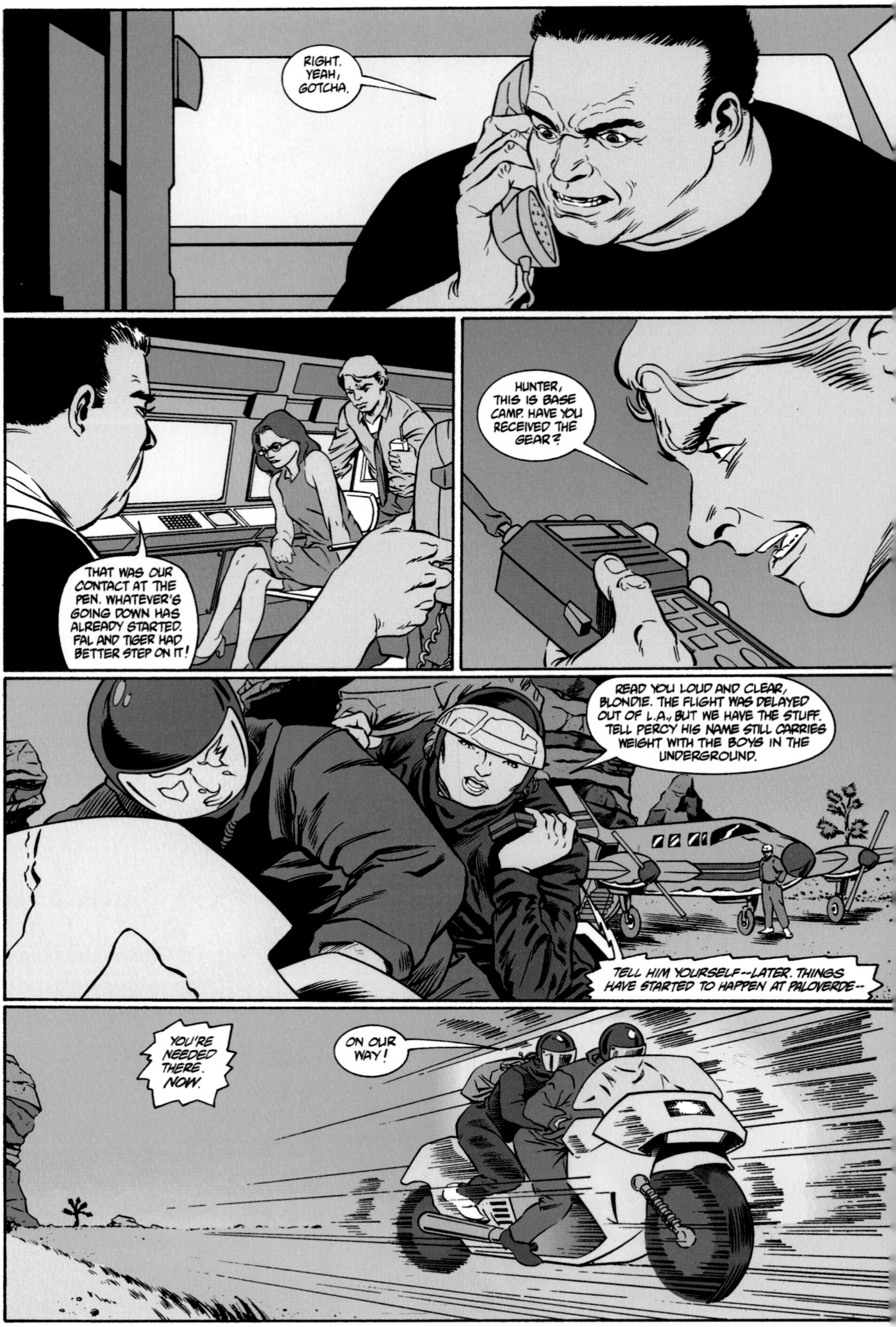
RIGHT. YEAH, GOTCHA.
THAT WAS OUR CONTACT AT THE PEN. WHATEVER'S GOING DOWN HAS ALREADY STARTED. FAL AND TIGER HAD BETTER STEP ON IT!
HUNTER, THIS IS BASE CAMP. HAVE YOU RECEIVED THE GEAR?
READ YOU LOUD AND CLEAR, BLONDIE. THE FLIGHT WAS DELAYED OUT OF L.A., BUT WE HAVE THE STUFF. TELL PERCY HIS NAME STILL CARRIES WEIGHT WITH THE BOYS IN THE UNDERGROUND.
TELL HIM YOURSELF--LATER. THINGS HAVE STARTED TO HAPPEN AT PALOVERDE--
YOU'RE NEEDED THERE. NOW.
ON OUR WAY!

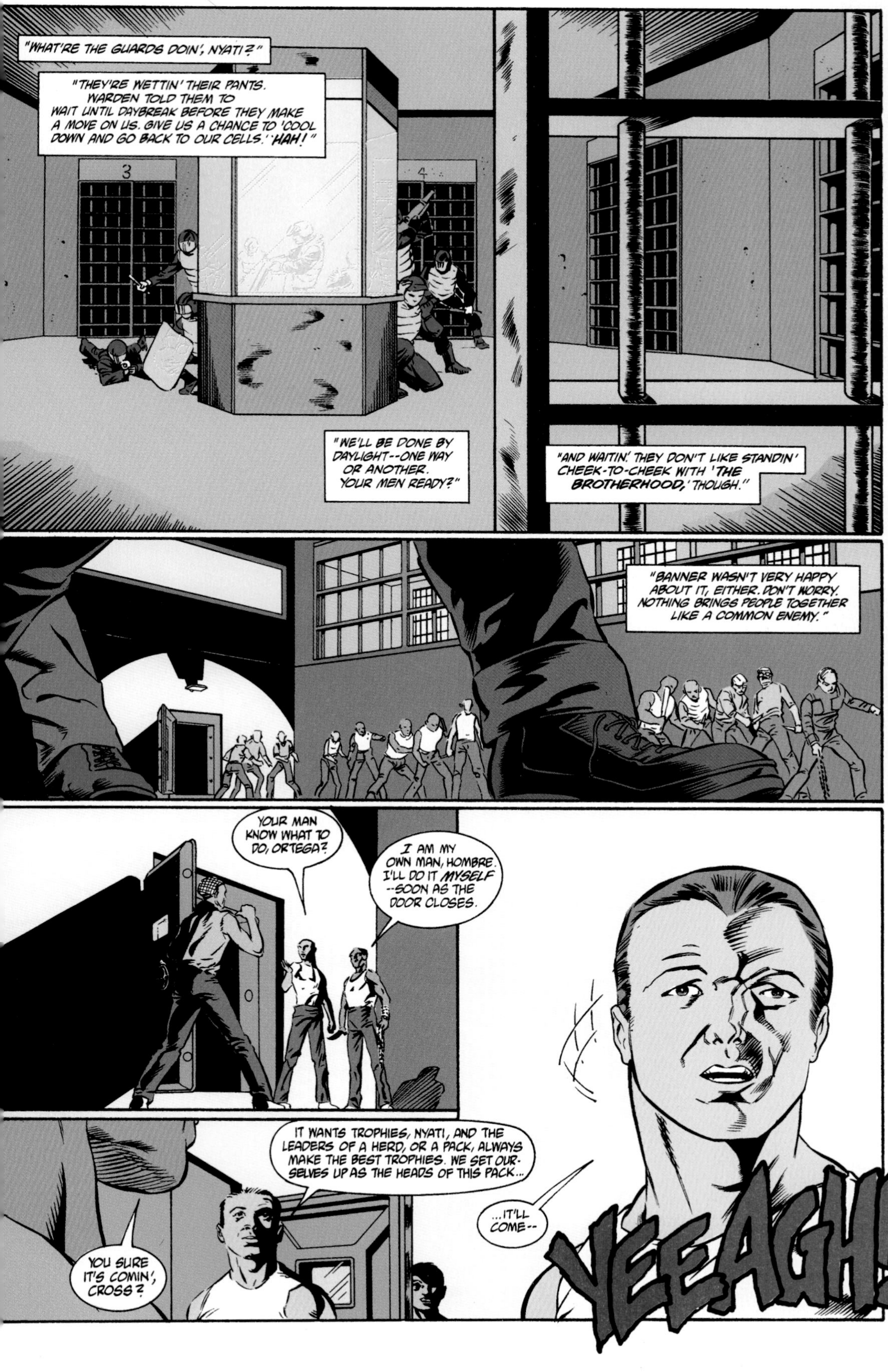
"WHAT'RE THE GUARDS DOIN', NYATI?"
"THEY'RE WETTIN' THEIR PANTS. WARDEN TOLD THEM TO WAIT UNTIL DAYBREAK BEFORE THEY MAKE A MOVE ON US. GIVE US A CHANCE TO 'COOL DOWN AND GO BACK TO OUR CELLS.' HAH!"
3
4
"WE'LL BE DONE BY DAYLIGHT--ONE WAY OR ANOTHER. YOUR MEN READY?"
"AND WAITIN.' THEY DON'T LIKE STANDIN' CHEEK-TO-CHEEK WITH 'THE BROTHERHOOD,' THOUGH."
"BANNER WASN'T VERY HAPPY ABOUT IT, EITHER. DON'T WORRY. NOTHING BRINGS PEOPLE TOGETHER LIKE A COMMON ENEMY."
YOUR MAN KNOW WHAT TO DO, ORTEGA?
I AM MY OWN MAN, HOMBRE. I'LL DO IT MYSELF --SOON AS THE DOOR CLOSES.
IT WANTS TROPHIES, NYATI, AND THE LEADERS OF A HERD, OR A PACK, ALWAYS MAKE THE BEST TROPHIES. WE SET OURSELVES UP AS THE HEADS OF THIS PACK...
YOU SURE IT'S COMIN', CROSS?
...IT'LL COME--
YEEAGH!

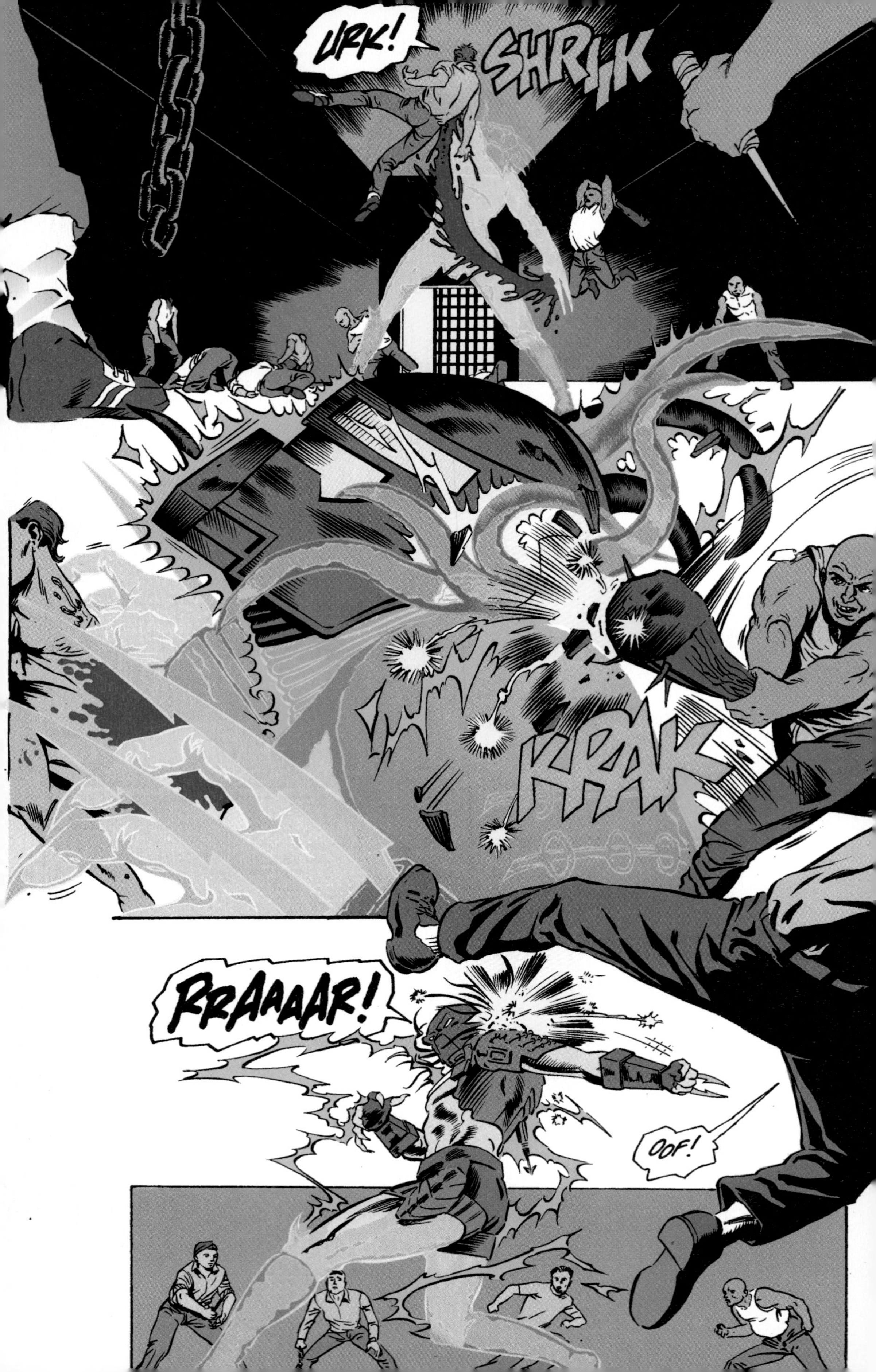
URK!
SHRIIK
KRAK
RRAAAAR!
OOF!

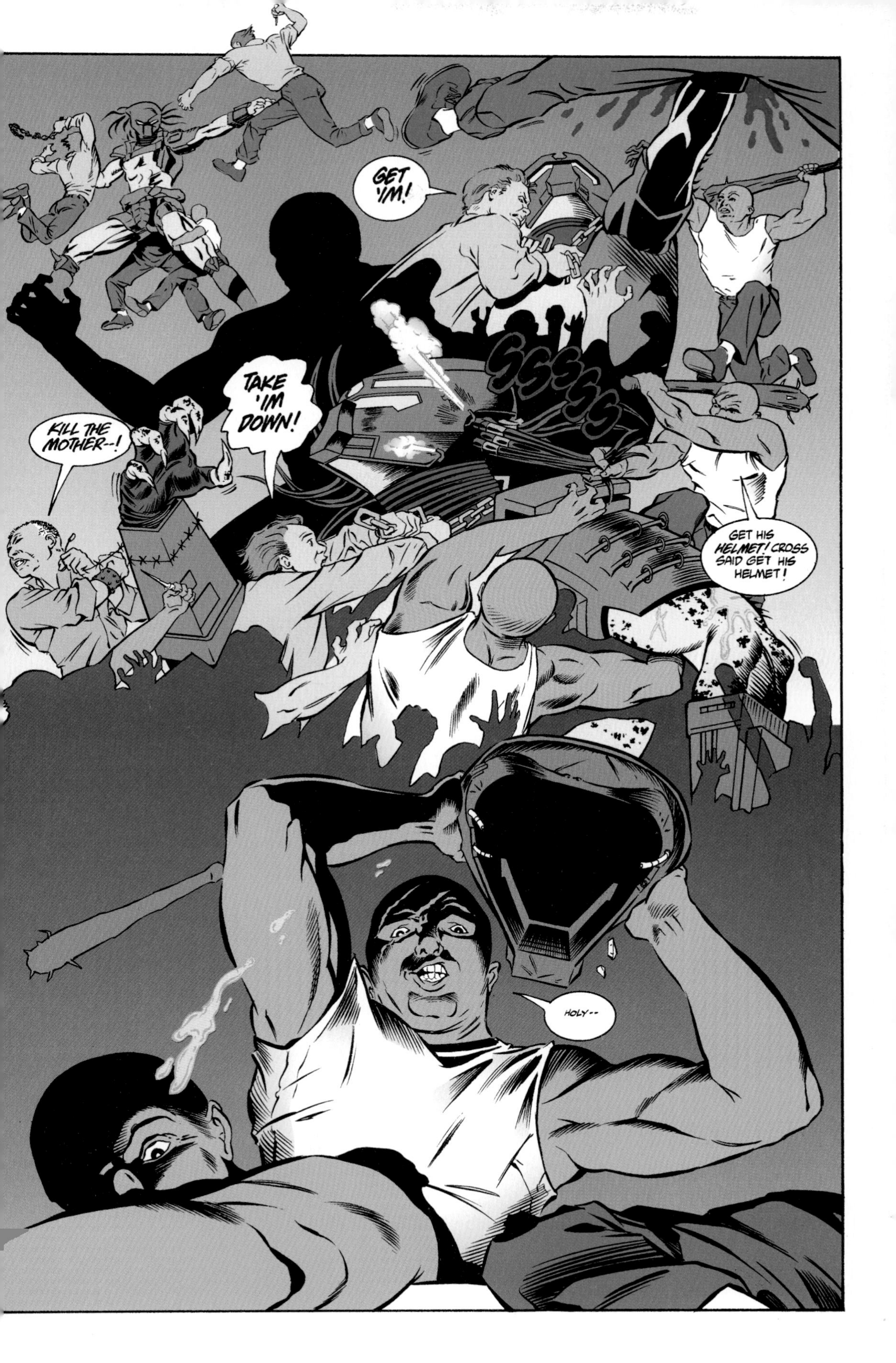
GET 'IM!
SSSSSS
TAKE 'IM DOWN!
KILL THE MOTHER--!
GET HIS HELMET! CROSS SAID GET HIS HELMET!
HOLY--

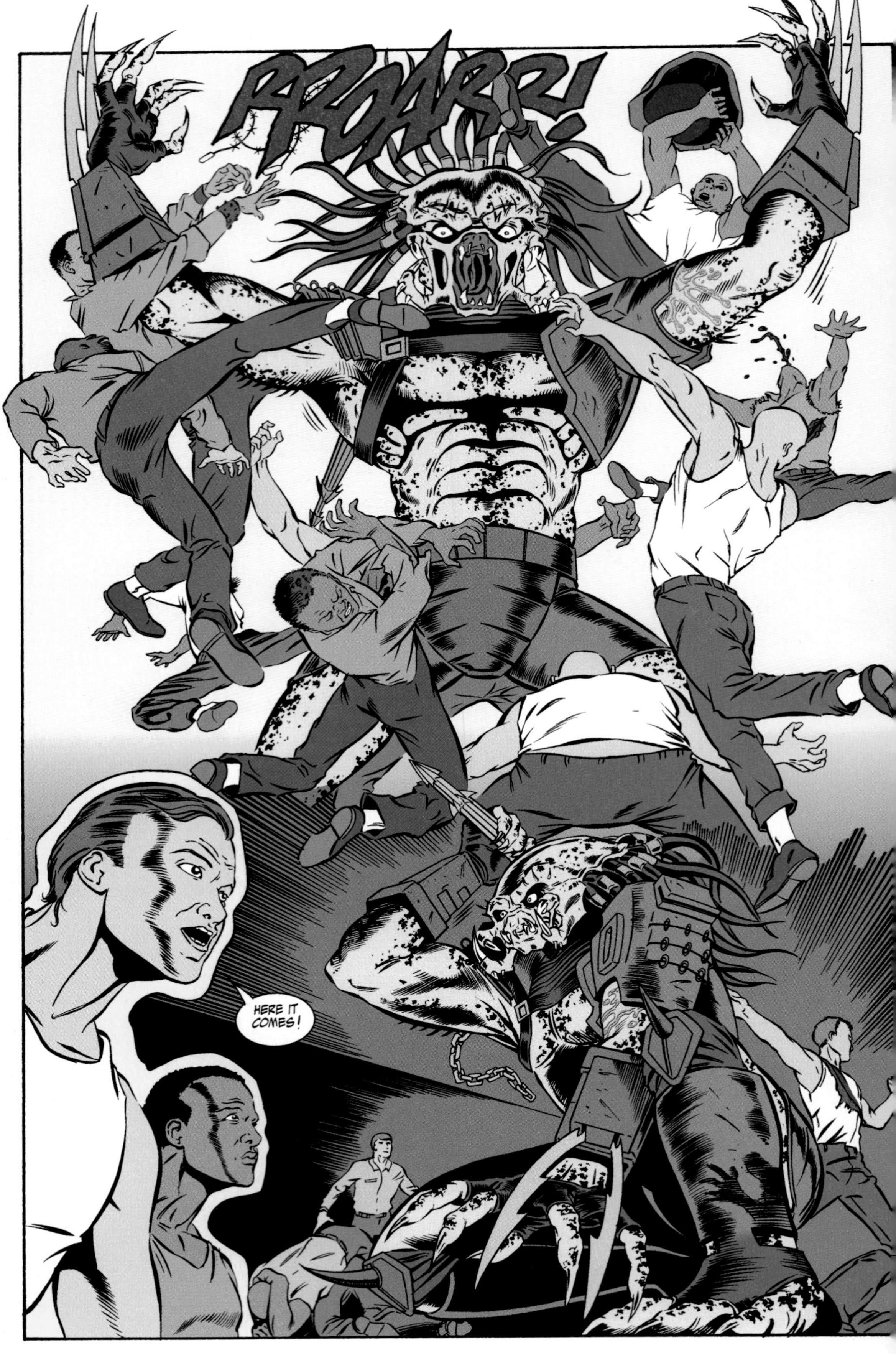
BRRAARR!
HERE IT COMES!

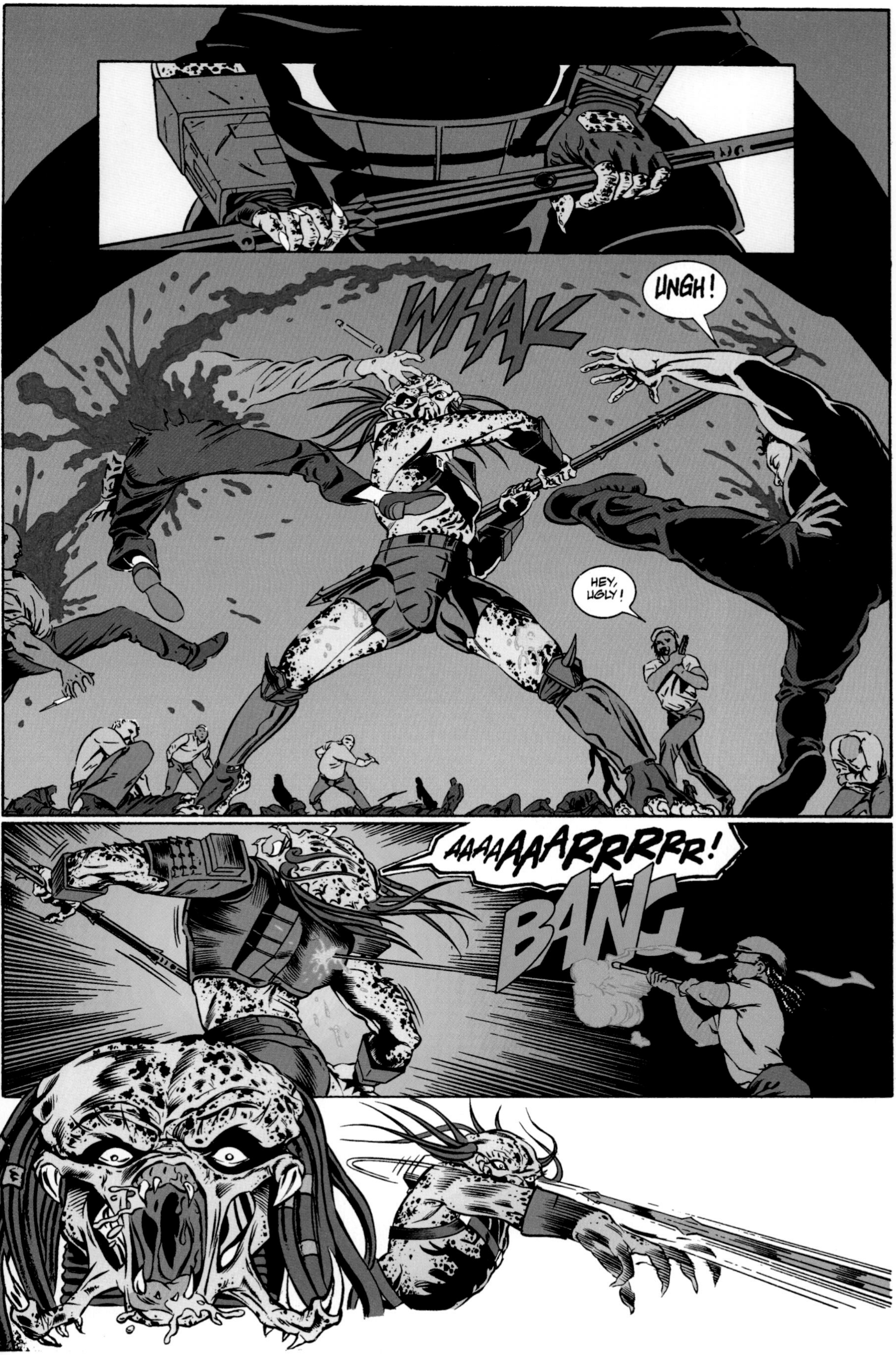
WHAK
UNGH!
HEY, UGLY!
AAAAAAARRRRR!
BANG

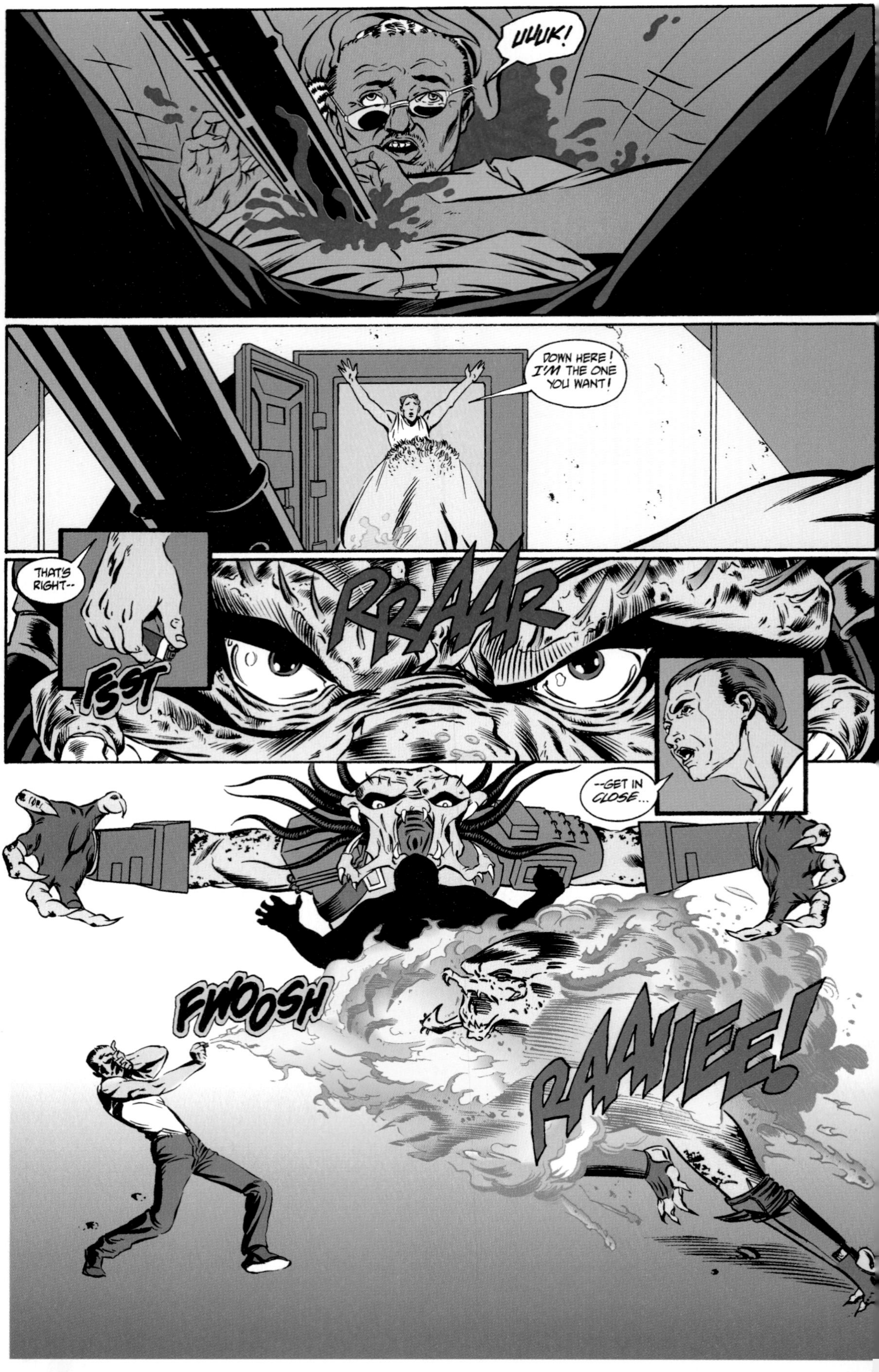
UUUK!
DOWN HERE! I'M THE ONE YOU WANT!
THAT'S RIGHT--
RRAAAR
FSST
--GET IN CLOSE...
FWOOSH
RAAIEE!

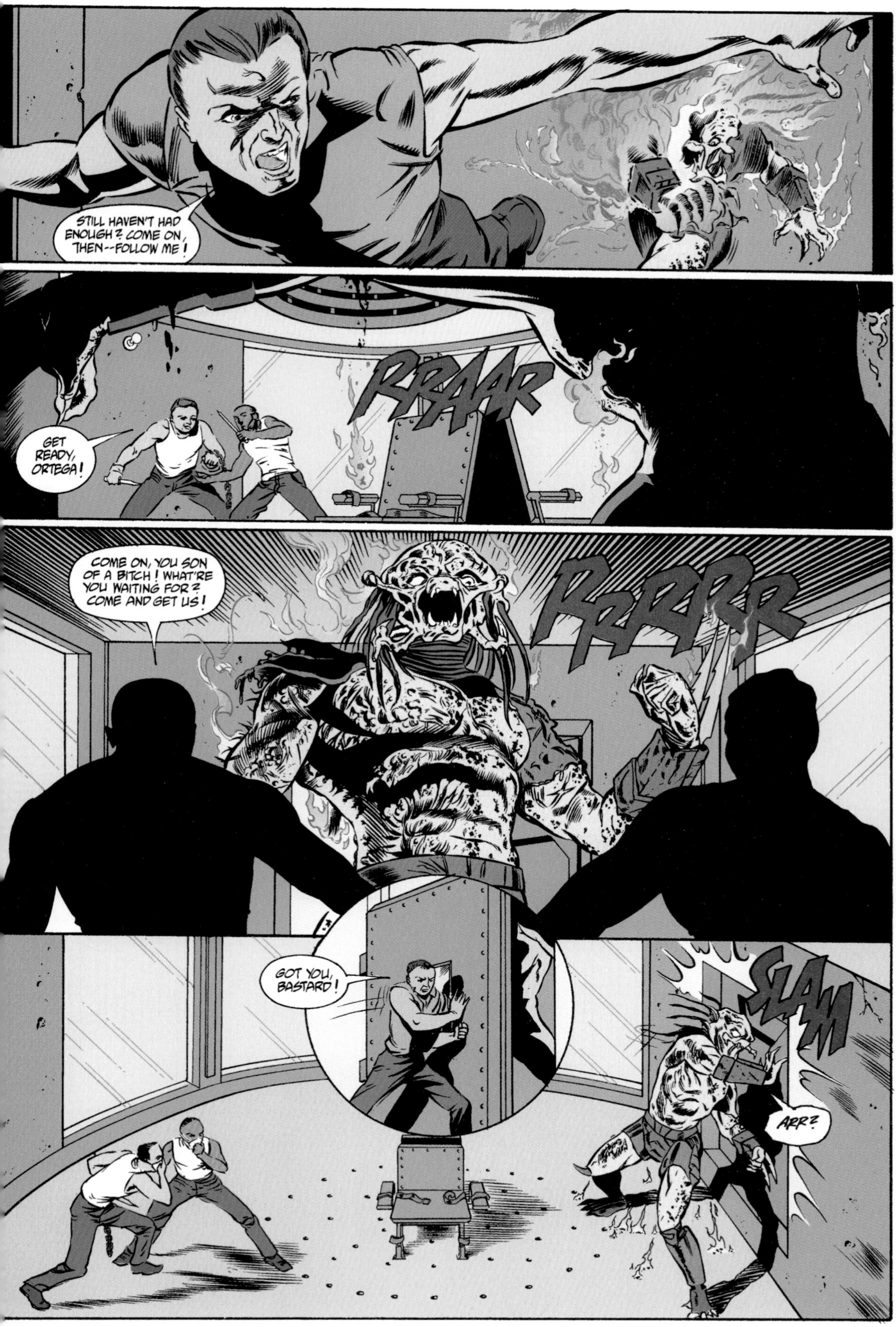
STILL HAVEN'T HAD ENOUGH? COME ON, THEN--FOLLOW ME!
RRAAR
GET READY, ORTEGA!
COME ON, YOU SON OF A BITCH! WHAT'RE YOU WAITING FOR? COME AND GET US!
RRRRR
GOT YOU, BASTARD!
SLAM
ARR?

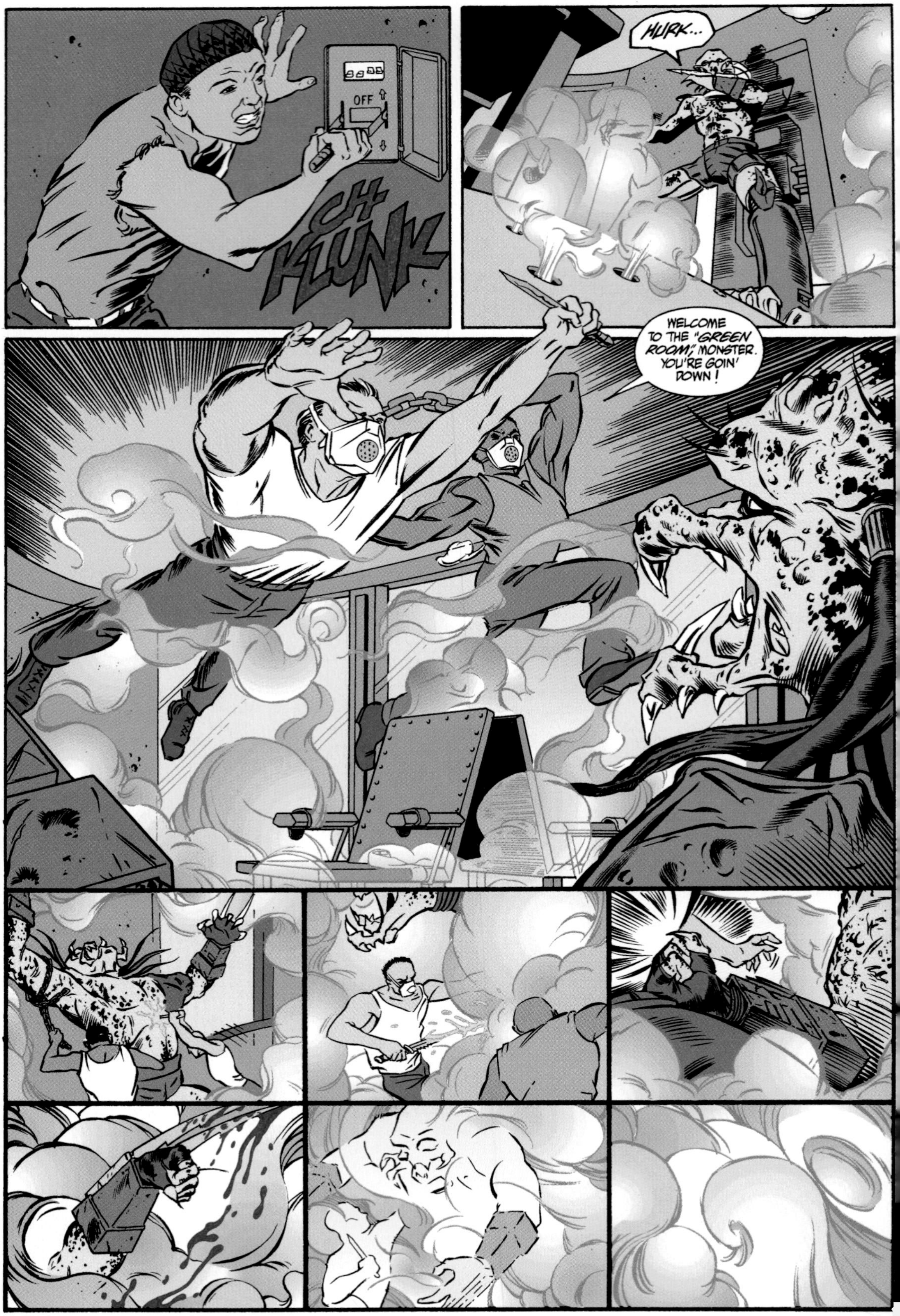
OFF
CH KLUNK
HURK...
WELCOME TO THE "GREEN ROOM," MONSTER. YOU'RE GOIN' DOWN!

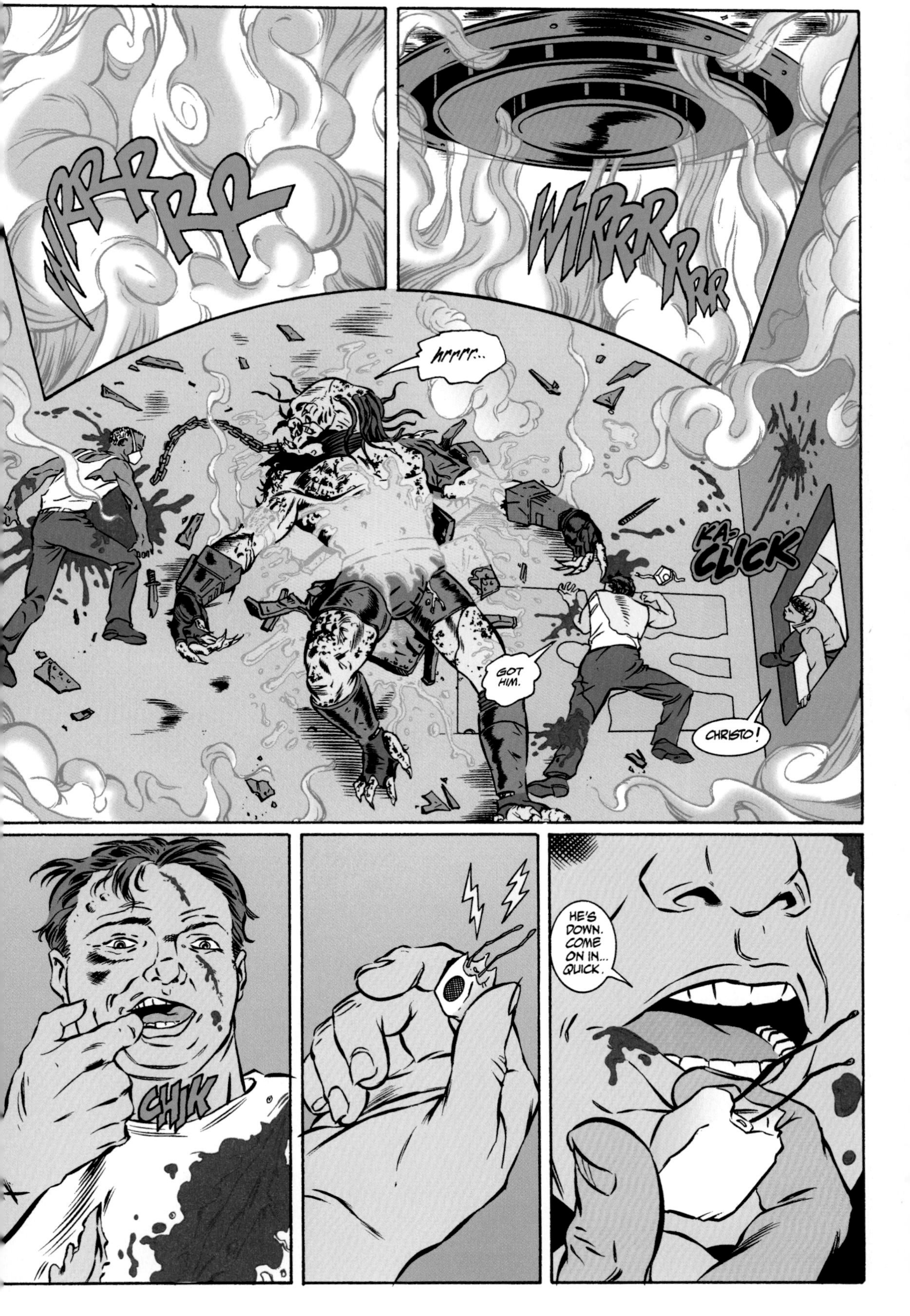
WARRRR
WIRRRRRR
hrrrr...
KA-CLICK
GOT HIM.
CHRISTO!
CHIK
HE'S DOWN. COME ON IN... QUICK.

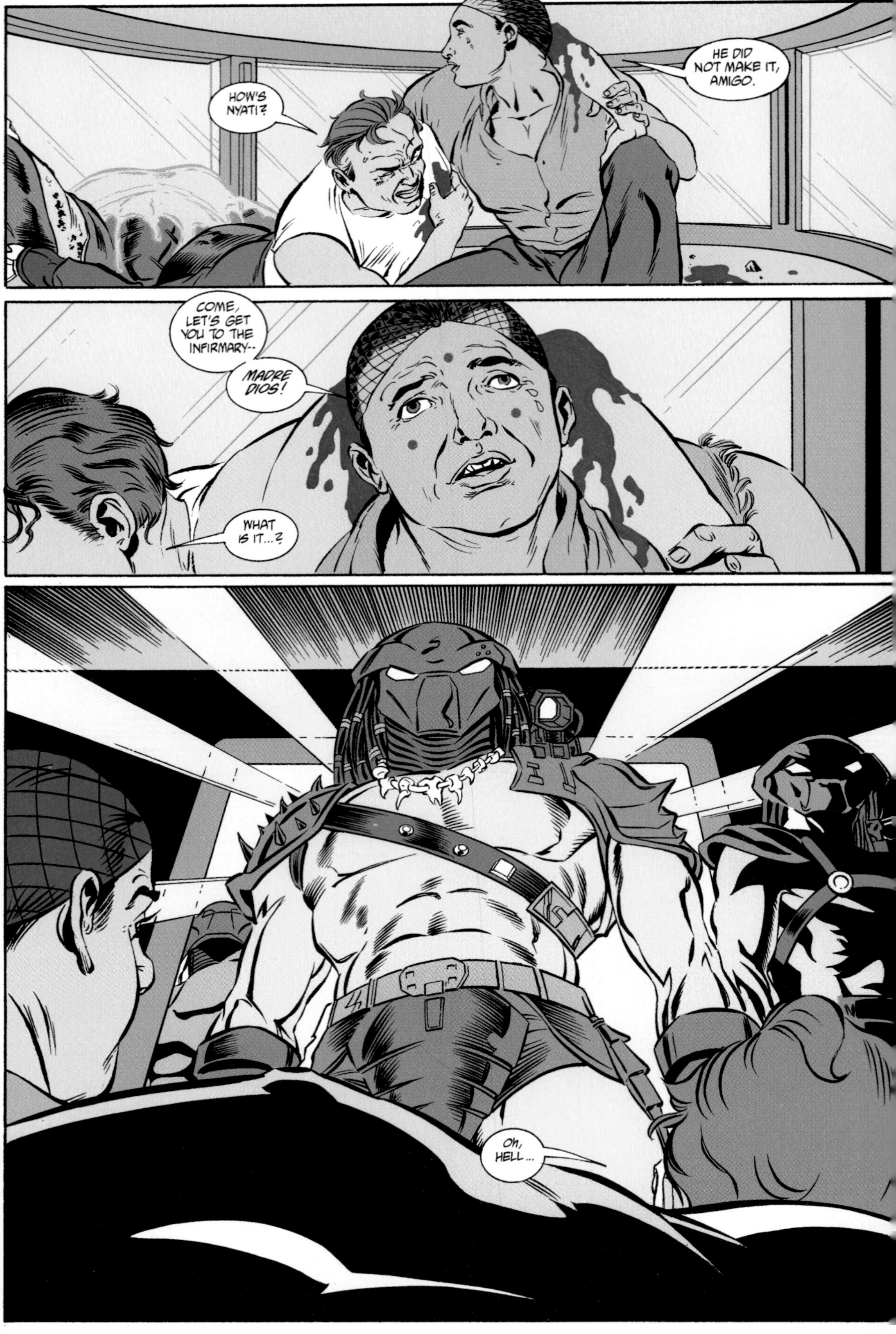
HOW'S NYATI?
HE DID NOT MAKE IT, AMIGO.
COME, LET'S GET YOU TO THE INFIRMARY--
MADRE DIOS!
WHAT IS IT...?
Oh, HELL...

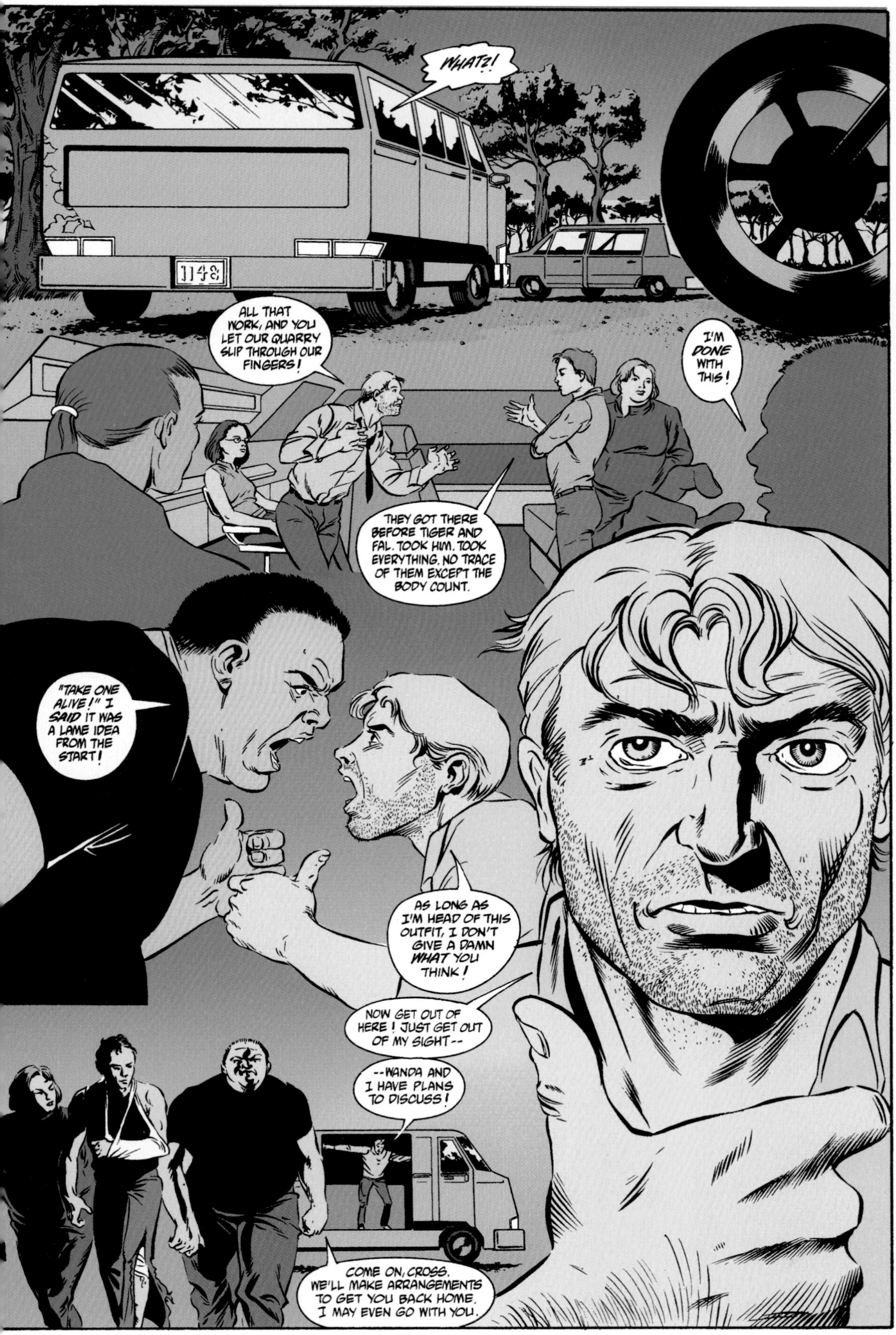
WHAT?!
ALL THAT WORK, AND YOU LET OUR QUARRY SLIP THROUGH OUR FINGERS!
I'M DONE WITH THIS!
THEY GOT THERE BEFORE TIGER AND FAL. TOOK HIM. TOOK EVERYTHING. NO TRACE OF THEM EXCEPT THE BODY COUNT.
"TAKE ONE ALIVE!" I SAID IT WAS A LAME IDEA FROM THE START!
AS LONG AS I'M HEAD OF THIS OUTFIT, I DON'T GIVE A DAMN WHAT YOU THINK!
NOW GET OUT OF HERE! JUST GET OUT OF MY SIGHT--
--WANDA AND I HAVE PLANS TO DISCUSS!
COME ON, CROSS. WE'LL MAKE ARRANGEMENTS TO GET YOU BACK HOME. I MAY EVEN GO WITH YOU.

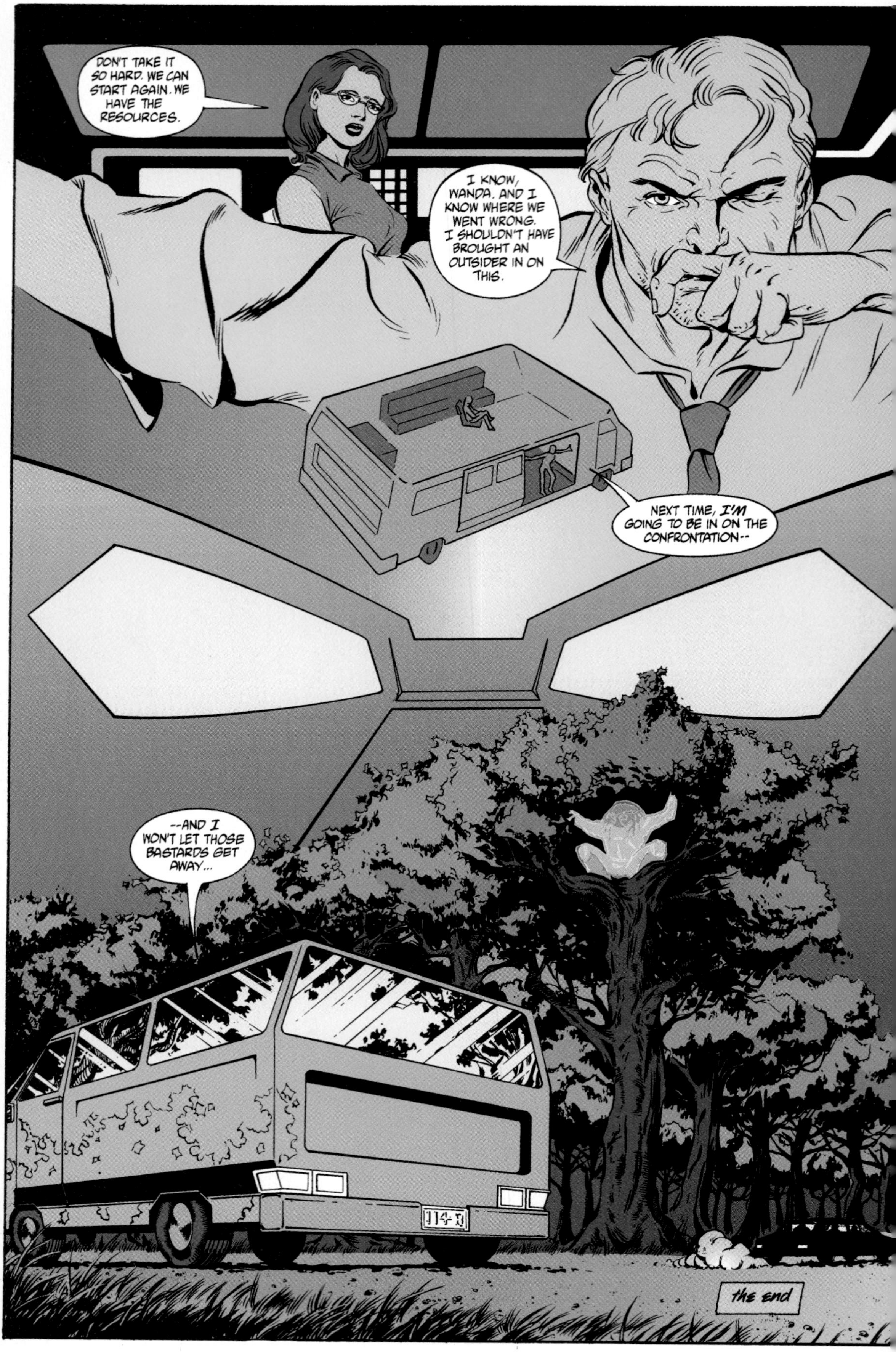
DON'T TAKE IT SO HARD. WE CAN START AGAIN. WE HAVE THE RESOURCES.
I KNOW, WANDA. AND I KNOW WHERE WE WENT WRONG. I SHOULDN'T HAVE BROUGHT AN OUTSIDER IN ON THIS.
NEXT TIME, I'M GOING TO BE IN ON THE CONFRONTATION--
--AND I WON'T LET THOSE BASTARDS GET AWAY...
the end

BACKGROUND

by Randy Stradley

After Dark Horse began publishing Predator stories (sometime in 1988, I believe), I, as senior editor, received a number of proposals that revolved around a Predator hunting a serial killer. With any established character, certain ideas will naturally occur — almost simultaneously — to more than one person. And, for the Predator, a character who intentionally seeks out and attacks other predators, the idea of one of them coming after a serial killer is a natural one indeed. So, I had these proposals, two of which were under serious consideration, in which Predators hunt serial killers — forcing the serial killers (as the stories' primary representatives of the human race) into the role of hero. Dope that I was (some would say, still am), no alarms went off in my head.

It took Andrew Vachss to set off the alarms. "The serial killer's the *hero*?" His tone spoke far louder than any degree of volume.

Of course. The most obvious thing in the world. People who routinely (or ritually) prey on other people are not — and should not be made out to be — anything but the scum that they are. Within a few minutes, Andrew had outlined an idea for a story. Within the next few weeks, he delivered a hundred-page manuscript for the story you have just read. And because I had answered, "me," when Andrew asked who was Dark Horse's resident Predator "expert," I was given the opportunity to adapt Andrew's prose story to comics.

It was one of the most exciting — and certainly the most difficult — jobs I have undertaken in all my years in the business. Exciting, because I was getting to work with one of my all-time favorite writers. Difficult, because (and, if you've ever read any of Andrew's prose, you know exactly what I mean) there is no "fat" in anything Andrew writes. There is nothing that can be cut without destroying the meaning or point of some other portion of the story. Every scene somehow links to, or dovetails into, another. Truncate one event, and you rip the guts out of a later one. Somehow though, I was able to fit his story into a nearly equal number of comic-book pages.

The story, as you now know, centers around a man called Cross. Cross is a hunter and a killer. His environment is largely responsible for who and what Cross is, but he fiercely maintains a spark of individualism — and, at least, *business* ethics — regardless of what fate throws his way. In these respects, Cross is like the Predator, with its strictly observed codes of the hunt. But the parallels between Cross and the Predator stop there. The Predator kills for sport and glory — making its motives similar to the those of Towers, the serial killer in the story. Cross may kill, but for reasons of survival or profit; there is no joy in it, and certainly no honor. Unlike the Predator and the serial killer, Cross has no illusions about what he is. He knows he's no hero. He's a predator, in the purest sense of the word, and that makes him the natural target for the Predator.

Readers of Andrew Vachss' *Hard Looks* (also published by Dark Horse), or the short-story collection *Born Bad*, may already be familiar with Cross. Though the character isn't always named in the stories in which he appears, there are unmistakable clues as to his identity in many. For instance, the scene in the pool hall in *Race War* also takes place in the short story "Statute of Limitations" — *and* in the upcoming *Cross* comic-book series from Andrew Vachss and fellow novelist James Colbert (Dark Horse, scheduled for late '95). Also in the *Cross* series is another look at the scene between Cross and Enrique Cerezo, and the explosion of Cerezo's limo (as well as the events, six years prior, that lead up to that confrontation). Finally, you'll see Fal and Tiger the way they were originally envisioned — not the way they were depicted in *Race War*.

If this is your first exposure to Andrew Vachss' work, some background: all of author-attorney's best-selling crime-fiction novels (nine at last count, *Footsteps of the Hawk* and *Batman: The Ultimate Evil* — both prose and comic-book versions — being the latest) revolve around the central theme that we, as a society, create our own "predators," first by allowing abuse, then by ignoring its effects on the abused. The money Andrew earns from the sales of his novels allows him to do what he calls his "real work": interceding for, and representing in court, the victims of abuse.

GALLERY

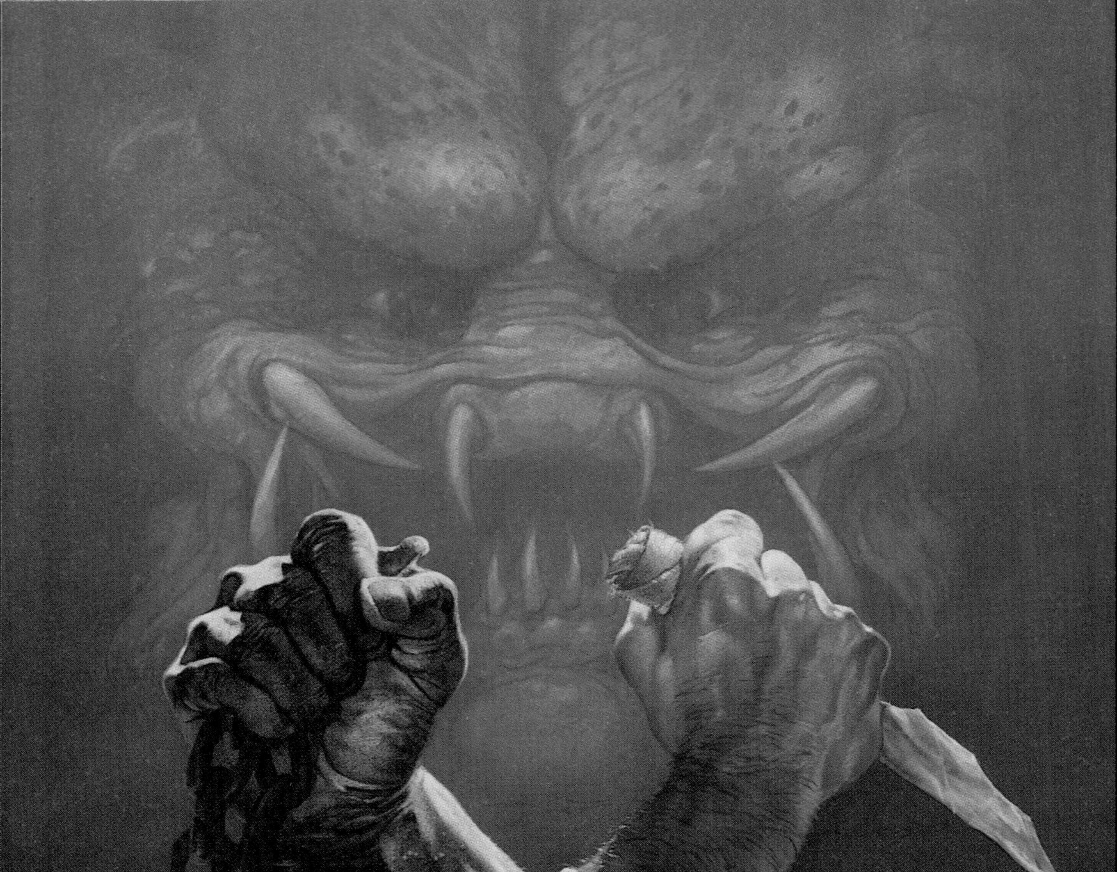
DORMAN

PAINTED COVERS BY DAVE DORMAN

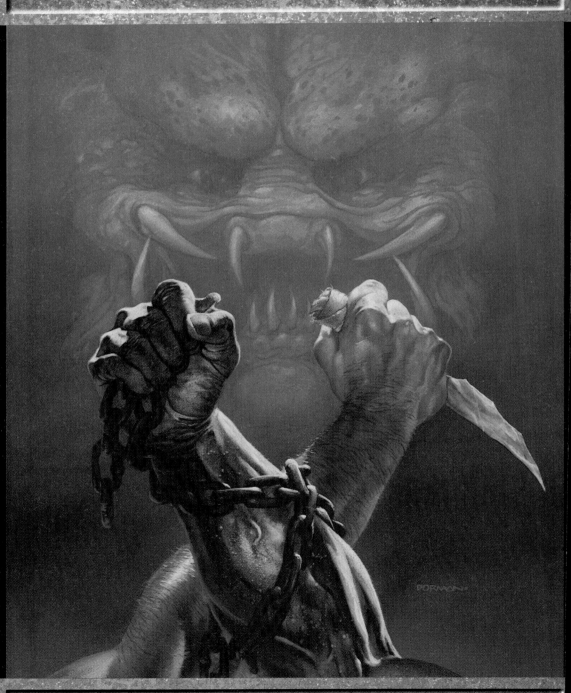

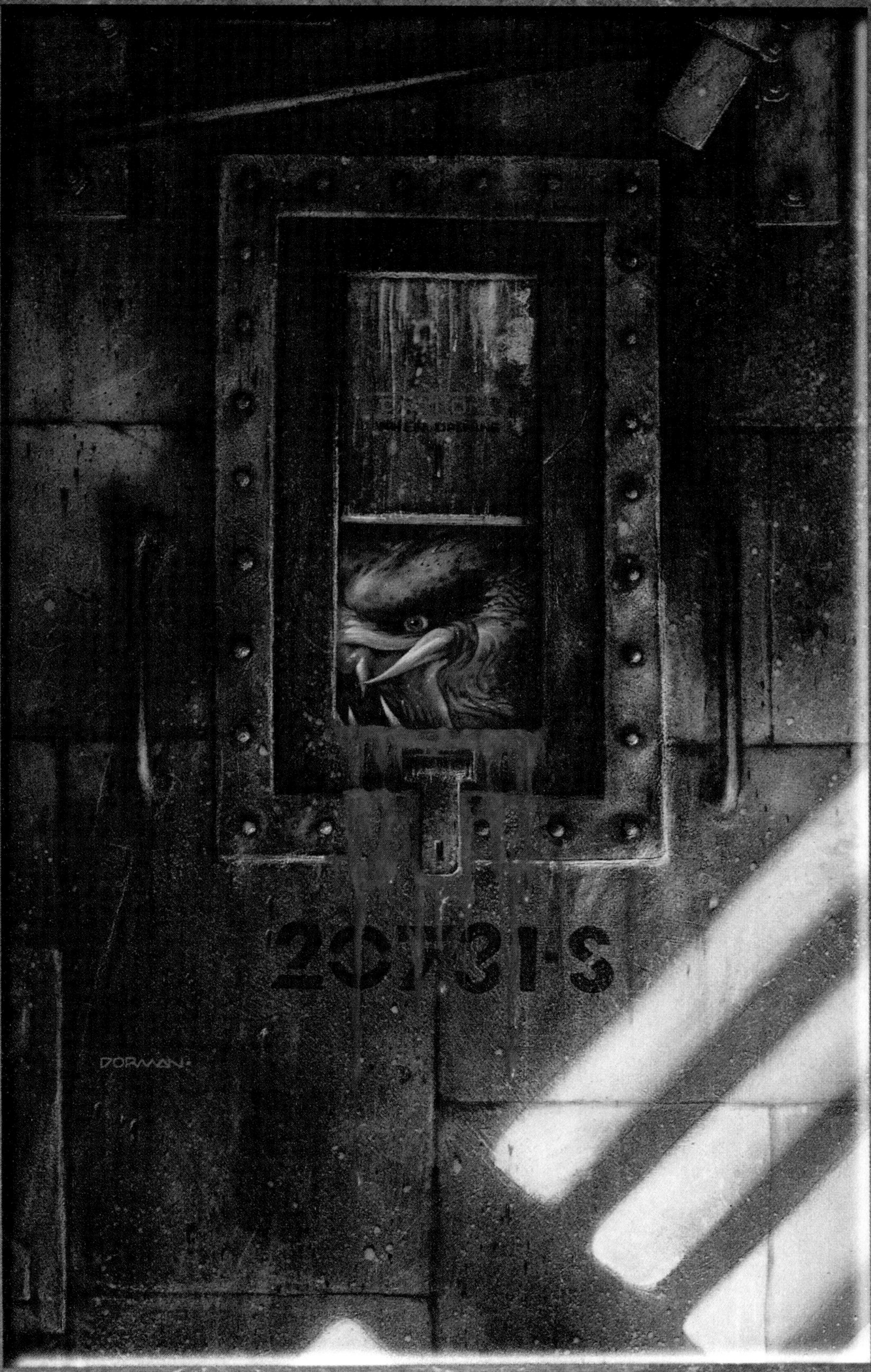
DORMAN

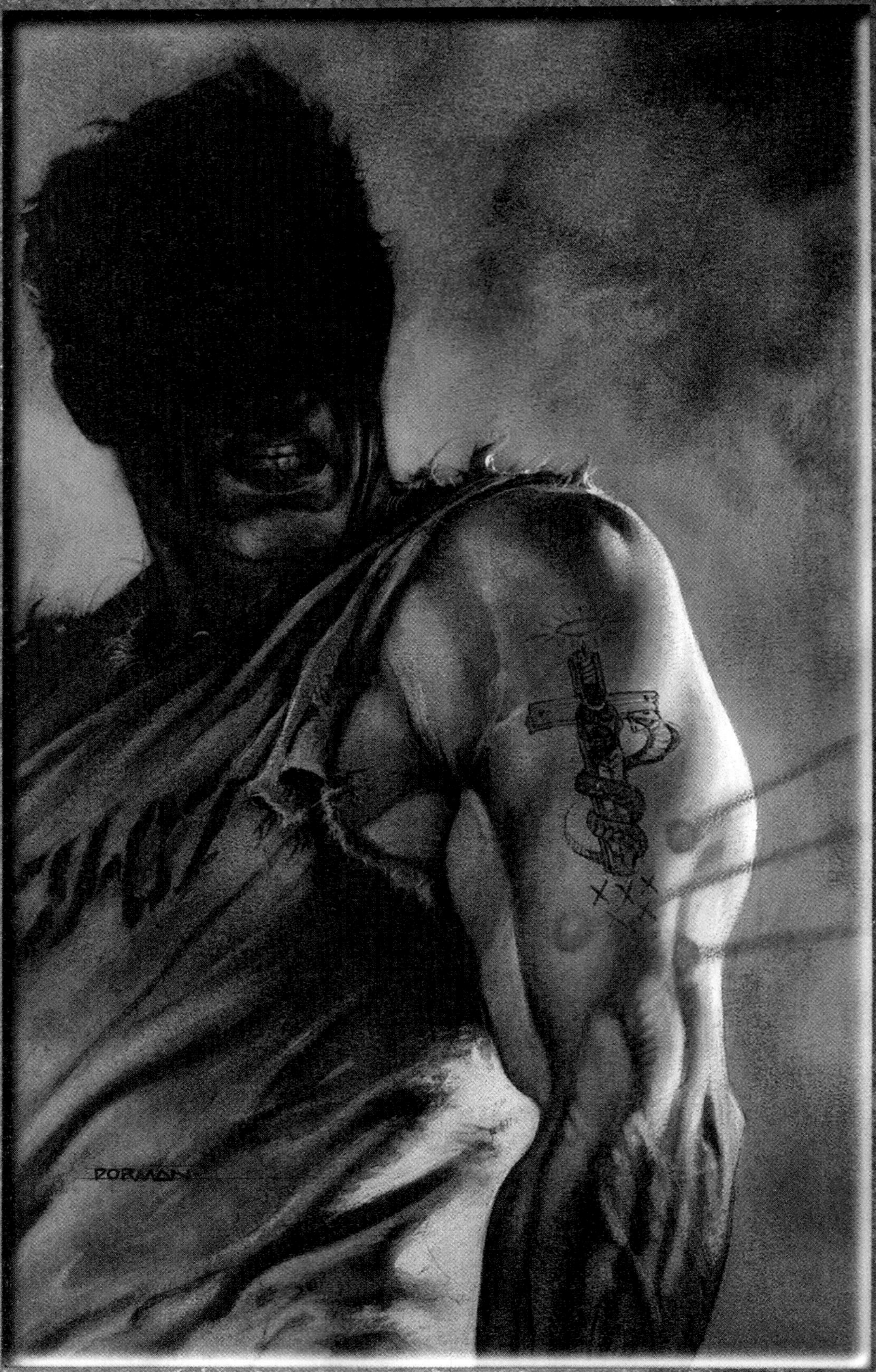
DORMAN

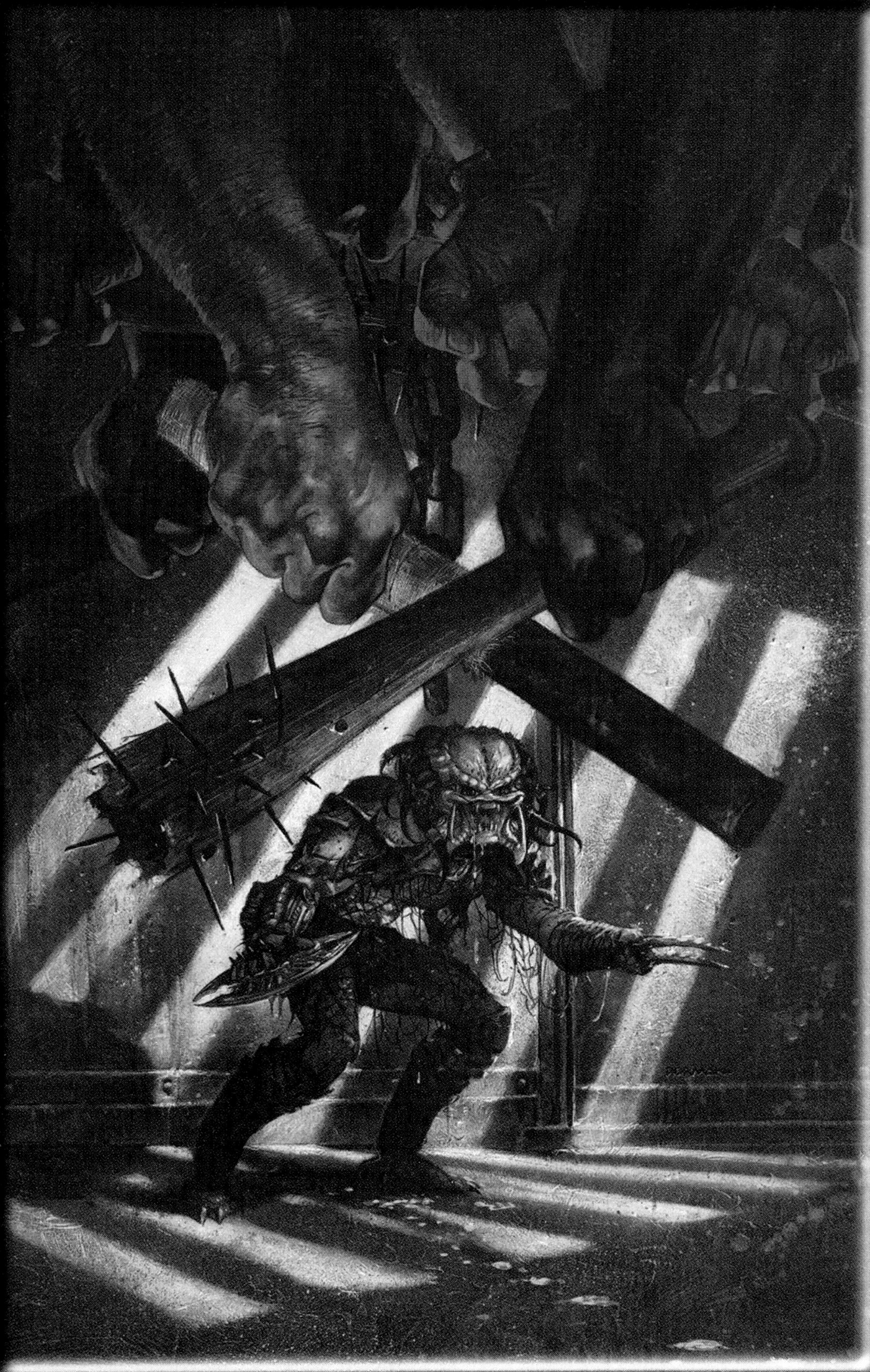

ALIENS™ AND PREDATOR™ PAPERBACK BOOKS AVAILABLE FROM DARK HORSE

ALIENS

VOLUME ONE: OUTBREAK
Verheiden • Nelson
176-page color paperback
ISBN: 1-56971-174-7 $17.95

VOLUME TWO: NIGHTMARE ASYLUM
Verheiden • Beauvais
112-page color paperback
ISBN: 1-56971-217-4 $16.95

EARTH WAR
Verheiden • Kieth
112-page color paperback
ISBN: 1-878574-23-X $13.95

GENOCIDE
Arcudi • Willis • Story
112-page color paperback
ISBN: 1-56971-123-2 $14.95

HIVE
Prosser • Jones
112-page color paperback
ISBN: 1-56971-122-4 $14.95

LABYRINTH
Woodring • Plunkett
136-page color paperback
ISBN: 1-56971-110-0 $17.95

ROGUE
Edginton • Simpson
112-page color paperback
ISBN: 1-56971-023-6 $14.95

TRIBES
Bissette • Dorman
72-page color paperback
ISBN: 1-878574-68-X $11.95

STRONGHOLD
Arcudi • Mahnke • Palmiotti
112-page color paperback
ISBN: 1-56971-154-2 $14.95

ALIENS VS PREDATOR

ALIENS VS PREDATOR
Stradley • Warner
176-page color paperback
ISBN: 1-56971-125-9 $19.95

WAR
Stradley • Warner
200-page color paperback
ISBN: 1-56971-158-5 $19.95

PREDATOR

BIG GAME
Arcudi • Dorkin • Gil
112-page color paperback
ISBN: 1-56971-166-6 $14.95

CONCRETE JUNGLE
Verheiden • Warner • Randall
112-page color paperback
ISBN: 1-56971-165-8 $14.95

COLD WAR
Verheiden • Randall • Mitchell
112-page color paperback
ISBN: 1-878574-79-5 $13.95

RACE WAR
Vachss • Stradley
144-page color paperback
ISBN: 1-56971-112-7 $17.95

PREDATOR VS MAGNUS ROBOT FIGHTER
Shooter • Ostrander • Weeks
64-page color paperback
ISBN: 1-56971-040-6 $7.95